RESPONSE TO INTERVENTION AND PRECISION TEACHING

Also from Kent Johnson

Enhancing Instructional Problem Solving:
An Efficient System for Assisting Struggling Learners
John C. Begeny, Ann C. Schulte, and Kent Johnson

Response to Intervention and Precision Teaching

Creating Synergy in the Classroom

Kent Johnson
Elizabeth M. Street

THE GUILFORD PRESS
New York London

A Division of Guilford Publications, Inc.
72 Spring Street, New York, NY 10012
www.guilford.com

Printed in the United States of America

This book is printed on acid-free paper.

Last digit is print number: 9 8 7 6 5 4 3 2 1

Library of Congress Cataloging-in-Publication Data

Johnson, Kent R.
Response to intervention and precision teaching : creating synergy in the classroom / Kent Johnson.
pages cm
Includes bibliographical references and index.
ISBN 978-1-4625-0761-0 (pbk. : alk. paper) — ISBN 978-1-4625-0762-7 (hardcover : alk. paper)
1. Remedial teaching. 2. Response to intervention (Learning disabled children)
3. Effective teaching. I. Title.
LB1029.R4J66 2012
371.9'043—dc23

2012035298

*For his years of service to the profession of school psychology,
his encouragement to us to write this book, and his gentle spirit,
we dedicate this book to the late Dr. Kenneth W. Merrell,
whose life well lived was an inspiration to so many.*

About the Authors

Kent Johnson, PhD, founded Morningside Academy, in Seattle, Washington, in 1980, and serves as its Executive Director. Morningside is a laboratory school for elementary and middle school children and youth. Morningside investigates effective curriculum materials and teaching methods, and has provided training and consulting in instruction to over 125 schools and agencies throughout the United States and Canada since 1991. Dr. Johnson has published many seminal papers and books about research-based curriculum and teaching methods, including *The Morningside Model of Generative Instruction: What It Means to Leave No Child Behind,* with Elizabeth M. Street. The Morningside Model of Generative Instruction focuses on foundation skills in reading, writing, mathematics, thinking, reasoning, problem solving, studying core content, and project-based learning. Over 40,000 students and over a thousand teachers have used this model. Dr. Johnson is also a cofounder of Headsprout, Inc., now Mimio, a company that develops web-based, interactive, cartoon-driven instructional programs, including *MimioSprout Early Reading* and *Mimio Reading Comprehension Suite.* He received the 2001 Award for Public Service in Behavior Analysis from the Society for the Advancement of Behavior Analysis; the 2010 Edward L. Anderson Award in Recognition of Exemplary Contributions to Behavioral Education from the Cambridge Center for Behavioral Studies; the 2009 Ernie Wing Award for Excellence in Evidence-Based Education from the Wing Institute; the 2006 Allyn and Bacon Exemplary Program Award from the Council for Exceptional Children, Division for Learning Disabilities; and the 2011 Ogden R. Lindsley Lifetime Achievement Award in Precision Teaching from the Standard Celeration Society.

Elizabeth M. Street, EdD, is Professor Emerita of Psychology at Central Washington University, where she served as a faculty member and administrator for 33 years. Prior to joining Central Washington University, she was a teacher and research assistant at the University of Illinois Child Behavior Laboratory; she directed the Champaign,

Illinois–based HEED (Help and Education for the Emotionally Disturbed) School, the first day-treatment program in Illinois for children diagnosed with challenging behaviors; directed the adolescent unit at Adolph Meyer Mental Health Center in Decatur, Illinois; and served on the faculty of the University of Wisconsin–LaCrosse. She began her tenure at Central Washington University in 1979, beginning in the Department of Education and moving to the Department of Psychology in 1983. Dr. Street also was an AAAS–APA Congressional Science Fellow and served on Senator Edward Kennedy's education committee staff. From 1999 to 2009, she was the assistant to the president of Central Washington University under several different titles. She has consulted to numerous programs that serve children diagnosed with autism spectrum disorders, in addition to her more than 30 years of service as a consultant, trainer, and coach for Morningside Academy. Dr. Street is a board-certified behavior analyst and has coauthored several papers and a book, *The Morningside Model of Generative Instruction: What It Means to Leave No Child Behind,* with Kent Johnson.

Preface

For over 40 years, we have used and benefited from a technology known as Precision Teaching (PT). As the response-to-intervention (RTI) framework began to emerge and take hold, it was obvious to us that PT and RTI share an emphasis on optimizing a child's learning trajectory in its early stages to create the greatest learning benefits throughout the child's school career. We realized almost immediately that incorporating PT technology into the framework could increase RTI's potential to improve learning outcomes for students. With encouragement from our friend and colleague the late Dr. Kenneth W. Merrell, we submitted a proposal for this book that describes the RTI framework and PT technology and suggests ways to combine them for maximum effectiveness.

MORNINGSIDE ACADEMY

Much of what we describe in this book comes from our more than 30 years working at Morningside Academy (where Kent Johnson is the founder and Executive Director, and Elizabeth M. Street is a consultant and trainer) and its subsidiaries, Morningside Teachers' Academy and Morningside Press. Morningside Academy is a nonprofit, private laboratory school, located in Seattle, Washington. The school serves learners in grades 1–9 of average to above-average intelligence who struggle in school because of deficits in the basic skills of reading, writing, and math; in reasoning and problem-solving skills; and in learning skills such as listening, organizing materials, participating in instruction or discussion, and studying. Some of these learners have mild special education diagnoses such as learning disabilities and attention-deficit/hyperactivity disorder (ADHD), but a special education diagnosis is not a requirement for attending.

Morningside Academy has been the site for developing and refining the Morningside Model of Generative Instruction (Johnson & Street, 2004), a model that combines the power of good instructional design and implementation with optimal practice on the critical tool and component skills that make up "the three Rs"—reading, writing, and arithmetic. The model also directly teaches critical thinking and builds repertoires that position learners to engage in important academic capstone activities. You can read more about Morningside Academy at *www.morningsideacademy.org*.

Morningside Academy also partners with public schools to transfer its model to general education classrooms. Over 125 public schools and agencies with over 40,000 learners have implemented the Morningside Model of Generative Instruction. Morningside Teachers' Academy is the arm of Morningside Academy that implements curriculum and instructional protocols developed or selected by and proceduralized at the laboratory school in schools and agencies throughout the United States and Canada and beyond. Go to *www.morningsideteachers.org* to read more about Morningside Teachers' Academy.

We encourage readers who are interested in implementing PT in their district, school, or classroom to contact Kent Johnson at Morningside Academy (*kent@morningsideacademy.org*) to discuss and negotiate a consulting and coaching partnership. In addition to establishing formal partnerships with schools and agencies, we have hosted hundreds of teachers at our Seattle-based Summer School Institute (SSI) each July, and at other times throughout the school year. Those interested in arranging a visit or in participating in SSI may also contact Kent Johnson.

Morningside Press is the publication arm of Morningside Academy. It publishes, among other materials, many of the PT practice materials that are referenced in this book. You can learn more about the materials that Morningside Academy administrators and teachers have developed at *www.morningsidepress.org*.

Throughout this book, we describe performance standards that Morningside has established for various practice sets. These standards have been informed by the work of thousands of precision teachers around the world and represent Morningside Academy's evidence of the performance rates that predict maintenance, endurance, stability, application, and generativity—the hallmarks of fluency. We also mention a number of instructional programs that have been particularly effective in achieving the front-end accuracy of skills for which PT practice sets are designed. Although the list is by no means exhaustive, each of the programs we describe has been tested with students in the laboratory school, and some have been successfully implemented in schools and agencies that adopt the Morningside Model of Generative Instruction.

THE BOOK

In this book, we recommend a marriage of two highly effective approaches to improving learners' academic skills: RTI and PT. RTI has emerged over the past 30 years to ensure that all learners receive the levels of support they need to make academic gains. It is a framework for combining elements of good practice to meet the needs of all children without being unduly prescriptive about instruments or interventions to use or the specific measures to employ. The approach triages learners into three tiers, with each tier characterized by increased teacher support, a more specialized curriculum, and more specific and frequent assessment. Tier 1 consists of the core curriculum and instructional programs/practices that occur in the general education classroom; Tier

2 comprises evidence-based supplemental instruction designed for small groups of students whose progress lags behind that of same-age peers; and Tier 3 is made up of evidence-based interventions to meet the needs of individual students. RTI typically includes the following components, each of which is briefly reviewed in this text: (1) early identification; (2) early intervention; (3) high-quality, evidence-based core instruction and interventions; (4) increasingly intensive interventions; (5) continuous and increasingly frequent progress monitoring; and (6) data-based decision making.

PT provides a technology for practicing skills in a time-efficient manner to achieve performance rates that predict maintenance, endurance, stability, application, and generativity. The technology, which has been improving the lives of learners for more than half a century, is perfectly suited to meeting the requirements of RTI for progress monitoring and data-based decision making. The PT approach to practice is designed to build rates on tool skills and component skills, as a means to ensure that they will be recruited in the context of composite skills. *Tool skills* are the building blocks of any content area, while *component skills* integrate two or more tool skills in preparation for learners to engage in the highest skill levels—composite skills, which typically require application of learned repertoires to novel situations. PT also emphasizes rate building within learning channels. *Learning channels* describe the input and output for curricular objectives, using common descriptors. For example, *see/say* tasks are all of those where one sees a stimulus and says the name. (For example, "See/say letters of the alphabet" is a shortcut for saying "When you see the letters of the alphabet, say them.") Precision teachers have provided evidence that building rates on a subset of see/say tasks improves the ease with which learners will build rates on all other see/say tasks, regardless of content area.

PT and RTI share an emphasis on optimizing a child's learning trajectory in its early stages to create the greatest learning benefits throughout his or her school career. This book first describes the RTI framework and PT technology and then suggests ways to combine them for maximum effectiveness. In the book's subtitle, we've used the word *synergy* in its contemporary meaning of increased effectiveness produced by combined action to suggest that these two approaches, used in combination, can produce a greater result than either one used alone. In the text, we expand this notion and make the case that RTI and PT, when used in combination with a well-designed curriculum, give advantages to learners and provide teachers with effective strategies to solve any learning problems that emerge.

This book will be particularly useful to teachers, school psychologists, and administrators who have adopted the RTI framework but continue to struggle to identify effective procedures for continuous and increasingly *frequent* progress monitoring, as well as data-based decision making. It introduces them to another tool that, like RTI, has been demonstrated to make a difference in the lives of learners. The difference is that PT provides the micro-level progress monitoring that predicts performance on macro-level assessments and prompts teachers about when and how to intervene when less-than-optimal gains are predicted.

Most chapters of this book include vignettes of the struggles teachers face in working in classrooms full of very diverse learners. The chapters then provide recommendations for how teachers can use RTI and PT together to address the challenges they face and to meet the needs of each learner. Chapter 1 describes the RTI history and framework. Chapter 2 describes the history and practices involved in PT. Chapter 3 describes aspects of content analysis that inform PT, including component–composite analysis, types of learning, and learning channels. Chapter 4 suggests ways to blend the PT technology with the RTI framework, while Chapter 5 includes how PT looks in practice, with special attention to a peer coaching model that allows students to practice different skills simultaneously and frees the teacher to act as monitor and trainer. In Chapters 6–8, the role of PT in the content areas of reading, mathematics, and writing are separately addressed; in addition, these chapters provide examples of well-designed curricula and practice sheets. Chapter 9 addresses the use of PT practices in the content areas, and Chapter 10 describes how PT contributes to learners' abilities to engage in project-based learning.

This text is ideal as a supplemental text for preservice and practicing teachers, school administrators, and school psychologists whose learners vary in their learning trajectories and who are seeking ways to serve them more appropriately.

THE CHALLENGE

What we propose here is not easy, nor is it a quick fix. Like all good teaching, PT is hard work. Still, the payoff is tremendous. Using the PT technology in combination with evidence-based instruction has radically improved the academic performance of children and adolescents, many of whom come to Morningside well behind their same-age peers. Not only do they catch up; they move ahead of their peers. The benefits of PT technology result not only from the practice regimen we prescribe, but also from the careful content analysis that provides a clear understanding of the tool and component skills underpinning important academic activities. The strength of PT lies in practicing these tools and components. The combination of content analysis with PT is akin to building one's house on a foundation of rock rather than sand! The result is solid learning. In this book, we provide guidance on both how to practice and what to practice.

The type of practice we propose here is different from what students experience in many classrooms. The difference requires that our teachers spend much of the first month of school teaching the technology. Students and teachers need to change their way of thinking about practice, which is facilitated by practicing a different way. At Morningside, we keep no secrets from students, and so we not only teach them how to monitor and chart their own practice; we also teach them why. As a result, students who have been with us for a year or more become very conversant with the instructional and practice protocols we implement. In fact, when some of them return to more typical public schools, they are often concerned that the same protocols aren't used! Many simply continue to practice the way they've practiced at Morningside and continue to accelerate the pace of their learning. In other words, they learn about how to learn and apply the strategies widely.

Still, it's worrisome to some teachers that they need to set aside their curriculum while they teach the practice protocol. We want to assure readers that, when implemented with fidelity, PT practice on the tools and components we prescribe results in more rapid and more thorough skill mastery than students achieve in its absence. In addition, strengthening tools and components for many Tier 2 learners and for some

Tier 3 learners can bring them in line with their peers and enable them to benefit from the core curriculum.

CURRICULAR RECOMMENDATIONS

Throughout the book, we mention instructional programs and practice sets that have proven particularly effective to teachers at Morningside Academy and at schools and agencies that implement the Morningside Model of Generative Instruction. Although we don't intend this to be an endorsement of these materials over others, we do intend that they become the model for the kinds of materials you choose in your schools and districts. In other sources, we've provided greater detail about the criteria we use to choose instructional materials. You'll notice that some of the instructional materials we cite are dated. That's because they continue to be the best we've found to achieve student learning outcomes.

ACKNOWLEDGMENTS

We want to acknowledge especially our colleague Dr. Warren Street, who served as our editor and fact checker, and whose careful review and feedback on this book improved it immensely. This book could not have been completed without the professional assistance of The Guilford Press staff. Natalie Graham was with the project from start to finish and was available to hold our hands and answer our questions with patience and grace. Mary Beth Wood provided invaluable assistance in seeking and obtaining permission to reproduce materials that are used in the book. We also benefited enormously from Anna Nelson's wise counsel and the outstanding copy editing of Marie Sprayberry. Marie brought an attention to detail to the project that is unparalleled in our experience. We are also indebted to our colleagues—many of whom are no longer with us—from whom we learned the science of human behavior, most particularly Dr. B. F. Skinner, Dr. Ogden Lindsley, Dr. Julie Vargas, Dr. Sidney Bijou, Dr. Ellen Reese, Dr. Beatrice Barrett, Dr. Beth Sulzer-Azaroff, Dr. Susan Markle, Dr. Thomas Gilbert, Dr. Charles Ferster, Dr. Gil Sherman, and Dr. Hank Pennypacker, among others. Last, the teachers and students with whom we've worked over the years have provided the feedback that has allowed us to hone our craft, and so we are especially grateful to them.

We wish you the very best as you read about and try out these procedures. Should questions arise, don't hesitate to get in touch with either of us. You can reach us at *kent@morningsideacademy.org* (Kent Johnson) and at *streetl@cwu.edu* (Elizabeth M. Street).

Contents

CHAPTER 1

The Response-to-Intervention Framework

ORIGINS

Response to intervention (RTI) is a framework of strategies that has proven effective for improving academic and behavioral outcomes for students in the K–12 schools. According to Brown-Chidsey and Steege (2010), the RTI framework expands on Evelyn Deno's (1970) cascade model of special education service delivery, which was popular in the 1970s and 1980s. The RTI model is also an outgrowth of the normalization movement of the 1970s (Wolfensberger, 1972); the Regular Education Initiative (Will, 1986), a federal policy the goal of which was to maintain students in regular education if at all possible; and the inclusive education movement (Villa & Thousand, 1995), an outgrowth of the civil rights movement that favored opportunities in general education for all students, regardless of race, ethnicity, or disability. In his foreword to VanDerHeyden and Burns (2010), Ysseldyke adds that

> RtI has its roots in the work on diagnostic teaching, and specifically in Ogden Lindsley's (1972) work on precision teaching. It also has as its origin a negative reaction to the use of ability measures and other process tests to diagnose and then remediate within student deficits, dysfunctions, disorders, and disabilities. (p. xii)

George Sugai, in a presentation to the December 6, 2007, Response to Intervention Summit, identified the following early influences on the development of the framework: applied behavior analysis, Precision Teaching (PT), curriculum-based measurement (CBM), prereferral interventions, teacher assistance teaming, diagnostic prescriptive teaching, and behavioral and instructional consultation. He further suggested that RTI developed out of a perceived need for comprehensive screening, early and timely decision making, data-based decision making, support for nonresponders, instructional accountability and justification, assessment–instruction alignment, and resource and time use (Sugai, 2007). Frank Gresham (2007) traces the basis of the approach back to a

National Research Council report (Heller, Holtzman, & Messick, 1982), which evaluated the validity of the special education classification system according to three criteria: "(a) the quality of the general education program, (b) the value of the special education program in producing important outcomes for students, and (c) the accuracy and meaningfulness of the assessment process in the identification of disability" (Gresham, 2007, p. 11).

Batsche et al. (2006) credit Stanley Deno (2002) for the problem-solving approach that is foundational to the RTI framework. They also credit John Bergan's (1977) consultation model and Sharon Vaughn's three-tier model applied to reading (University of Texas System/Texas Education Agency, 2005) as critical underpinnings of the framework. They acknowledge Bergan for promoting the use of the problem-solving approach with struggling learners; Deno for providing a standard, research-based way to monitor learners' progress in basic skill areas of reading and math; and Vaughn for including all learners in such a way that the approach is both preventive and remedial.

In sum, it isn't possible to credit a single person, report, or movement for the development of the RTI framework. Rather, it emerged from the work of several scientists and practitioners, and it gathered steam as a result of the shared interests of three primary groups of educators and psychologists. They sought the adoption of classroomwide practices—including curriculum, instruction, and management—that provided data-based evidence of effectiveness in enabling the large majority of students to achieve academic and behavioral goals; the earliest possible identification of students who were not making progress; and increasingly structured practices to improve their success.

- The first group—the evidence-based group—included Douglas Carnine, Edward Kame'enui, Robert Horner, and George Sugai at the University of Oregon, among others.
- The second group—the specific learning disabilities (SLD) group—included James Ysseldyke, Lynn Fuchs, and Douglas Fuchs, among others.
- The third group—the "no child left behind" (NCLB) group—included Amanda VanDerHeyden, Thomas Kratochwill, and Kent Johnson, among others.

The evidence-based group was especially interested in ensuring that curriculum, instruction, and management practices—especially in basic skills instruction—were based on sound evidence. Its followers were concerned that many practices widely used in the K–12 schools were untested. They noted that evidence-based practices were often set aside in favor of those that were consistent with a particular philosophical view, regardless of their impact. They fundamentally favored the use of curricular, instructional, or management practices or packages that had been carefully tested on those they were meant to serve, and that had shown a positive and substantial impact on the academic performance or conduct of learners.

The SLD group was increasingly dissatisfied with the slow responsiveness inherent in the discrepancy model's diagnostic approach and the resultant poor outcomes for learners. Its supporters were disenchanted by continued adherence to the aptitude–treatment interaction approach in the face of its failure to remedy learning deficits of students with SLD (D. Fuchs & Fuchs, 2006; Ysseldyke, 1973). The SLD group was concerned that the use of a discrepancy model to qualify learners for special services under the SLD category resulted in extreme delays in providing the level of support these learners needed. Specifically, the discrepancy model, which came to be known sardonically as the "wait-to-fail" model (Reynolds & Shaywitz, 2009) required students to be (1) of average intelligence, and (2) a full 2 years behind same-age peers on standardized tests (D. Fuchs & Fuchs, 2006) to qualify for services under an SLD diagnosis. This meant that by the time they could avail themselves of special services, students were already woefully behind and had accumulated a considerable failure history that didn't bode well for their eventual academic success.

The NCLB group was concerned about the large number of students who were not progressing in the K–12 system; the tendency to maintain students in the core curriculum long after evidence of their failure to thrive had emerged; the racial and ethnic bias that had emerged in special education placement; and the largely unimproved learning trajectories of learners placed in special education (Johnson & Street, 2004; VanDerHeyden & Burns, 2010). Those aligned with this group noted that despite considerable investment by state and federal legislative bodies, too many children in both general and special education were not mastering basic skills by third grade, and too many continued to struggle with literacy and numeracy well into high school. Such data raise concerns not only for the well-being of individual children, but also for society: Children who fall behind academically have a greater likelihood of dropping out of high school and of dropping into the penal system. Proponents of the NCLB position were also troubled that those most likely to be left behind came from low-income and from racial and ethnic minority families (Newell & Kratochwill, 2007; VanDerHeyden & Burns, 2010).

Although the RTI framework had its beginnings in the latter decades of the 20th century, it took on new life with enactment of the Individuals with Disabilities Education Improvement Act in 2004. According to D. Fuchs and Fuchs (2006),

> On December 3, 2004, President Bush signed into law the Individuals with Disabilities Education Improvement Act (IDEA, 2004). The revised law is different from the previous version in at least one important respect. Whereas practitioners were previously encouraged to use IQ–achievement discrepancy to identify children with learning disabilities (LD), they now may use "Response to Intervention," or RTI, a new, alternative method. It is also a means of providing early intervention to all children at risk for school failure. IDEA 2004 permits districts to use as much as 15% of their special education monies to fund early intervention activities. (p. 93)

The online RTI Network (*www.rtinetwork.org/learn*) reflects the long-term hope of all who implement the system when it says, "RTI holds the promise of ensuring that all children have access to high-quality instruction, and that struggling learners—including those with learning disabilities—are identified, supported, and served early and effectively."

WHAT IS RESPONSE TO INTERVENTION?

Response to intervention is variously abbreviated as RtI or RTI. We use the latter throughout this text, except in quoted material that uses RtI. RTI is variously described as a method, a practice, a movement, and a framework. For our purposes, we refer to it as a framework, because it provides just that: a framework for combining elements of good practice to meet the needs of all children without being unduly prescriptive about instruments or interventions to use or the specific measures to employ.

Many definitions of the RTI framework have emerged in the literature. According to Brown-Chidsey and Steege (2010), "RTI is a systematic and data-based method for identifying, defining, and resolving students' academic and/or behavior difficulties" (p. 3). Batsche et al. (2006) include two key elements in their definition: (1) the provision of high-quality instruction and/or intervention that is matched to student needs, and (2) the use of learning rate over time and level of performance to make important educational decisions. Ysseldyke (2008) describes RTI as a process that "involves assignment of evidence-based instruction or interventions, monitoring of student progress, and the making of instructional or eligibility decisions based on progress-monitoring data" (p. 3).

From reading between the lines of these and other definitions or descriptions, it quickly becomes apparent that the framework contains, at a minimum, the following components:

- Early identification.
- Early intervention.
- High-quality, evidence-based core instruction and interventions.
- Increasingly intensive interventions.
- Continuous and increasingly frequent progress monitoring.
- Data-based decision making.

The primary purpose, then, of the RTI framework is to ensure that schools use skill-specific screening to place learners in programs, measure the effects of the core curriculum or instructional practices on all learners' academic and behavioral responding, use measures at the earliest possible time to detect inadequate progress toward specified goals, select evidence-based interventions for a given learner or group of learners, monitor their progress on clearly identified learning objectives, and change instruction as needed to ensure a positive learning trajectory.

VanDerHeyden and Burns (2010)—who witnessed the rise of the discrepancy model and its fallout, the poor results of the search for aptitude–treatment interactions, and the doctrinaire dismissal of effective teaching strategies—describe their own frustration for which the RTI framework brought new hope. They say, "We remembered the values that brought us to our field: the desire for all students to learn, efficient and responsible resource allocation to support student learning, and the idea of a great public education being central to social justice and equity" (p. xix). VanDerHeyden and Burns took comfort in the RTI framework in part because it substituted a risk model (identifying students who were at risk for failure and intervening early) for a deficit model (determining who had failed and intervening only at that point).

The RTI logic is visualized by the Office of Special Education Programs (OSEP) Center on Positive Behavioral Interventions and Supports (*www.pbis.org*) as a bottom-heavy triangle (Figure 1.1) divided vertically down the middle, with each side depicting a different area of emphasis and divided horizontally into three tiers. The two areas of emphasis are *academic* behavior systems and *social* behavior systems. Although

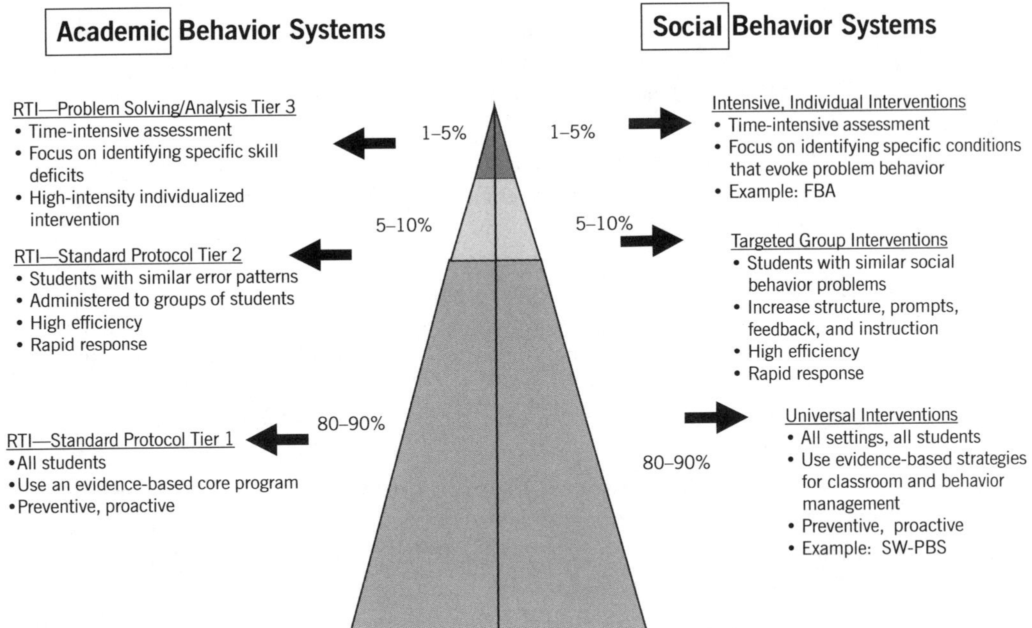

FIGURE I.1. RTI logic as conceptualized by the U.S. Department of Education Office of Special Education Programs (OSEP) Center on Positive Behavioral Interventions and Supports (*www.pbis.org*). FBA, functional behavioral assessment; SW-PBS, schoolwide positive behavior support. Based on Sugai and Horner (2008).

academic and social behaviors respond to the same behavioral principles, evidence-based interventions for each have developed along separate lines and are therefore separately represented.

According to Sugai (2007) and others (Walker et al., 1996; Walker & Shinn, 2002), the triangle isn't new to RTI. Rather, it has been adapted from a similar model used in public health and disease prevention (Larson, 1994). As described by the National Center on Response to Intervention (2010), the elements of this model are as follows:

- *Primary* medical services are made available to all and attempt to prevent the development of disease.
- *Secondary* medical services treat those for whom prevention was unsuccessful; specifically, this is a smaller subset of the entire population that has acquired a given disease.
- *Tertiary* services treat an even smaller number of individuals who have developed complications or acquired a particularly virulent form of a disease.

Gresham (2007) agrees. He notes that "RTI is not a new concept in other fields. The field of medicine provides a particularly salient example of how physicians utilize RTI principles in their everyday practice to treat physical disease" (p. 11). He points to four important principles that undergird the use of this framework in medicine: (1) Increases in intervention intensity are based on a patient's unresponsiveness to current practice; (2) treatment decisions are based on continuously collected objective data; (3) the data are proven indicators of good health; and (4) frequency and type of data increase as treatment intensifies.

The concept of *triaging*—dividing sick or wounded individuals into three groups—also has its roots in the medical profession. According to the *Concise Dictionary of Modern Medicine* (Segen, 2006), triaging is

> a method of ranking sick or injured people according to the severity of their sickness or injury in order to ensure that medical and nursing staff facilities are used most efficiently; assessment of injury intensity and the immediacy or urgency for medical attention. (p. 701)

Mirroring the public health model, the RTI model is first and foremost a prevention model. Ideally, educators prevent academic and social failure by providing comprehensive and evidence-based programs for all learners, by intervening at the earliest signs that educational or social behaviors are not keeping pace with expectations, and by providing the level of support necessary to ensure normative progress. Also parallel to the medical model, the RTI model triages learners according to their levels of skill development and their rates of progress through the curriculum. However, unlike the framework that dominated special education since its beginnings in the United States—a framework that triaged students through placement (e.g., in reading, a student might be placed in general education, Title I programs, or special education)—the RTI framework triages through intervention. In addition, while the framework focuses on learning and behavior for all learners, it inspects effects of interventions at the level of the individual. According to Gresham (2007), "RTI is used to select, change, or titrate interventions based on how the child responds to that intervention" (p. 10).

Schools that adopt the RTI framework are encouraged to select practices in all three tiers that are evidence-based and learner-verified. As Begeny, Schulte, and Johnson (2012) explain, *evidence-based* means "that the program incorporates key ingredients that research has shown to be effective" (p. 215), whereas *learner-verified* means "that research demonstrates that the program itself produces significant gains in student achievement" (p. 215). The important standard is that programs and practices have been tested on populations similar to those with whom they will be employed and are accompanied by evidence that the large majority of children at a particular age or grade make adequate yearly progress with them (according to mutually agreed-upon standards).

THE THREE TIERS

Triaging occurs for both academic and social behavior, and both are included in the RTI framework. Effective procedures for social behavior triaging have been developed by proponents of positive behavior support (see, e.g., *www.pbis.org*), and this collection of procedures is often referred to separately as PBS. Still, the similarities to RTI are apparent. Sandomierski, Kincaid, and Algozzine (2007) note that both RTI and PBS have their foundations in differentiated instruction, and that both identify factors and components that should constitute three tiers: a universal tier, a targeted group tier, and an individualized support tier.

About multi-tiered instruction, D. Fuchs and Fuchs (2006) say:

> The nature of the academic intervention changes at each tier, becoming more intensive as a student moves across the tiers. Increasing intensity is achieved by (a) using more teacher-centered, systematic, and explicit (e.g., scripted) instruction, (b) conducting it more frequently, (c) adding to its duration, (d) creating smaller and more homogeneous student groupings, or (e) relying on instructors with greater expertise. (p. 94)

VanDerHeyden and Burns (2010) add that measurement becomes more frequent and precise, and problem analysis becomes more detailed and costly, at each successive tier.

Tier I

Both the academic and social sides of the framework assume that curricular, instructional, and management practices exist that, when used with fidelity, should result in adequate yearly progress for the large majority of students in every general education classroom. Thus, in the ideal scenario, 80–90% of the students in a classroom are represented in the bottom tier, Tier 1.[1] In the framework, this tier and these programs and practices are referred to variously as *general instruction and assessment* or *universal interventions*. For the model to work, the programs and practices adopted for use in Tier 1 must have been demonstrated to prevent failure for most children and must actively engage learners. That is, each must have an empirical basis supporting its use, must identify what is to be learned, and must specify how it will be measured. According to the University of Texas System/Texas Education Agency (2005) model, Tier 1 is defined as the " 'core' curricular and instructional programs and strategies in the general education setting" (p. 11).

To ensure that the majority of learners are making expected progress, and to allow for fine-tuning of classroom practices and/or assigning students to supplementary or specialized instruction, measures that predict annual growth (*meta-level assessment* measures; see section on progress monitoring below) are administered periodically. Students whose performance on these measures predict inadequate growth if Tier 1 or "universal" practices are used may be provided with evidence-based supplemental instruction in Tier 2.

The relation between teaching and assessment is beautifully described by Ysseldyke, Burns, Scholin, and Parker (2010):

> Educators typically make decisions about *what* to teach (instructional level or content) and *how* to teach (the particular instructional approach, content, instructional strategies, or tactics that work best). Tests are helpful tools in making decisions about what to teach, but they do not help us decide how to teach. . . . The best way to make decisions about how to teach is to teach, and gather data on the relative effectiveness of alternative instructional approaches

[1] These percentages may obtain in classrooms of children who are well prepared for academic instruction when they enter school, but there is some doubt about the degree to which they can be expected in more typical classrooms without considerable support beyond the core curriculum.

> or interventions. Essentially, the task is to monitor progress and use data to make instructional modifications; such is the thinking that underlies precision teaching . . . , data-based program modification . . . , and RTI. (p. 54)

Assessment also allows teachers and districts to estimate the fit and adequacy of programs and practices within the school environment. Should the results of assessment reveal that the practices aren't working for at least 80–90% of learners in a school or district, it serves notice to the teachers, the building-level administrators, and the district either that the practices aren't being implemented with fidelity, that they are not adequate to teach the knowledge and skills for which they've been adopted, or that they are not well suited to the demographic mix in the classroom. Before any further action is taken, it's incumbent on the school or district to decide whether one or more of these conditions exist. We discuss the matter of treatment integrity later in this chapter. Suffice it to say here that unless programs and procedures are implemented consistent with their design and instructions, it's impossible to determine whether weaknesses in learners' performances are a function of their learning or of the instruction. It's also possible that a school or district has adopted a program that is simply not capable of achieving district goals. This makes the selection process critical—not only because poorly designed programs disadvantage learners, but also because they use resources that could be turned to better advantage. Last, the intervention must fit the learners. For example, a reading comprehension program that works well for learners from high-income families may be effective and efficient because of the background knowledge the students share. However, that same program may be less effective or efficient with learners from low-income families (VanDerHeyden & Burns, 2010). This is why it's important for a district staff to look at evidence of effectiveness with its particular population.

Tier 2

Most typically offered within the regular education classroom, *supplemental* or *targeted group* instruction is designed to strengthen particular areas of weakness that have emerged among a small group of students with similar error patterns (academic) or similar social behavior problems (social). For example, students who are not mastering sound–symbol associations in grade K or 1 (academic) may spend a portion of the classroom time assigned to reading in an evidence-based supplemental curriculum—or, if they have achieved accuracy on the task but respond so slowly that the skill doesn't transfer to word reading, they may participate in frequency-building exercises. Similarly, students with organizational problems (social) may participate in a study skills program. Grouping in Tier 2 is almost always homogeneous and based on skill level. Ideally, Tier 2 instruction will complement Tier 1 activities. That is, learners will continue to participate in Tier 1 activities, but part of the time or additional time will be allocated to Tier 2 activities. This works particularly well when assessment is sufficiently frequent that students don't lose a lot of ground before an intervention is employed. Because the goal is to move students back to the core curriculum as quickly as possible, there is a special incentive for schools to select supplementary instructional materials that are both effective (i.e., teach the skill to some determined level of mastery) and efficient (i.e., do so in a timely manner). According to the OSEP Center on Positive Behavioral Interventions and Supports (*www.pbis.org*), the materials and practices selected for Tier 2 should be characterized by high efficiency and rapid response.

Many supplementary programs, procedures, and practices advocate a designated length of intervention, but the lengths vary considerably. For example, Dixon, Boorman, Conrad, Klau, and Muti's (2008) *Reading Success* is designed to be used for 30 minutes a day, 3–5 times per week, for an entire academic year. Research findings by Lynn and Douglas Fuchs and their colleagues favor Tier 2 interventions of 30 minutes or fewer for three sessions a week that typically last for 16 weeks (see L. S. Fuchs et al., 2009). Koutsoftas, Harmon, and Gray (2009) report good outcomes for a Tier 2 intervention to improve phonemic awareness in young children with 20-minute twice-weekly sessions lasting 6 weeks.

Should continued progress monitoring suggest that learners in Tier 2 are not reaching designated aims within a reasonable period of time, the teachers and district are faced with the same questions we have noted above: Is the Tier 2 curriculum being implemented with fidelity? Is it inappropriate to address the needs of these particular learners? As we discuss in more detail later in this chapter, the importance of professional development related to evidence-based practices from the start cannot be overemphasized. To do otherwise risks failure that is costly to the school or district and to each learner that is affected by it. In addition, adopting practices without adequate teacher training, coaching, and assessment virtually guarantees that they won't be implemented with fidelity.

Tier 3

When evidence exists that the program has good support for its effectiveness and that it is being implemented with fidelity, learners who are not progressing in Tier 2 may move to Tier 3, or *specialized instruction*. In some cases, the placement team may recognize during screening or at the time of the first meta-level assessment that the general education curriculum and even the Tier 2 specialized programs are not suited to an individual learner's deficits. In these cases, the learner may be assigned immediately to the highly specialized and individualized interventions that characterize Tier 3.

Here the focus is on time-intensive assessment to identify specific skill deficits (academic) or the conditions that evoke problem behaviors (social). Academic instruction in this tier is intensive and individualized, and is typically informed by thoroughgoing task analyses and more detailed assessment to determine the best jumping-off point for instruction. Management practices in Tier 3 are often informed by a *functional behavioral assessment*[2] to determine the function of troublesome behaviors.

In the remainder of the current chapter and in the succeeding chapters of this book, we focus on RTI as it applies to *academic* deficits, although readers are encouraged to review the work of Sugai and Horner as it relates to RTI applied to *social* behaviors

---

[2] According to Steege and Watson (2009), "functional behavioral assessment is an investigative process that results in an understanding of why behaviors occur . . . a set of assessment procedures that results in the identification and description of the relationships between the unique characteristics of the individual and the contextual variables that trigger, motivate, and reinforce behavior" (p. 9).

(e.g., Sugai et al., 2000; Sugai & Horner, 2005). Their work with PBS provides an outstanding parallel to the work we describe here.

KEY COMPONENTS OF THE REPONSE-TO-INTERVENTION FRAMEWORK

Although there is some disagreement about the number of components that make up the RTI framework, most proponents agree that the five components displayed in Figure 1.2 are essential: (1) early identification through *brief, universal screening*; (2) the use of comprehensive evidence-based or learner-verified *core curriculum* and practices to teach agreed-on grade-level or content-specific skills; (3) increasingly intensive and early intervention through the use of evidence-based supplementary and specialized *intervention programs* based on the specific needs of small groups of students or individual students; (4) thoroughgoing and frequent *progress monitoring*; and (5) *data-based decision making.*

Brief, Universal Screening

In the slides accompanying his webinar posted on the National Center on Response to Intervention website, David Heistad (2009) defines screening as the use of "brief assessments that are valid, reliable, and evidence-based. They are conducted with all students or targeted groups of students to identify students who are at risk of academic failure and, therefore, likely to need additional or alternative forms of instruction to supplement the conventional general education approach" (p. 3). VanDerHeyden and Burns (2010) add to the list three other important characteristics of universal screening instruments: They should "reflect future performance without intervention, accurately and efficiently discriminate between students at risk and students not at risk, and be tied to local expectations for student learning" (p. 19). These authors also point out that teacher nomination is not a good predictor of a given student's need for intervention, because "teachers tend to identify students who do not need intervention at high rates and also fail to identify those who do need intervention" (p. 19).

The Core Curriculum

A district or school should use at least two criteria in selecting its core curriculum. First, it should be comprehensive; that is, it should provide evidence that it is based on, and provides instruction reflecting, a thorough analysis of the content. Although it isn't necessary that one program cover the entire content in the area (e.g., reading), this is the most parsimonious approach. Begeny et al. (2012) note that while very little empirical evidence exists to support core curricular programs, content analyses and positive results from state review committees suggest that some are better than others. They provide a list of the most thorough and effective reading and mathematics programs, at the same time noting that none of them is perfect. They further state that "far fewer evidence-based programs and published studies on effective instruction exist for writing than for reading and math. . . . To our knowledge, no evidence-based core writing

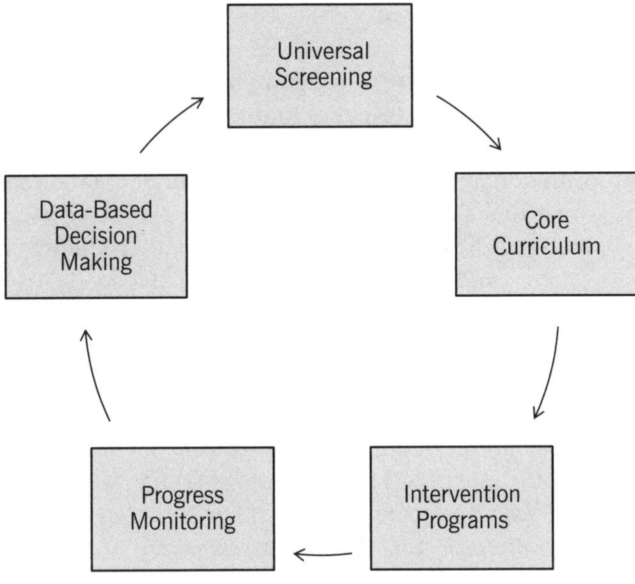

FIGURE 1.2. Five key components of the RTI framework.

program exists that includes instruction in each of the three areas of writing described in our content analysis" (p. 240).

Recommendations for evidence-based curricula are also available from the U.S. Department of Education Institute of Education Sciences What Works Clearinghouse website (*http://ies.ed.gov/ncee/wwc*). In addition, teachers interested in selecting evidence-based reading programs may review Simmons and Kame'enui's (2003) consumer's guide to evaluating core reading programs.

Second, the curriculum should be accompanied by evidence that, in its entirety or with respect to individual components, it is effective in achieving school, district, state, and/or national goals by grade level for the large majority of students in the class. This too has proven to be a challenge, and little evidence to date suggests that any core curriculum is up to the task of ensuring that grade-level competencies are achieved by at least 80% of learners.

Intervention Programs

According to Begeny et al. (2012), intervention programs are "intensive, supplemental curricula that teach the struggling learner what a good core curriculum fails to teach him or her" (p. 215). Just as the core curriculum must be supported by evidence of its effectiveness in covering the entire scope of the area of study, intervention programs must also provide evidence that they can provide successful and timely remedy for specific skill deficits. For example, if a group of students is struggling with basic math facts, the intervention program should directly address math facts and should provide evidence that it has been effective in bringing similar students to mastery in an acceptable period of time.

Progress Monitoring

The purpose of progress monitoring is to identify learners who are not meeting criteria for content mastery, enabling teachers to provide them with additional support. Although many schools and districts accomplish progress monitoring by using benchmark assessments of student progress several times throughout the year, this is just one level of such monitoring that should inform data-based decision making.

Writing in Johnson and Street (2004), Sue Malmquist identifies three levels of monitoring: macro-, meta-, and micro-level assessments (Figure 1.3). *Macro-level assessments* are standardized norm-referenced or criterion-referenced tests that are typically administered annually and that provide the basis for determining whether students in a school or classroom are making adequate yearly progress. Commonly used macro-level assessments include state tests and national tests. Examples of state tests include Washington's Measurements of Student Progress (MSP) for grades 3–8 (*www.k12.wa.us/assessment/statetesting/MSP.aspx*) and High School Proficiency Exam (HSPE) for the high school grades (*www.k12.wa.us/assessment/statetesting/HSPE.aspx*), as well as Oklahoma's Core Curriculum Test (*http://sde.state.ok.us/acctassess/core.html*). National tests include the Woodcock–Johnson (WJ III) Tests of Achievement (*www.riverpub.com/products/wjIII-Achievement*), the Iowa Tests of Basic Skills (ITBS; *www.riverpub.com/products/itbs*), and the Stanford Achievement Test Series, Tenth Edition (*www.pearsonassessments.com/HAIWEB/Cultures/en-us/Productdetail.htm?Pid=SAT10C*).

Meta-level assessments are typically administered weekly, monthly, or quarterly. In the best possible scenario, these assessments are publisher- and teacher-independent. That is, while they are broadly aligned with the curriculum that the school has adopted, they provide standardized content that is based on state or federal benchmarks. They are also characterized by standardized format, administration, and scoring guidelines. *Curriculum-based measurement* (CBM; S. L. Deno, 1985; Shinn, 1989) is the gold standard for meta-analysis. A good CBM instrument should reliably predict performance on macro-level assessments. That is, it should provide information to the teacher and other district personnel about the likelihood that staying on the current growth trajectory will result in appropriate grade-level or criterion-level gains in the content area by the end of the year. An ideal CBM instrument requires performance on a subset of skills that best predict mastery of related skills. Typically mastery of these tool or component skills is prerequisite to mastery of component skills and composite repertoires that the macro-level assessments may measure. CBM instruments record rate as well as accuracy of performance, because a learner's facility with a skill predicts how effectively he or she will be able to employ it in compound (composite) repertoires.

The best-known CBM instrument is arguably Dynamic Indicators of Basic Early Literacy Skills (DIBELS; Good & Kaminski, 2002). A product of the Center on Teaching and Learning at the University of Oregon, DIBELS provides evidence of progress in reading at least three times each year. Although it provides assessments for other skills related to reading, it emphasizes two tool skills that, when mastered, improve performance in other important reading skills and strategies: oral reading fluency and retelling.

Another product of work at the University of Oregon is *www.easyCBM.com*, which provides similarly standards-based measures for mathematics. Both provide data that

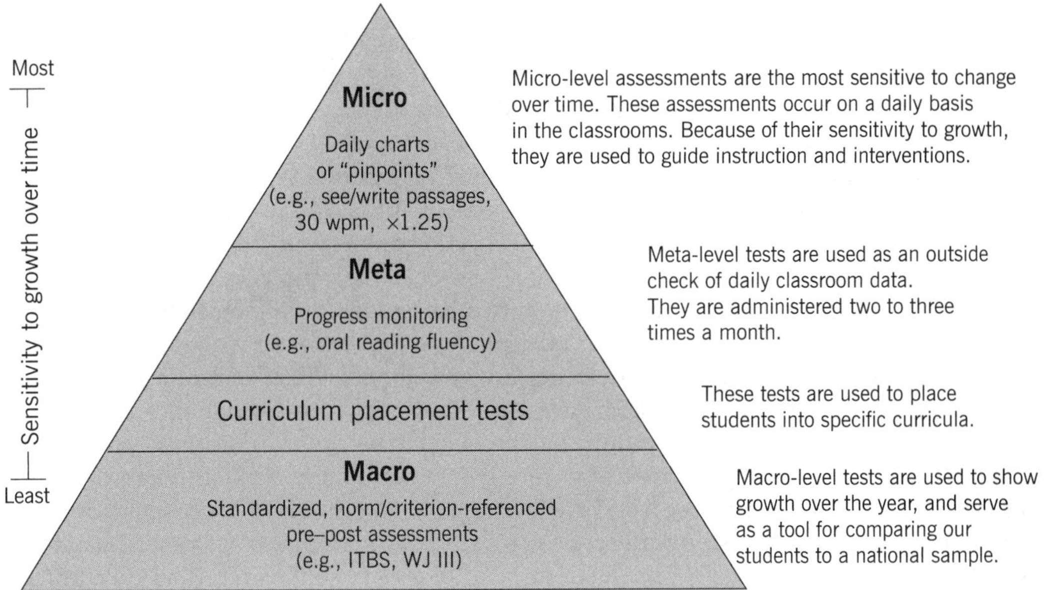

FIGURE 1.3. Morningside Academy's levels-of-assessment triangle.

allow teachers to make midyear instructional corrections to ensure that all students stay on track. These corrections run the gamut from greater focus on a student learning objective in the core curriculum (if many students are not progressing as expected) to specialized or individualized programs (if only one or a few students are struggling).

Another meta-level assessment tool that has proven useful for assessing growth in reading is the Scholastic Reading Inventory (SRI; Scholastic, 2007). The SRI can be administered up to five times each academic year without damaging its validity. Awarded the highest rating for reliability and validity in 2009 by the National Center on Response to Intervention, the SRI receives particularly high marks for predicting performance on high-stakes, end-of-year tests.

Clearly, it is important for districts to select meta-level assessment instruments that are valid (they measure what they say they measure) and reliable (they yield the same or consistent results each time they are administered). In Appendix A of their outstanding CBM resource, *The ABCs of CBM: A Practical Guide to Curriculum-Based Measurement*, Hosp, Hosp, and Howell (2007) provide references for validity and reliability studies for CBM instruments in reading, spelling, writing, and mathematics. AIMSWeb (2006) also describes validity studies of progress-monitoring tools.

Some schools use CBM more frequently than quarterly. Clearly schools need to determine the point at which more frequent monitoring improves overall outcomes to such a degree that it justifies the time and cost of the higher frequency. Hosp et al. (2007) recommend screening or benchmarking all students at least three times per year. However, they suggest that more frequent benchmarking may be justified for students who are at greatest risk for academic failure.

Curriculum-based assessment (CBA) has also gained popularity among publishers who provide measures for periodic monitoring of student progress. As the term indicates, CBA measures are curriculum-based; however, they often lack the independence from specific curricula that characterize CBM instruments, rarely include standardized administration and scoring criteria, have not been normed on specified populations, and frequently don't reliably predict performance on macro-level assessment. Table 1.1 identifies meta-level assessment instruments currently used at Morningside Academy.

Micro-level assessments are typically teacher- or publisher-made assessments that correspond directly to individual curricular lessons. For example, in mathematics, the teacher might assign a page of two-column, two-row addition problems with and without "carrying" at the end of a lesson on the carrying process. Although items included in these practices may correspond to those in the meta-level assessment, they often don't predict performance on these measures because of both format and procedure. For instance, learners are commonly given considerably more time to complete the assignment than would be needed if normative frequency criteria were established or than they will have during meta-level assessment. Furthermore, the items may or may not correspond to formats typically chosen for meta- and macro-level assessments. The teacher would ideally use the results of these measures to determine whether learners require additional support to master the objective, but this doesn't always happen. The teacher both administers and scores the measure, sometimes according to prescribed criteria and sometimes not. In addition, the instruments chosen and the scoring rubric may or may not be linked to end-of-year assessments. Last, teachers may or may not account for explicit or implicit prompts that assist the learner in achieving a correct response. Moors, Weisenburgh-Snyder, and Robbins (2010) describe an elegant systematic application of the three levels of assessment—macro, meta, and micro—in a Precision Teaching (PT) approach to mathematics instruction.

In the remainder of this book, we build a case for the use of PT as the ideal micro-level assessment for students who are not keeping pace with performance expectations.

TABLE 1.1. Meta-Level Assessment Instruments Currently Used at Morningside Academy

Academic area	Instrument
Reading	• Dynamic Indicators of Basic Early Literacy Skills (DIBELS) (*https://dibels.uoregon.edu*) • Scholastic Reading Inventory (SRI) (*http://teacher.scholastic.com/products/sri_reading_assessment/index.htm*) • Qualitative Reading Inventory (*www.sedl.org/cgi-bin/mysql/rad.cgi?searchid=193*)
Writing	• Genre-specific writing samples (samples and rubrics available from *kent@morningsideacademy.org*)
Mathematics	• MBSP Concepts and Application, Computation (*www.proedinc.com/customer/productView.aspx?ID=1431*)

PT is a technology for which Ogden Lindsley (1972, 1990) developed the Standard Celeration Chart to standardize measurement and recommended policies for its use in the late 1960s. We also show how this chart is the ideal graph for charting, monitoring progress, and recording benchmark data, instead of typical equal-interval graph paper. Students and colleagues of Lindsley, as well as thousands of teachers who implemented his policies, have refined its use over the last half century. As we describe in Chapter 2, the chart is especially designed to provide easy-to-read pictures of learning trajectories based on timed assessments of critical tool and component skills. Precision teachers record daily performance rates, typically for 1 minute, on the chart. Experienced teachers use the chart to project trajectories of growth for skills and to intervene daily when learners' performances don't match projected trajectories. In Chapter 5, we describe how learners also develop proficiency in charting their own performances and learn how to intervene to keep learning trajectories on track. PT is a particularly good companion to CBM, which has its own roots in PT technology.

Data-Based Decision Making

Meta- and micro-level analyses are only useful to the degree that they form the basis for decision making about level of support and placement. Data-based decision making serves two purposes. First, it allows for adjustments to the intensity and nature of the intervention, depending on each individual student's responses. Second, it provides confirmation of each student's placement within the tiers. To determine each student's responsiveness to treatment, teachers and school psychologists review data to decide whether the student's progress is on a trajectory that will result in expected annual performance growth. When learners are not keeping pace with grade-level expectations, districts typically choose between two decision-making methods within the RTI framework: the problem-solving method and the standard protocol method.

While acknowledging that the problem-solving method varies among districts and schools, D. Fuchs and Fuchs (2006) suggest that in most of its versions, "practitioners determine the magnitude of the problem, analyze its causes, design a goal-directed intervention, conduct it as planned, monitor student progress, modify the intervention as needed (i.e., based on student responsiveness) and evaluate its effectiveness and plot future actions" (p. 95). Although a single problem-solving episode could be used simultaneously to resolve more than one student's failure to progress, it is more typically an individualized approach. Fuchs and Fuchs (2006) say, "Its popularity among practitioners is no doubt due to its idiopathic nature: For each child, an effort is made to personalize assessment and intervention" (p. 95). They also note that this individualized approach is potentially challenging because it "presupposes considerable expertise among practitioners in assessment and intervention" (p. 95)—expertise that not all practitioners may possess.

The standard treatment protocol method differs from the problem-solving method in that standard treatments are described for various skill deficits. They are individualized not by learner, but by the nature of the presenting problem. The typical course would be that students who are not keeping pace as evidenced by performance during meta-level analyses would be assigned to a fixed-length course of treatment that had been predesigned.

As D. Fuchs and Fuchs (2006) note, the problem-solving method is more popular with practitioners, while the standard protocol method is preferred by researchers. Schools may adopt and follow a standard problem-solving method in all cases, but the outcomes vary, depending on the staff members who are involved, their histories with students, and their preferences. The standard protocol method entails the use of predetermined interventions based on a learner's performance on meta-level assessments; all students with similar scores receive the same intervention.

Schools and districts are encouraged to select one of the two approaches, or perhaps to adopt a combination of the two. For example, the expectations for use of well-established programs and protocols in Tier 2 may favor the standard protocol method for movement between Tiers 1 and 2. However, the nature of the problems presented and the individual nature of the strategies that may be applied may favor the problem-solving method for movement between Tiers 2 and 3.

THE CHALLENGES

Most educators understand the benefits of a preventive approach like the one that underpins RTI. However, effective implementation of the model presents its own challenges, many of which have not yet been resolved. This movement is subject to the same concerns that Kauffman famously raised in his 1989 article about the regular education movement. Kauffman asserted then that "the primary objective should be more effective education; the secondary objective should be to provide that treatment in the least restrictive or most normalized setting. In pursuing both objectives, the achievement and socialization consequences of educational options must take precedence over the immediate consequences of place or location" (p. 274). Furthermore, as Reynolds and Shaywitz (2009) point out, it would be a shame if the challenges of the RTI model result in its being no more effective than the discrepancy model it replaced—as they put it, if a "wait-to-fail" approach is only succeeded by a "watch-them-fail" approach. To ensure that the RTI framework lives up to its potential, three key requirements must be met. First, general education teachers must pursue professional development to prepare them for the increased demands of their positions. Second, mechanisms must be in place to ensure the fidelity of the instructional intervention. Third, metrics and measures must be appropriate and must allow a teacher to affirm what a student has learned and the rate at which that learning has occurred.

Professional Development

RTI adoption places a significant responsibility on school and district administrators to provide professional development opportunities for general education teachers. Teachers in districts that adopt new, evidence-based core curricula will require professional development and coaching to master the idiosyncrasies of the new programs. In addition, most teachers will need assistance to develop facility with Tier 2 and, in some cases, Tier 3 interventions. Because a goal of the RTI model is to maintain a greater number of students in the general education classroom, general education teachers may need to become conversant with programs and procedures that heretofore were reserved for special education classrooms. Learners will also benefit from teachers who have facility with systems of micro-level assessment (e.g., daily measures) that predict performance on meta- and macro-level assessments. Along with increased monitoring of performance, teachers will need to develop facility with day-to-day decision making about student progress.

Professional development comes in many shapes and sizes, and some approaches are more effective than others. The research of the last half century provides convincing evidence that *in vivo* coaching increases the effectiveness of professional development activities (Joyce & Showers, 1980, 1995; Showers, Joyce, & Bennett, 1987). As teachers have opportunities to practice and receive feedback on new teaching and assessment strategies, their likelihood of adopting them and using them with fidelity increases dramatically. The research also confirms that even the best teachers need continuing professional development to prevent "treatment drift" (Cooper, Heron, & Heward, 2007).

Implementation with Fidelity

Choosing the right curriculum or intervention is only half the battle. To achieve desired results and match those that derive from formal and informal research, the curriculum or intervention must be implemented with fidelity. Gresham, MacMillan, Beebe-Frankenberger, and Bocian (2000) define *treatment fidelity* as "the degree to which treatment is implemented as planned or intended" (p. 198). Furthermore, they suggest that the importance of treatment fidelity extends not only to program implementation, but also to screening and progress monitoring and to the decision-making model.

The importance of ensuring treatment fidelity and preventing treatment drift is described in a comprehensive RTI handbook created for the State of Montana Office of Public Instruction (Beebe-Frankenberger, Ferriter-Smith, & Hunsaker, 2008). The authors note that "in order for schools to establish accountability for student outcomes, it is critical to evaluate and document fidelity of implementation" (p. 25). They identify several interchangeable terms related to fidelity of implementation, including *procedural fidelity, procedural integrity, treatment integrity,* and *treatment fidelity.* They define fidelity of implementation as "the accurate and consistent application of an agreed upon procedure" (p. 24) and emphasize the importance of periodic retraining to prevent drifting standards of assessment implementation and scoring.

Power et al. (2005) have identified five dimensions of treatment integrity that need to be assured: adherence, exposure, program differentiation, quality of delivery, and participant responsiveness. The case for treatment fidelity is made in a study by Ysseldyke and Bolt (2007), who compared classrooms that did and did not use technology-enhanced continuous progress monitoring related to math achievement, taking into account the degree of variability in teacher implementation of the program. Results on nationally normed tests of mathematics achievement revealed that "when teachers implemented the continuous progress monitoring system as intended, and when they used the data from the system to manage and differentiate instruction, students gained significantly more than those for whom implementation was limited or nil" (p. 453). However, they add that "failure to take into account intervention integrity would have made it look like continuous progress monitoring did not enhance math results" (p. 453).

VanDerHeyden and Burns (2010) note at least two influences on implementation integrity: antecedent conditions and performance feedback. They describe three types of antecedent conditions: "(a) ensure the intervention is acceptable to the teacher; (b) provide the teacher with a written protocol for implementation; and (c) train the teacher to implement the intervention with the student or students" (pp. 64–65). Even so, they cite research evidence suggesting that "under optimal antecedent conditions, intervention implementation occurs correctly less than 20% of the time" (p. 65). These data support the importance of ongoing professional development and coaching (Joyce & Showers, 1980) to ensure implementation fidelity.

To ensure that practices are being implemented with fidelity, according to VanDerHeyden and Burns (2010), the effects of interventions should be monitored weekly. When performance falls below expectations, a systematic program of performance feedback should be delivered by "a trained, competent, and diplomatic individual who knows how to implement the intervention" (p. 65). Monitoring for implementation integrity can be labor-intensive and may require resources that schools and districts don't have. That's why researchers are attempting to streamline the process. For example, Sanetti and Kratochwill (2009) reviewed the effectiveness of a three-stage process modeled on health psychology research, which suggests that "planning and self-regulation strategies are direct predictors of behavior initiation and maintenance for individuals who intend to engage in a new behavior" (p. 25) for its effectiveness in educational contexts. Specifically, they developed the Treatment Integrity Planning Protocol, a three-stage collaborative process during which teacher and consultant work together to calibrate the implementation for the setting and to develop a treatment integrity self-assessment. The results, which include comparisons to permanent products (e.g., charted data or student assessments), are promising. Schools and districts might also create a hedge against imperfect treatment integrity by selecting practices and programs that are very robust—in other words, somewhat forgiving of small failures in implementation.

To establish the level of oversight needed to ensure treatment integrity, and to determine areas in which teachers and other staff may require professional development, it is incumbent on schools and districts to identify who among the staff will serve as the instructional leader. Depending on knowledge and skills related to the content area(s) and his or her personal characteristics, the instructional leader may be the school psychologist, the principal, or a master teacher. The critical recommendation here is that someone be identified to watch over these important matters.

Appropriate Metrics and Measures

Another critical key to success for RTI programs is the use of appropriate metrics and measures. This includes selecting time-efficient measures for screening that produce acceptable levels of false-positive and false-negative errors. Ideally, screening instruments will identify those students who are at risk for failure in Tier 1 without also identifying those who are likely to thrive in Tier 1 (false positives) or failing to identify those who will need support (false negatives). Given that screening instruments must also allow for speedy assessment, this is a tall order.

It is also important that those using the RTI framework select instruments to use for meta-level analyses that accurately predict performance on macro-level assessments.

That is, districts are advantaged when they have an early warning system for identifying learners whose progress falls below the trajectory needed to meet annual goals. Such a system allows for early intervention to improve the prognosis.

A third feature critical to the success of the RTI framework is a district's or classroom teacher's ability to identify key tool or component skills that, when mastered, predict mastery of the important composite skills in a field of study. Such knowledge allows teachers to focus effort on building mastery on these key indicators, rather than spending time on activities that don't have a good track record.

SUMMARY

The RTI framework holds great promise for ensuring that all learners receive the type and level of intervention they require to meet academic and social goals. To be implemented successfully, it requires well-trained and supportive instructional leaders, general education teachers who are willing to expand their roles, evidence-based instructional practices, thoroughgoing assessment practices, and a highly trained placement team. Furthermore, its effectiveness can be substantially enhanced by the addition of more frequent progress monitoring than is typically recommended in the framework.

In the remainder of this book, we describe PT, a technology that has nearly a half-century of evidence of effectiveness in improving student learning through frequent progress monitoring. Ysseldyke et al. (2010) note that

> other forms of data are collected more frequently (e.g., moment-by-moment, daily, once or twice each week) and are used to assess specific skills rather than general outcomes, a process typically referred to as *progress monitoring*. Although most or all children require annual and periodic data, continuous data are usually only collected for students whose needs warrant them. However, preliminary research found that data derived from continuous monitoring of students' daily performance was highly predictive of their performance on annual high-stakes state tests (Ysseldyke, 2006), suggesting that continuous assessment of all students can be useful. (p. 57)

PT provides a parsimonious approach to the kind of frequent progress monitoring that Ysseldyke and his colleagues recommend.

CHAPTER 2

Concepts and Principles of Precision Teaching

Precision Teaching was the name that its founder, Ogden Lindsley, a psychologist and professor of educational administration at the University of Kansas, gave to a measurement system he designed for teachers to track the learning and performance of their students. He envisioned that teachers using his measurement system, which includes methods for observing and graphing performance, would be much more precise in their work—hence the name *Precision Teaching*. The pure, general case of PT specifies five steps (Johnson, 2008b; Johnson & Street, 2004; Lindsley, 1990). First, the teacher defines a learning objective, or *pinpoint*, of what the learner is to accomplish. Second, the teacher arranges materials and procedures for learning and practicing the pinpoint. Third, the teacher and the learner time the student's performance and count its frequency. Typically 1–5 minutes in length, *timings* may be as short as 10 seconds or as long as 15 minutes or more. Fourth, the learner and the teacher chart the learner's performance on the most common version of the Standard Celeration Chart, the Daily per minute Chart.[1] Fifth, the teacher and learner review performance trends on the chart and make decisions about possible interventions to improve performance. The PT motto is *Pinpoint, time, record and chart, decide, and—as needed—try, try again* (Lindsley, 1972, 1990). Figure 2.1 illustrates a portion of a Standard Celeration Chart with performance data.

The beauty of the general PT case is that it can incorporate a variety of instructional methods while maintaining its integrity. Teachers can try different teaching procedures and interventions; as long as they measure and chart student performance, they can know whether their teaching approach is working or needs to be revised. Lindsley

[1]Lindsley eventually created a family of charts (see *www.behaviorresearchcompany.com*), each appropriate to a specific application: Daily per minute, Daily per day, Weekly per week, Median count per minute per week, Monthly per month, Median count per minute per month, Yearly per year, and the Timings Chart. In this book we discuss only the Daily per minute Chart and the Timings Chart.

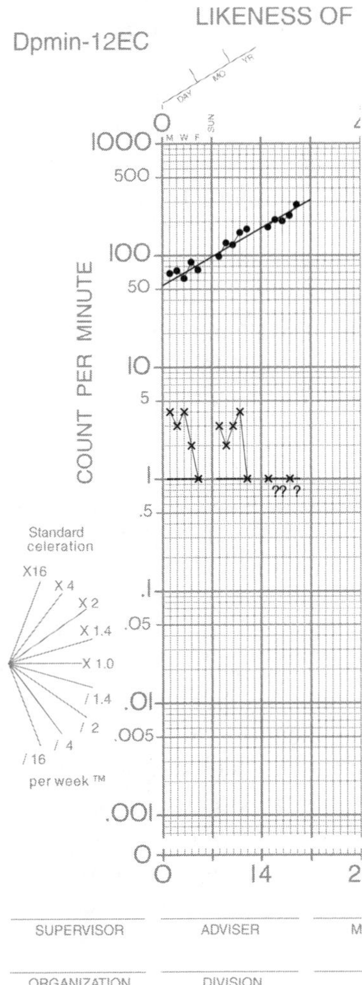

FIGURE 2.1. Likeness of a portion of a Daily per minute Standard Celeration Chart with corrects and errors plotted. Used with permission of the Behavior Research Company.

envisioned a teacher-as-scientist approach to teaching, which he thought would revolutionize the teaching profession.

COMPONENT TEACHING TO MASTERY

The focus of PT is upon building the *frequency* or *rate* of performance[2] of component skills and concepts to mastery. Although more complex behaviors can be measured and charted, component skills and concepts most easily illustrate the general case of PT. As we describe in Chapter 3, complex performances can be broken into component skills, each of which can be taught and practiced until the learner achieves mastery. A complex repertoire such as engaging in book club discussions can be broken into component

[2]In the PT tradition, we use the terms *frequency* and *rate* interchangeably to mean "number over time."

skills such as maintaining a certain reading rate, saying opinions, writing critiques, and taking turns. Likewise, applying math skills to carpeting a room can be similarly analyzed into components such as measuring feet and inches, determining the area, and selecting carpet within a budget. The charted performance data can be quickly analyzed, and new teaching and practice interventions can be tried until a learner successfully meets the criteria specified in a state standard or an instructional objective.[3] The explicit focus in PT is upon discrete component *performance*.

In reading, typical component skills and concepts include sounds of letters and word parts; pronunciation of words (decoding); meanings of words and phrases (vocabulary); rhythm and cadence (prosody) of reading text; meaning of comprehension concepts (e.g., author's purpose, main idea, drawing conclusions, making predictions); and application of specific comprehension skills and strategies during reading. In writing and language arts, typical components include writing and typing words legibly; spelling words correctly; using adjectives for nouns in sentences; using punctuation in sentences; sequencing sentences in paragraphs; and writing paragraphs in various genres (e.g., fiction, sensory descriptions, spatial descriptions, persuasion, summarizing, comparing and contrasting). In mathematics, typical components include writing legible numbers; saying math facts; reading numbers; identifying a digit's place value; applying computation algorithms (e.g., column addition with carrying, regrouping during subtraction, adding fractions with unlike denominators); solving standard word problems with algebraic equations; converting among fractions, decimals, and percents; and factoring numbers. In teaching content areas, typical components for any content course include describing and locating parts of a textbook; pronouncing terms; defining terms and principles; writing questions based upon headings and captions; answering questions (e.g., factual, conceptual, and procedural questions); and describing knowledge in short-answer essays. In social studies, examples might include locating places on a map; saying the countries that make up a continent; and discriminating between socialism and communism. In science, saying the elements in the periodic chart and describing the steps in the scientific method might serve as examples.

Precise analysis of academic content areas is critical to determining the components to be selected for instruction and practice and the sequence for combining them until complex performance is achieved. Chapter 3 is entirely devoted to content analysis and other aspects of instructional design for PT. Later chapters on PT in reading (Chapter 6), writing (Chapter 7), and math (Chapter 8) define the components in those areas.

By focusing on component skills, precision teachers have discovered an important mantra: *The problem that a learner presents is not necessarily the problem to solve.* For example, a learner who is having trouble in algebra may not need instruction intensified at the level of algebra algorithms, but may need instruction and practice in prerequisite components such as multiplication and division, or even math facts. A learner's problems in comprehension may not need interventions for comprehension skills; rather, the learner may need more instruction and practice in decoding multisyllabic words. This nonlinear, systemic perspective is also important in the practice of medicine. For

[3]The Standard Celeration Chart can also be used outside a PT context—for example, to graph complex performance in order to examine trends in social phenomena (e.g., oil consumption in a country or population trends), and to record aspects of self-management projects (e.g., number of cigarettes smoked or steps walked during exercise).

example, a patient may have a rash on his or her wrist. Although a linear solution (i.e., addressing the presenting problem) such as cortisone cream may be helpful in attenuating the itch and redness of the rash, the patient's rash may be a symptom of liver damage, and the problem to be solved may involve systemic treatment directed at that organ. We return to this perspective frequently in this book.

THE FLUENCY CONCEPT

One primary assumption behind PT is that true mastery of a performance includes not only its quality or accuracy, but also its pace (Eric Haughton, 1971). *Fluency* is the PT concept for performance that is flowing, flexible, effortless, errorless, automatic, confident, second nature, and masterful. An individual who is fluent in a performance is said to be able to perform it "with his hands tied behind his back" or "with her eyes shut." Individuals who can perform fluently know what it must feel like to be an Olympic athlete. All other things being equal, fluent performances are more likely to occur in the future than nonfluent behaviors. As behaviors become fluent, they take on new dimensions. They are fun, energetic and energizing, and naturally reinforcing. Fluent behaviors are also streamlined, not requiring self-prompts such as mnemonics, thoughtful pauses, or other memory strategies or devices. Most people understand the everyday usage of the term *fluency*, but many don't know how to achieve it, and some don't think it's teachable. However, behavioral and cognitive psychologists alike have disputed that position, providing a great deal of evidence that expert performance is the result of deliberate (Ericsson, 1996, 2006) and well-designed (Binder, 1996) practice. PT is a thoroughgoing approach to practice with nearly half a century of data to support it.

The primary indicator of fluency for precision teachers is performance frequency. They set *criterion rates* or *frequency aims* for component skills. These are rates that predict fluency, which includes skill and concept maintenance, successful application of those skills and concepts, and the ability to combine them to solve novel problems. Of course, fluency is not synonymous with building high frequencies. Many other characteristics of instruction and practice promote fluency, such as the breadth and variety of the practice materials, chunk size of the curriculum, and the opportunity for both massed and distributed practice. These are also essential to building a fluent repertoire. For precision teachers, building frequency is the key aspect of building fluency.

FREQUENCY AS FUNDAMENTAL

Many people associate PT with speed of performance because of its focus on building rate or frequency. A look at the history of behavioral psychology may clarify why behavioral frequency has come to serve as a proxy for fluency in PT. Ogden Lindsley (1972, 1990), who created the Standard Celeration Chart to measure performance rates, was a student of B. F. Skinner, the most famous behaviorist of the 20th century. Skinner adopted rate as the primary datum for his laboratory work in determining basic principles of behavior because of its sensitivity to changes in performance and slight modifications in interventions, and the continuous, orderly data that it produces (Ferster & Skinner, 1957; Skinner, 1938, 1953).

Perhaps the most important feature of frequency for pragmatists and behaviorists alike is that it can very accurately represent the probability of future action (Ferster, Culbertson, & Boren, 1975; Ryle, 1949; Skinner, 1953). In everyday talk, terms such as *habit, disposition, tendency,* and *personality* are used to attempt to predict what someone will do, based upon the frequency with which they have behaved that way in the past. For example, a person who "has a habit" of whistling tunes does so regularly and will probably do so in the future. Someone who "has a high disposition" or "tendency" to speak out about politics will do so when occasions arise, such as the presence of listeners who speak about politics. Someone who "has an addictive personality" engages in behaviors that may be detrimental at high frequencies, such as taking drugs or gambling. Thus building high frequencies of performance may make them more likely to occur in the future! All teachers hope that what they teach will have a long-lasting effect on their learners, and that learners will engage in those performances throughout their lives. By building frequency, teachers can be more confident that they will achieve these desired effects.

Frequency is not only an important dimension of behavior to measure; it is also a fundamental property or dimension of behavior itself (Lindsley, 1991). Behaviors occurring at higher rates are functionally different from those occurring at lower rates. High-rate behaviors look different to a casual observer, feel different to the behaver, and have a different impact on the environment. As we have mentioned in our discussion of fluency, high-frequency behavior is streamlined, not requiring self-prompts such as mnemonics, thoughtful pauses, or other strategic memory strategies or devices.

The predominant measure of performance in classrooms today is *percent correct.* Precision teachers resist the temptation to describe performance in terms of percents. Percent only spuriously predicts future probability of performance and is very insensitive to individual differences in performance. Barrett (1979) provocatively illustrated the wide range of frequencies possible at the same percentage. Three groups of people—developmentally delayed state school learners ages 12–54, public school learners ages 5–7, and typical adults—achieved 100% correct performance on a variety of tasks such as hammering pegs into pegboards, copying the numerals 0–9, naming numerals, and counting tiles into a can. Figure 2.2 shows that the average frequencies of performance for each task varied widely across the three groups. However, as Figure 2.3 indicates, when we graph the average percent correct of each group, performance across the three groups looks identical! Regardless of the data, our intuitions tell us that the performance of these three groups cannot possibly be identical.[4]

DEFINING FLUENCY WITH PRECISION

In the early days of PT, teachers devised three norm-referenced ways to set frequency goals for their students. Some calculated the average frequency that students had achieved in the past. For example, some measured the frequency with which typical third graders could see/say math facts, and used that frequency as the criterion for fluency in math facts. If typical third graders could answer math facts at a rate of about

[4]The same criticism of percent measures applies to several recording methods in applied behavior analysis, such as interval recording and time sampling.

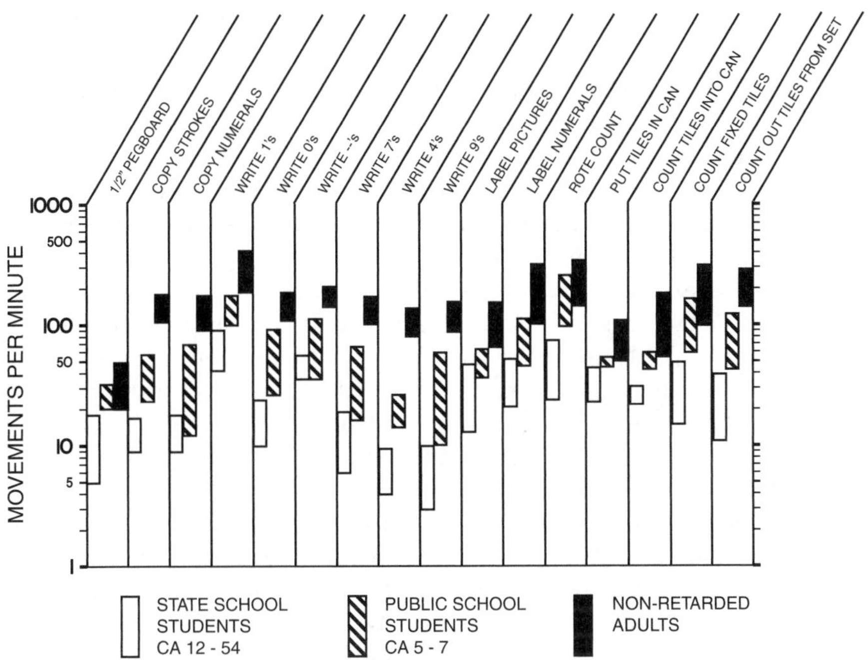

FIGURE 2.2. Comparison of performance frequencies across three groups from an unpublished pilot study conducted by Frances George and Deborah Pease, published in Barrett (1979). This replication of the original, created by Scott Born, is reproduced with permission of The Association for the Severely Handicapped.

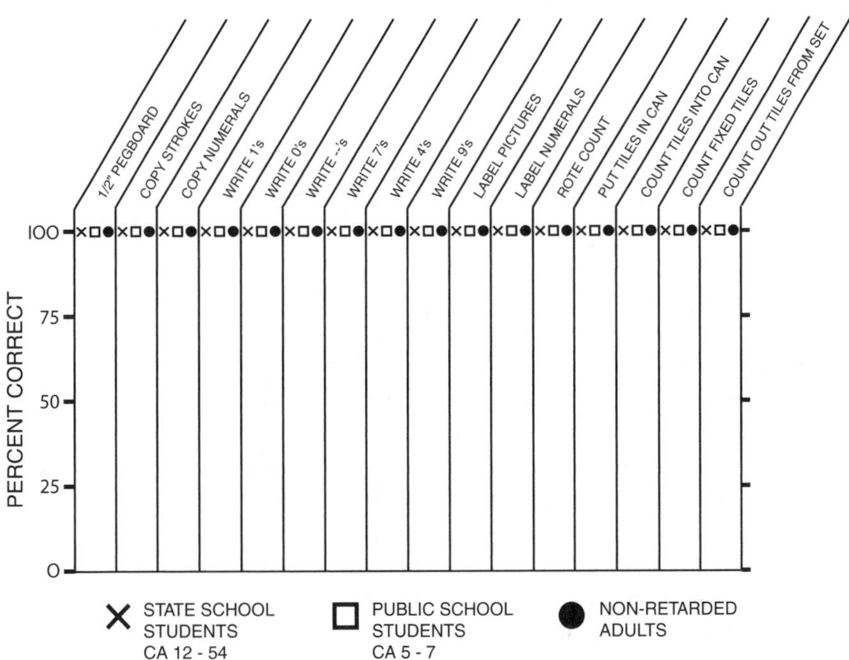

FIGURE 2.3. Comparison of performance accuracies across three groups from an unpublished pilot study conducted by Frances George and Deborah Pease. This figure is a reproduction by Scott Born of the original, created by Carl Binder, who has granted permission for its use.

30 per minute, a third-grade teacher used that fluency criterion. Other teachers measured the top 10% of math students in a grade and used those rates as fluency aims. For example, if the top 10% of third graders answered math facts at 50 correct per minute, a third-grade teacher would use that criterion. Still other teachers measured math facts experts, such as middle school math teachers or even bank tellers, and used their average frequency as a fluency aim.

The problem with these norm-referenced approaches is that they do not guarantee important learning outcomes of practice. Practice for practice's sake harkens back to the traditional "drill-and-kill" sessions that teachers would routinely include in their lesson plans; in fact, practice has all but disappeared in education today, due to its tedium and misapplication. Over time, when precision teachers became convinced that frequency served as a proxy for fluency, they began to define fluency more precisely. Eric Haughton (1972, 1980) first proposed setting frequency aims that predicted *retention* and ease of *application* of the objective being practiced. He used an acronym to express his goals: RA/PS, for Retention and Application Performance Standards. Although he initially described RA/PS as a challenge for teachers, his proposal attracted a lot of empirical interest in discovering just what these frequencies were. People began measuring retention effects: If learners did not practice for a significant period of time (say, a month or a summer), would they still be able to engage in the performance at the same frequencies, without errors? A few years later, Carl Binder (1993, 1996) added another learning outcome to the acronym—*endurance*. His doctoral dissertation showed that students who performed at low frequencies per minute were not able to maintain their performance over an increasingly longer period of time (up to 15 minutes). However, students who could perform the objective at high frequencies were able to maintain their rates. Specifically, the faster that students could write legible numbers, the longer they were able to write them without fatigue. The acronym was expanded to REA/PS, for Retention, Endurance, and Application Performance Standards. Others began expanding the acronym further. Johnson and Layng (1992, 1994, 1996) added *stability* of performance: Students should be able to perform the objective in the face of distraction, without needing an environment in which you could hear a pin drop—a noble, real-world goal. The acronym was now RESA/PS: Retention, Endurance, Stability, and Application Performance Standards.

Johnson and Layng (1992, 1994, 1996) also added *adduction* to the acronym: Students should practice until novel performances emerge, as needed, to engage in objectives not directly taught. For example, learners should not need to be taught how to solve fraction word problems if they have learned whole-number word problem skills and fraction computation skills. If components are well taught and automatic, students can adduce many new skills without instruction! Now precision teachers were accounting for adduction in their list of learning outcomes—new performances characterized as figuring out, insight, and problem solving. The acronym was now RESAA/PS.

At Morningside, we have recently modified the acronym in two more ways. First, in order to determine empirically whether a student's performance meets the learning outcome of retention, we must deliberately prevent a performance from occurring. Usually this is clinically undesirable. For example, when we are teaching subject matter such as mathematics, in order to determine that a student is retaining math facts, we would have to prevent him or her from performing math facts for a month or more—not realistic when we are teaching computation skills! So, instead of anchoring our frequency aims to the laboratory research concept of retention, we use the term *maintenance*. It is far more relevant in the real world that skills be maintained in an academic environment and used as they are needed, than that they show retention after a specified period of no practice. Second, there is some confusion over the second A (adduction) in the RESAA/PS acronym, so we've replaced it with the more easily understood concept *generativity*. Our acronym is now MESAG/PS: Maintenance, Endurance, Stability, Application, and Generativity Performance Standards. An easy mnemonic for remembering these five attributes of fluency is "Get the MESsAGe" (Johnson & Street, 2012).

Let's look at each of these learning outcomes in greater detail.

- *Maintenance* refers to the learner's ability to perform a task in the future, on demand, without additional practice. Everyday and oft-cited examples include the ability to sit down at a piano and play a song that a person hasn't played for years, or the ability to ride a bike after many years of not practicing. Similarly, schools expect that, once acquired, accuracy with math facts is unaffected by the passage of time. Even so, many students who can recite math facts correctly do not maintain the skill in the face of extended periods of time without practice (e.g., over summer break). When performance is fluent, however, skills are maintained across natural breaks without practice, or occur within seconds after engaging in the performance.

- *Endurance* refers to the ability to meet real-world requirements for how long the behavior should be performed. Many everyday examples of endurance come from physical activities; for example, people often need to be able to type words at some designated rate for a designated period of time. If their endurance is limited to 1-minute or even 5-minute timings, they are unlikely to be able to keep pace with job expectations. The same is true with academic tasks. A learner is expected to maintain accuracy and rate of responding on an academic task such as reading a chapter in a textbook for as long as the task typically requires.

- *Stability* refers to the ability to continue to perform a skill amidst distractions. Many of us are impressed when a pianist continues to play a song even while talking to a friend who drops by. That is, the pianist's accuracy and rate of performance are largely unaffected by distraction. Similarly, we're quite impressed by a bank teller who can correctly input all of the information to complete a transaction while carrying on a casual conversation with a customer. Many academic tasks require this kind of stability or unflappability in the face of distraction.

- *Application* refers to the ability to use a skill in a real-world context that requires it—a context that is different from the typical classroom task. When we learn how to separate a series of adjectives with commas in a language arts class exercise, and when we become fluent at it, whenever we write we will separate a series of adjectives with commas, no matter which adjectives or nouns they modify. When we learn how to sound out words in a first-grade reading class, we do it whenever we read, regardless of whether we're reading the newspaper, magazines, comic books, or e-mail. And so on.

- *Generativity* is the emergence of complex behavioral repertoires without explicit instruction (Johnson & Street, 2004). The term *contingency adduction*, coined by Andronis, Layng, and Goldiamond (1997), describes the same phenomenon in a research laboratory context. In their account, contingency adduction is a process in which new performance requirements recruit behaviors learned in other situations. Generativity and contingency adduction go beyond simple application of the same performance to a new example, and instead describe situations in which the learner figures out a new performance in response to a very different situation by blending and combining already learned performances, without prior training. Johnson and Layng (1992) report one example: Students who had mastered whole-number word problem solving and computation of fractions were able to solve word problems involving fractions without additional instruction. Generativity involves figuring things out, creativity, and learning through discovery. Generativity allows teachers to move more quickly through a curriculum by simply assessing for the emergence of new, untrained skills as part of the instructional process.

In sum, the goals of practice and fluency building can be defined as follows:

- Easily executed whenever necessary (Maintenance).
- Executed for as long as necessary (Endurance).
- Not easily disrupted or distracted (Stability).
- Easily applied in new situations (Application).
- Easily combined with other performances as necessary to solve novel problems or create something new (Generativity).

Table 2.1 illustrates frequency aims that have been empirically tested and shown to pass the MESsAGe test.

Though they didn't appeal to the functioning of the brain, neither Skinner nor Lindsley would have been surprised to learn that cognitive psychologists and neuroscientists have come to similar conclusions about fluency and offer evidence that the brain "behaves" differently as increased practice gives rise to the hallmarks of fluency—for example, the ability to respond in the face of distraction (Poldrack et al., 2005).

Virtually all educators agree that practice is the key to achieving these important characteristics of fluency, although practice procedures, what is chosen for practice, and

TABLE 2.1. Examples of Frequency Aims Employed at Morningside Academy That Pass the MESsAGe Test

Skill	Correct	Errors
Math facts	80–100/minute	0
Word problems with whole numbers	12–15 in 15 minutes	0
Computation of fractions	80–100 steps in 5 minutes	0
Oral reading	250–300 words/minute	0–2
Finding main idea in passage (75 words)	8–10 main ideas in 10 minutes	0
Sentence combining	20–25 words in 3 minutes	0

the terminal goals for practice vary. PT has developed a systematic and standardized approach to practice that (1) assists teachers in calibrating practice materials; (2) identifies practice strategies that result in greater practice opportunities per unit of time; (3) establishes standards for behavioral frequencies (rates); and (4) recommends not only desired behavioral rates, but also desired growth trajectories.

STANDARD CELERATION CHARTING

After several years of observing teachers explaining how to read their individually designed graphs of learner performance frequency during data-sharing sessions in his seminars at the University of Kansas, Lindsley (1972, 1990) decided to design a universal, standardized chart to make communication of results simpler and clearer. The outcome of these efforts, the *Standard Celeration Chart* (Daily per minute Chart), is presented in Figure 2.4. Let's examine it closely. Because the chart is standardized, one can easily compare charts to observe differences in the learning of various skills and

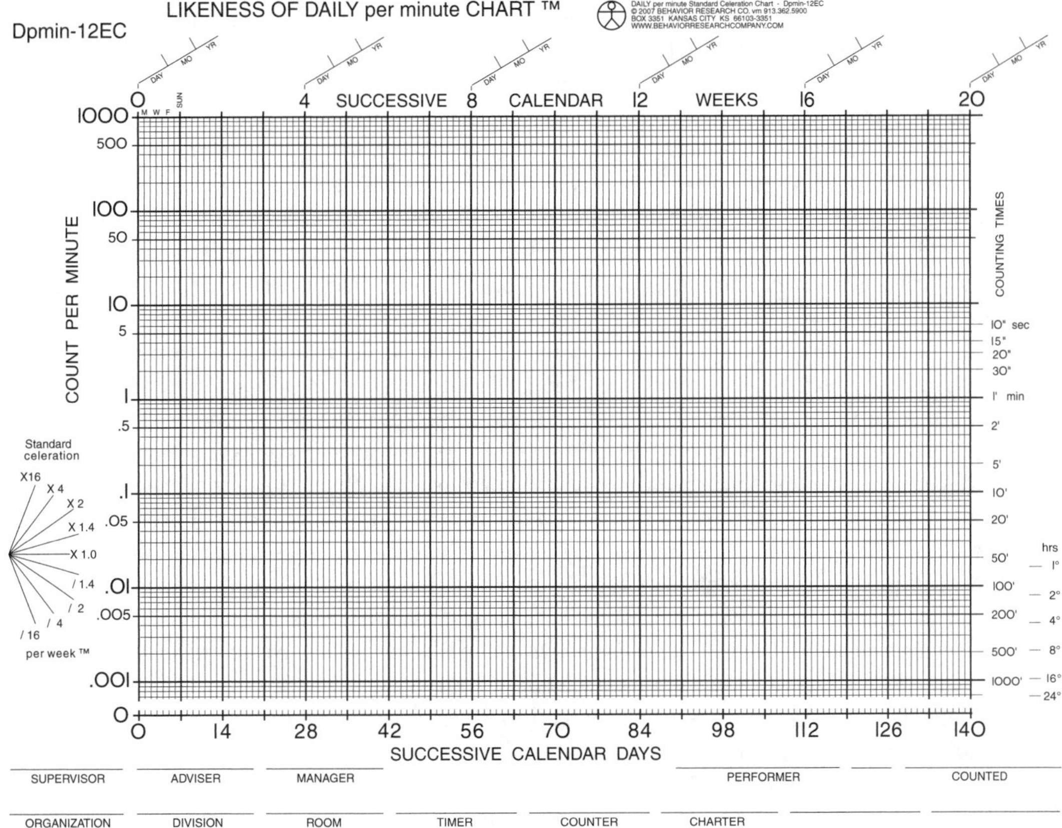

FIGURE 2.4. Likeness of a Daily per minute Standard Celeration Chart. Used with permission of the Behavior Research Company.

concepts, to determine how learning one skill can influence learning other skills, and to compare the relative effectiveness of different programs. The chart Lindsley designed is also *calendar-based,* showing the effects of performance across days when a program is in place and days when it is not (such as weekends and vacations). The chart also focuses on learning, growth, change, and progress over time, not performance on a given day. *Learning,* as expressed by change in frequency over time, becomes the criterion by which we maintain what we are doing or change to something more effective.

Many different graphic designs could incorporate these four features of Lindsley's chart: (1) standardized, for easy communication, and chart and program comparison; (2) calendar-based, not session-based, to show the effects on performance of programs when they are in place and when they are not; (3) focused upon frequency, not percent correct; and (4) focused on learning, not performance. What sets the Standard Celeration Chart apart from other possible instruments—what makes it uniquely the chart of choice—is its *logarithmic* or *ratio* scale up the left side.

Most graphs show growth in equal intervals. When a learner's frequency grows from 5 per minute to 10 per minute, we simply move up 5 equally distant lines on the graph, from 5 to 10. When a learner's frequency grows from 25 per minute to 30 per minute, we also move up five equally distant lines, from 25 to 30. When a learner's frequency grows from 105 to 110 per minute, we also move up the same distance: 5 equally distant lines, from 105 to 110. Expressing growth in this way—how much is added or subtracted to a rate—is called *absolute change* (White & Haring, 1980).

After charting the performance of thousands of individuals across time, Lindsley noticed that changes in their frequencies, or how their rates "grew," were not absolute but relative. Charting progress in terms of how much is added or subtracted to rate (i.e., absolute change) did not produce the smooth, linear, or consistent curves that we see when we chart that same growth as *relative* change in count over time. The growth that learners make is proportional to their previous growth. Proportional growth is much more representative of the way people really learn.

It makes behavioral sense that a learner's history of learning should be taken into an account of progress. Learners are changed as they study a subject, and they bring their cumulative histories to the learning table each time they study the next part. The assertion that progress is proportional to previous progress is also consistent with teachers' casual observations about children's performance, such as "Lesley seemed to have trouble getting started, but once she began to grow, she really took off!" Parents concur as well. Mothers and fathers are usually elated when their babies take their first steps. They applaud each additional step a baby makes, from steps 1 to 2 to 3. However, when the baby advances from step 99 to step 100, the additional step is often not even noticed and is rarely praised; in fact, the parents are more likely to ask the baby to sit down! It is often easier to learn once learners gain basic skill in a task, and a measurement system that reflects this is much more likely to lead to good decisions about whether a program is working or not working.

Relative change or growth is represented on a chart with a *ratio scale,* not a chart with equal intervals. The Standard Celeration Chart is sometimes referred to as a *multiply–divide chart,* and the "absolute scale" charts that are frequently used in educational circles are referred to as *add–subtract charts.* Ratio or logarithmic scales are very commonly used in most areas of science. Apparently almost all things in nature change proportionally (White & Haring, 1980).

Decision Making with Ratios and Intervals

In fact, looking at progress in terms of absolute changes in frequencies leads to poor decisions about whether interventions are having their desired effects. Specifically, charts of absolute frequencies usually underestimate the power of an intervention when performance is occurring at low frequencies, and overestimate the power of a program when performance is occurring at higher frequencies.

For example, look at Figure 2.5. The equal-interval chart on the left shows progress as absolute changes in frequencies. The ratio chart on the right shows relative progress—progress based upon and *proportional* to previous progress. In the absolute chart on the left, progress at low frequencies looks as if it is at a near standstill. Industrious teachers are likely to change their procedures to produce more progress. However, when the same data are plotted on the relative chart on the right, we see that the program is working; progress is just fine, given the early stage of learning.

Likewise, in the absolute chart on the left, progress at high frequencies looks as if it is soaring. No change in procedures seems to be necessary. However, that analysis is flawed because progress is represented in equal intervals. When the same data are plotted on the relative chart on the right, we see that progress is slowing way down, and that it may be time to change the program.

Notice also that the data in the absolute graph on the left reflect very inconsistent growth. However, when the data are recharted on the relative chart on the right, performance looks quite consistent. And imagine these data to represent a child's progress in mathematics, your choice of stock investment based upon the growth rate of the company's earnings, or whatever will drive home the point that poor decisions to keep doing or change what you are doing can be costly!

It turns out that a chart with a ratio scale up the left has another advantage: A much wider variety of behaviors with a much wider variety of frequencies can fit on the same

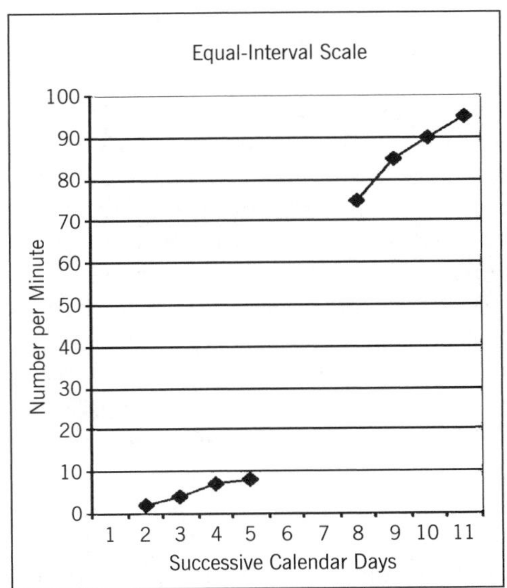

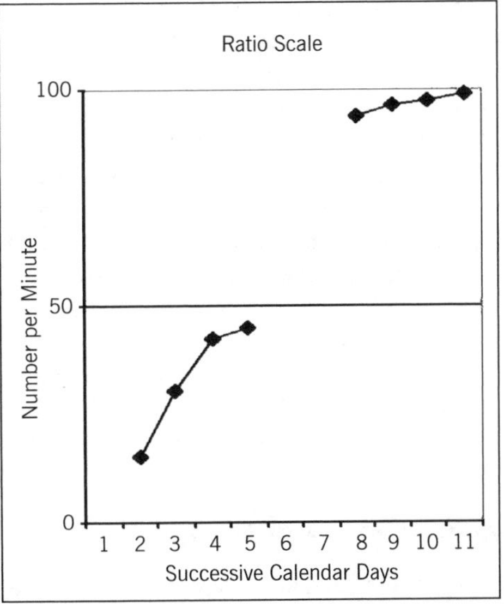

FIGURE 2.5. Comparison on data plotted on an equal-interval graph and a ratio chart.

chart! We can compare a learner's rate of classroom talk-outs, which may occur once every 5–10 minutes, to the learner's rate of math facts answers, which may occur 80–100 times per minute, on the same chart. With an equal-interval scale, you'd probably need three or four of pieces of equal-interval graph paper taped together to compare the growth of both performances on the same graph. Speaking rate often occurs at 250 words per minute. White and Haring (1980) observed that to examine talk-outs and speaking rates on the same chart would take several thousand sheets of equal-interval graph paper!

Fortunately, Lindsley developed the Standard Celeration Chart to reflect these facts about learning. Reexamine Figure 2.4. The chart uses a vertical ratio scale that repeats in six cycles of ten units. Changes in frequency of performance on the chart are multiplicative, not additive. The distance between 1 and 10 is the same as the distance between 10 and 100, reflecting the fact that it is as easy to accelerate from 1 to 10 responses per minute as it is to accelerate from 10 to 100. This ratio property of the Standard Celeration Chart accurately represents rate of change as proportional to previous change. Lindsley targeted a doubling of growth as desirable, and made it easy to spot by scaling the dimensions of the chart to show that doubling—which precision teachers abbreviate as a "×2," or "times 2," rate of change—starting at any frequency on the chart would be parallel to a diagonal line drawn across the chart from the bottom left to the upper right corners.

The PT community was an outgrowth of those who used Ogden Lindsley's Standard Celeration Chart to record performance frequency. Precision teachers tend to be teacher-scientists, who plot learners' frequency data on the chart to discover procedures and materials that produce the greatest improvements for each individual learner. They do not collect data only for record-keeping purposes, although the data certainly serve that purpose as well. Instead, they have learned how to use data for self-correction. They are very creative and inventive about their practices, letting the data guide their teaching. Precision teachers are risk takers who "try, try again" when the learner isn't learning. The sensitivity of frequency, combined with some powerful features of Lindsley's chart, has produced an impressive database.

Johnson and Layng (1992) say that the Standard Celeration Chart has a

> logarithmic, count-per-minute scale "up the left" (y-axis) [that] enables students to measure and chart data on frequencies of correct responses as well as on frequencies of errors. Each data point is equivalent to the average of 1 minute of responses in a cumulative record slope (Ferster & Skinner, 1957; Skinner, 1938). Accordingly, as data points increase in value over time, they indicate increasing rates of change. Because growth is proportionate to previous growth, the chart's ratio scale produces straight accelerating lines if the student's rate of change is being maintained. Curves indicate faster or slower rates of change. Because rate of change, not absolute frequency, is used as the critical property of progress, the chart makes it easy for students and teachers to make quick, daily, timely decisions about whether a student is progressing to fluency.... [Students] quickly learn how to improve their performance through daily practice, self-monitoring, decision-making, and self-correction. (p. 1478)

The Mechanics of Charting

To provide a bird's-eye view of what it takes to become a fluent charter, Figure 2.6 features a Morningside Academy "placemat," which Morningside coaches use during

Morningside Academy
Teacher Coaching Form
Fluency Building

Level 3

Name ____________ Date ____________
School ____________
Task/Name of Tool ________ Lesson #______ # of Students ______
Observer ____________
Duration of Observation ____________

Rating Scale

4 = All the time (95–100%)	2 = Some of the time (40–74%)	0 = Never (0%)
3 = Most of the time (75–94%)	1 = Rarely (≥ 39%)	DK = Don't Know

Teacher Behavior

Yes/No Assigned practice pairs/trios have similar repertoires
Yes/No Assigned practice pairs/trios have dissimilar repertoires (stronger with weaker)

Teacher clearly states:
__ Rules/directions for practicing
__ Points for reaching aim, and other consequences (time until students are practicing: ________)

__ Practice pairs/trios sit in optimal seating arrangements
__ Each practice session dated and labeled by lesson
__ Students draws an aim box on the last practice line
__ Each student plots her first timing on the first practice line
__ Students draw line from the first timing to the aim box
__ First student performer completes successive timings until reaching the fluency aim
__ Each timing begins in a new place
__ Students do not alternate practices
__ Coaches use a follow-along sheet to track the performer's corrects and errors on say outputs
__ Immediately after performer completes each timing, student coach(es) count(s) data and plot the frequency
__ After reaching fluency aim, performer asks teacher for final verification timing
__ Final given within 2 minutes
__ Teacher and coach(es) provide final timing for verification that student reached the fluency aim
__ Teacher verifies correct and error frequencies with coach(es)
__ Student performer plots the final timing on the daily final chart
__ Teacher delivers points and other consequences as stated or understood at the beginning of the practice period
__ Students in practice pairs switch roles of performer and coach

Ongoing Fluency Building
__ Students determine aim by identifying the frequency that keeps them on the minimum celeration line of their daily final chart (blue chart)
__ Aim box accurately reflects daily aim

Teacher Performance
__ Teacher transition time between student pairs is as short as possible
__ Teacher enforces the "no waiting" rule
__ Teacher's tone of voice is conversational, variant, enthusiastic, and positive
__ Teacher provides praise several times per minute (see counts)
__ Teacher minimizes use of reminders for working (see counts)
__ Teacher's materials are well organized
__ Teacher provides more assistance for lower-performing practice pairs and equal opportunities for other pairs

Interventions
__ Practice pairs/trios ask for an intervention when 2 consecutive timings fall below the celeration line
__ Teacher selects appropriate intervention procedures
__ Teacher instructs students in intervention procedures, and explains why intervention was selected
__ Intervention took less than 3 minutes
__ Student moves to next Sunday line and draws new floor and aim box when endurance intervention made
__ Teacher returns within 3 minutes to determine success of intervention
__ Students in practice pairs/trios provide intervention for each other when needed
__ When intervention procedures go beyond tips and quips, teacher removes student from peer practice and provides additional direct instruction or sprinting on the skill

Student Performance During
__ Students' practice is paced, not rushed; breathing evenly
__ Students always practice with a timer
__ Students' materials are well organized
__ Students practice continuously

	1	2	3	4	5	6	7	8	9	10	Aim
Praise ↑											>4/ min
Reminders											0
Finals ↓											
Interventions											

Final Comments
Super performance!

Still to work on

FIGURE 2.6. Morningside Academy "placemat"—Teacher Coaching Form, Fluency Building. Used with permission of Kent Johnson. The Timings Chart is described in Chapter 5.

observations of teachers to ensure that they are implementing the PT procedures with integrity. During observations of novice teachers, coaches work with the novices to select a subset of the standards to be evaluated. As teachers become more comfortable, more standards are added, and eventually an "expert" precision teacher can perform all of them with great facility. However, it's always best to start at the very beginning by discussing the mechanics of charting.

Let's look at a few basic features of the Daily per minute Chart. Across the top of the chart are calendar dates to fill in. Each vertical line represents a day of the week, beginning with Sunday and ending with Saturday. Each Sunday line is in bold, separating one week from another. Each horizontal line represents a performance frequency. All data are charted as *counts per minute.* The chart allows us to plot data from once per day (~.001 per minute) at the bottom of the chart to 1,000 per minute at the top. All human performance frequencies can be plotted on the chart. Remember, the data multiply as they grow. The big numbers in the left margin indicate what to count by and what to count from. For example, find the frequency of 1, indicated by a big number 1 in the margin in the middle of the chart. The next frequency line is 2, the next is 3, and so on until we reach 10. To preserve a ratio or multiply scale, the numbers now grow by 10. Find the frequency of 10, indicated by a big 10 in the margin. The next frequency line is 20, the next is 30, and so on until we reach 100. To preserve the multiply scale, the next line is now 200, the next is 300, and so on until we reach 1,000. The chart works similarly on the bottom half of the chart, but in this overview we will save that for later learning.

Now we're ready to plot some data. Let's say we want to plot data on the Wednesday of the first week that a chart represents. A learner has completed a 1-minute timing on math facts and has completed 25 problems. Make a big dot on the intersection of the Wednesday line and a frequency of 25, which will be somewhere between the 20 line and the 30 line. Don't worry about the exact spot where the dot is plotted; remember, we are more interested in relative growth in frequency across days than in the exact, absolute frequency on any given day. The learner's performance can be scored as either correct or incorrect. We use a big dot to plot correct performance, and on the same day line we plot errors with an ×. Once we've plotted a series of data points, we can connect the dots and examine the trend of the student's learning line.

The Record Floor

When we are timing for 1 minute, the mechanics for charting data are straightforward, as illustrated in the math facts example just above. From looking at the charted data, however, we would not know whether the learner completed 25 math facts per minute for 1 minute, or 5 minutes, or 30 seconds. The data indicate only how many math facts were completed per minute. It's useful to know for how many minutes the learner stayed on that pace. Therefore, we must place a mark on the chart to indicate the length of the timing. This mark is called the *record floor.* To intuit the record floor, imagine the chart as a detection device. If we observe and record performance for 10 minutes, the lowest frequency of performance we can reliably detect is 1 every 10 minutes, or .1 per minute. If performance is occurring on average less than once every 10 minutes (say, once every 20 minutes), we cannot reliably detect each performance if we observe for only 10 minutes. We will need a longer timing period to detect those frequencies. The record floor indicates the lowest number per minute we can detect in the timing period we've chosen. We think the reference to a floor in the term *record floor* is apt.

Now we're ready to chart frequencies in timings longer than 1 minute. Suppose the learner in our previous examples took 10 minutes to complete those 25 math facts on that first Wednesday. How many math facts per minute, on average? Yes, 2.5 per minute. First we place a big dot at the intersection of the 2.5 frequency line and the first Wednesday line. (The 2.5 frequency line is between the 2 and the 3 frequency lines.) Next we place a horizontal dash on the Wednesday line at the .1 frequency line to indicate the record floor. Find that frequency line now. We place the dash on the .1 line because that is the lowest frequency per minute that we can reliably detect if we observe and record performance for 10 minutes. It's the floor or the bottom of our recording capacity. If the same floor is used each day, we extend the dashed line across each day (not Saturday or Sunday, of course, in a school).

Suppose we observe and record performance for 30 seconds. If we observe 1 performance in 30 seconds, how many performances per minute does that equal? Yes, 2 per minute. So we place the record floor on the 2 frequency line. It takes a while to get fluent at thinking about charting timed data—to automatically convert frequencies for different amounts of time into counts per minute.

We've provided a quick sketch of charting, which is really all you need to get started. There are many more fine points to learn about the Standard Celeration Chart, but never fear: Thousands of learners (and teachers!) from grade 2 to college level have learned how to use the chart. Appendices 1 and 2, written by our colleague Deb Brown, describe the relations between the timings chart and the daily chart and will serve as a good reminder for those who have some familiarity with the chart. In addition, our colleague Kris Melroe is writing a manual that teaches charting step by step.

Celeration of Performance Frequency over Time = Learning

You may be wondering why the charts used in PT are called Standard Celeration Charts. Although frequency is the best measure of *performance,* growth in rate of performance over time is the best definition of *learning.*

By measuring and graphing changes in rates of correct and incorrect performance over time, we can quantitatively describe learning and examine the learning pictures that evolve on a chart. Examining learning pictures allows us to predict precisely when a skill or concept will be fluent, or whether its rate of growth over time is insufficient and requires new teaching interventions. Lindsley coined the term *celeration* to indicate either rate of growth (acceleration) or deterioration of performance (deceleration) over time.

Celeration measures how much time it takes for a learner to reach the frequency aim. A *celeration aim* can be prescribed for each chart—for example, ×2, or doubling of growth in a week's time. To help learners reach fluency in a timely manner, precision teachers monitor celeration of learning and provide *celeration interventions* to "steepen the growth." Thus precision teachers build quicker learners by focusing upon building celeration. Figure 2.7 shows a chart that includes data and a celeration line at ×2 learning.

As Figure 2.7 shows, a celeration line is drawn through the data points to indicate their average progression across time. When drawing a celeration line through a set of

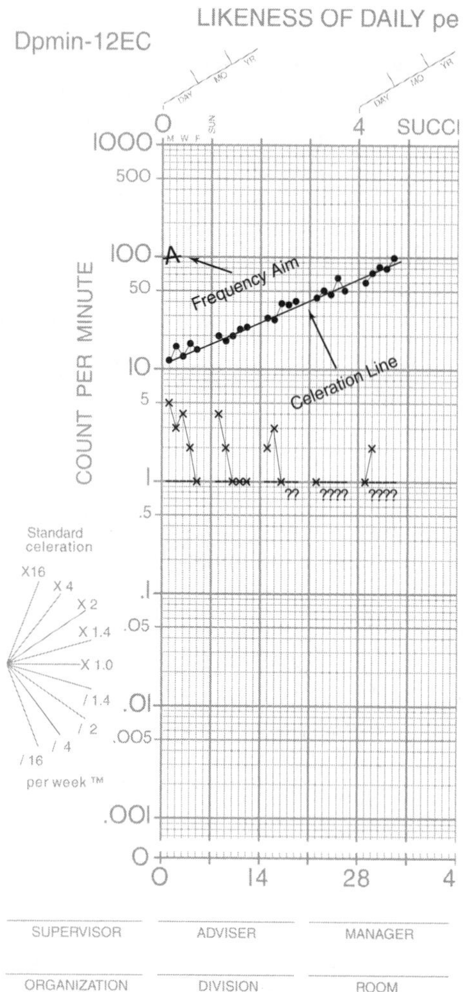

FIGURE 2.7. Likeness of a Daily per minute Standard Celeration Chart showing data, celeration line, and frequency aim. Used with permission of the Behavior Research Company.

data points, we make sure that there are equal numbers of dots above and below the line. When an *outlier dot* falls far above or below the frequencies of the remaining dots, we ignore it. Although statistical methods of precisely drawing celeration lines have been applied in PT (e.g., Pennypacker, Gutierrez, & Lindsley, 2003; White & Haring, 1980), data indicate that "eyeball" approximations produce equally effective data analysis and intervention (Haring, Liberty, & White, 1980). Celeration lines can be described by the *steepness* of the slopes they create—through either multiplying by a certain factor (e.g., ×2) or dividing by a certain factor (e.g., ÷4).

Setting celeration aims and providing interventions to meet them help us guarantee that fluency is reached in a timely manner. In his keynote address to the 1999 International Precision Teaching and Standard Celeration Conference, Ogden Lindsley (1999) used the analogy of *agility* to explain celeration. An agile learner is a fast, accurate learner. In business and other organizations, agility is the capacity to adapt rapidly and efficiently to changes. Business professionals in the technology industry talk about agile software development, for example. A goal for such organizations is to keep pace with the possibilities for newer and better ways of using the Internet. So too with agile performance in school: Fast, smooth, automatic, skilled learning demonstrates agility, the ability to learn new skills and concepts quickly and to adjust performance on the basis of new information. Once agile, a learner feels ready for any learning challenge. To paraphrase Charles Darwin, the ability to survive is based not on what learners know, but on their ability to adapt quickly to changes. PT incorporates the concept of agile performance into its measurement of celeration. Agile performances register as steep slopes on a Standard Celeration Chart. Celeration lines with steeper and steeper slopes show growth in agility. Celeration aims are set steep enough to predict high celerations in future learning. Agility is to celeration as fluency is to frequency.

PT RESOURCES

The entire family of Standard Celeration Charts, including the Daily per minute Chart and the Timings Chart discussed in this book, may be ordered from the Behavior Research Company (*www.behaviorresearchcompany.com*). The classic PT textbook for teachers is the second edition of White and Haring's (1980) *Exceptiotnal Teaching*. A third edition is currently in preparation. A more recent textbook is Kubina and Yurich's (2012) *The Precision Teaching Book*. The classic procedural handbook for PT is Pennypacker, Gutierrez, and Lindsley's (2003) *Handbook of the Standard Celeration Chart*.

Steve Graf and Og Lindsley's (2002) *Standard Celeration Charting* is a practical manual available in a three-ring binder at *www.behaviordevelopmentsolutions* or from Behavior Development Solutions, 80 Paper Mill Road, Woodbury, Connecticut 06798. In addition, Owen White and Malcolm Neeley's (2012) *The Chart Book*, an excellent and short manual on using the SCC, is available at *http://education.washington.edu/areas/edspe/white/precision/readings/chartbook.pdf*. White (2012) also has written an excellent manual—*The Finder Book*—which explains how to use a chart tool. It is available at *http://education.washington.edu/areas/edspe/white/precision/readings/finderbook.pdf*.

Finally, two software applications hold promise for PT enthusiasts. Erick Dubuque and Richard Kubina (2013) are publishing a tablet software application called *The Chart App* to assist in plotting, analyzing, and reporting on learning and performance. In addition, Vicci Tucci and Kent Johnson (2012) are publishing a tablet software application called *Fluency FlashCards* to assist in learning content from flashcards.

SUMMARY

In this chapter, we've provided a brief history of the PT technology that has been changing lives for a half a century. We've described the pure case of PT, which is summarized in Figure 2.8. We've also provided a brief introduction to the mechanics of charting. We have provided, for your convenience, a likeness of a blank Timings Chart in Appendix 3 and a likeness of a blank Daily per minute Chart in Appendix 4. In Chapter 3, we

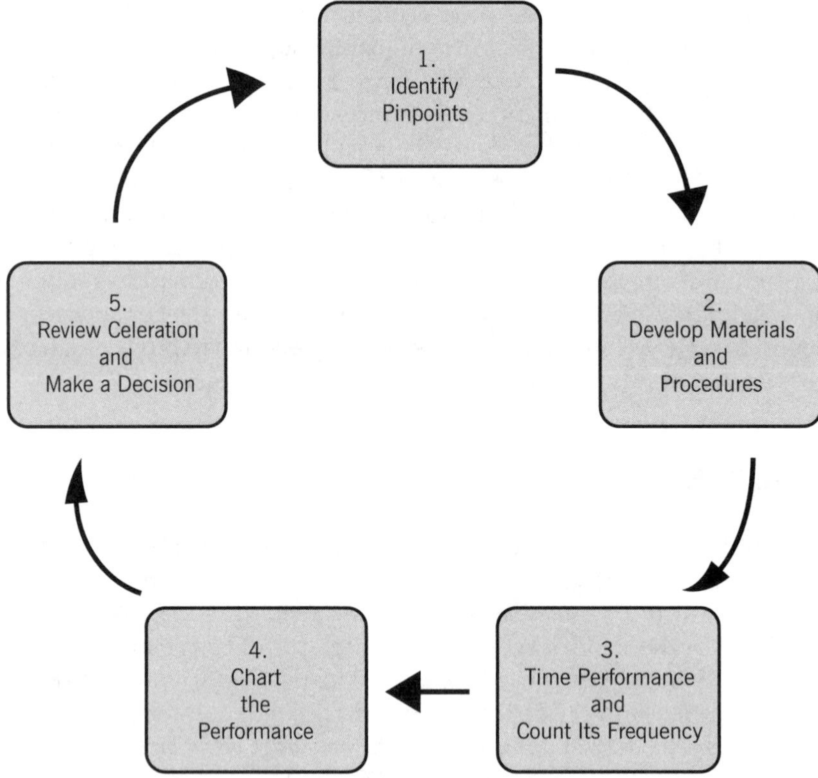

FIGURE 2.8. Five steps in the general case of PT.

recommend strategies for deciding what to practice; in Chapter 4, we describe the ways in which PT is a perfect accompaniment to the RTI framework. Then in Chapter 5, we get back to the nitty-gritty about how to make this approach work in whole-classroom (Tier 1), small-group (Tier 2), and individualized (Tier 3) settings.

CHAPTER 3

Instructional Design for Precision Teaching

MR. JOHANSON LEARNS A VALUABLE LESSON

Mr. Johanson's Tier 1 fifth-grade classroom* is made up of learners with a wide range of skills and abilities. To ensure that they are successful, he tries every strategy he has learned in his teacher training program. Still, some whom he thinks are capable aren't keeping up. For example, Misha continues to struggle with multiply–divide facts, and this is slowing down her performance on multiple-column multiplication problems and long division. Mr. Johanson has given her a "cheat sheet" with basic facts on it, but still she is taking so long to look up individual facts that she loses her place in the larger problem and makes mistakes. In reading, Samuel is struggling with multiple-syllable words, and this is slowing his overall reading rate and appears to contribute to his reading comprehension errors. And in history, Kaycee is so far behind in note taking that she simply gives up and asks a girlfriend for her notes. Ned can write the answers to math facts, but he can't do the work in his head when called on. Josiah is very good at answering multiple-choice questions about text, but he can't summarize a story either orally or in writing. Lorena remembers every example of erosion that Mr. Johanson talks about in class, but on the test she can't come up with a novel example.

The errors his students make have left Mr. Johanson scratching his head, and that's what has brought him to today's online interactive class about content analysis. He is intrigued by the flyer, which says, "Do your Tier 1 students have splinter skills, such that they do well on some tasks and poorly on others? Do they memorize quite well, but fail to get the concepts you're teaching? This workshop will help you analyze content and provide learning opportunities that will improve their performance."

The first thing the online instructor, Ms. Castell, talks about is how to analyze complex tasks (she calls them *composites*) into components and tool skills, and how to provide practice on each to ensure that students are prepared to meet expectations on these complex tasks. Mr. Johanson asks, "Are you saying I should take class time to provide practice on, let's say, math facts, even though it takes time away from students' time to practice computation?" Ms. Castell replies, "Yes. It may seem like you're taking time in the fifth-grade classroom to work on second- or third-grade skills, but doing so will pay off in the long run, particularly if you use timed practice that builds on a well-thought-out content analysis. It sounds like your students already 'know' the algorithms for long-division and multiplication computation, and that it's this piece that's slowing them down." Mr. Johanson realizes that this might be just the ticket for Misha, and that it might work for Samuel and Kaycee too.

Later Ms. Castell describes different kinds of learning, and when she gets to concepts, Mr. Johanson slaps himself on the forehead and says, "So that's the problem with Lorena. Erosion is a concept, and while I give examples of it in class, I don't give nonexamples. And students don't have to discriminate between them until the test. Duh!" Ms. Castell replies, "Don't be too hard on yourself. It's a common teaching error."

On the last day of the class, Ms. Castell talks about learning channels, and Mr. Johanson's life flashes before his eyes. He remembers when he was in his high school Spanish class, desperately trying to learn vocabulary. Eventually, he was able to remember the Spanish equivalents of the English words in the lesson—but then the teacher would give him the Spanish words and ask him to translate these into English, and he was hopelessly lost. Now he realizes that he either needed to practice both directions—Spanish to English and English to Spanish—or get speedy enough doing it one way that the other would emerge without practice. He almost wishes that he was back in high school so he could get it right, but at least now he knows how to help students like Ned!

---

*The teacher and students in this story are fictitious. The story is an amalgam of those we've heard and seen during our 30-plus years of working in schools.

THREE TECHNOLOGIES FOR CONTENT ANALYSIS

Well-designed instruction and practice are the keys to learner success. We've seen PT done very well and very poorly. This chapter will help you maximize the effectiveness of your PT implementation. Our PT programs build upon three instructional design technologies—*component–composite analysis, kinds-of-learning analysis,* and *learning-channel analysis*. Let us discuss each in turn.

Component–Composite Analysis

In a component–composite analysis, each teaching goal is parsed into sets of tool skills, component skills, and composite skills (Eric Haughton, 1972, 1980; Johnson & Street, 2004). *Tool skills* are those minimal responses that are at the core of many if not all of the skills and concepts inherent in the content areas. Each tool skill supports many different skills, analogous to the hub of a wheel with many spokes, with each spoke representing a skill that employs the tool. For example, tool skills for writing an essay include handwriting or typing speed and legibility. Tool skills are prerequisites for teaching other skills. At the very least, they should be built simultaneously with teaching a skill that employs them, although it is a better idea to begin building tool skills before teaching skills that require them.

We call the second-level building blocks that depend upon one or more tool skills *component skills*. For example, writing an essay includes many grammar and word usage component skills, such as subject–verb agreement and verb tense. Component skills are the building blocks for engaging in composite repertoires. *Composite skills* are the authentic, higher-level performances that socially validate a learner's mastery of a content area. The compound or composite repertoire in our example is the finished composition itself, incorporating all of the components and using all the tools necessary to complete it. Composite repertoires contain blends and combinations of component skills. Table 3.1 provides several examples of component–composite analysis in academic subjects.

The terms *component* and *composite* are relative concepts. A component of a larger composite is a composite of a smaller component. For example, decoding is a composite repertoire consisting of a sounding-out component and separate sound components. Decoding is also a component of active reading, a composite repertoire. Don't worry if we've lost you: Table 3.2 illustrates this relativity of tools, components, and composites in more detail. In the first column, a preschooler or a learner with motor skill deficits must master the motor skill of pinching a writing utensil (tool skill), in order to learn how to hold a pencil and make marks with it (component skills), in order to learn and practice writing numbers (composite skill). The prescription in the second column assumes that the learner can already pinch a pencil but needs to learn the tool skills of holding and making marks with it. Writing numbers is the component skill the learner must master in order to practice single-digit math facts, the composite skill. The prescription in the third column is typical of a kindergartener who can already write with a pencil but needs to practice writing numbers (tool skill), in order to learn single-digit math facts, a prerequisite component skill for learning basic computational algorithms such as column addition (composite skill).

Progressive educators especially favor teaching composite repertoires, and often devote the majority of their class time to real-world activities in *project-based learning* (PBL) formats. From their perspective, the lens for instructional design is aimed upward, at the broader contexts in which component skills are used—the *overlying* processes into which component skills fit. Instructional design for PT, on the other hand, is primarily focused on the *underlying* processes inherent in real-world activities. As we discuss in more detail in Chapter 10, progressive educators would do well to devote a portion of class time to using PT for teaching and practicing the components inherent in their composites. Chapter 10 is devoted to describing and illustrating how to use PT effectively to facilitate successful PBL and other progressive educational practices and learning in the real world.

TABLE 3.1. Academic Examples of a Component–Composite Analysis

Composites	Components	Tools
Understanding a text chapter (strategic, engaged reading)	Understanding the meaning of a word (vocabulary)	Sounding out a word (decoding)
Writing a research report	Writing complete sentences	Typing words
Solving a quantitative problem	Multiplying decimal numbers	Writing numbers, knowing math facts

TABLE 3.2. Relativity of Tool, Component, and Composite Skills

Tool skills:	Pinching	Holding a pencil Making marks	Writing numbers
Component skills:	Holding a pencil Making marks	Writing numbers	Single-digit math facts
Composite skills:	Writing numbers	Single-digit math facts	Basic computational algorithms (+, –, ×, ÷)

Kinds-of-Learning Analysis

After completing a component–composite analysis, we then perform a *content analysis* for each composite, component, and tool skill we have identified (Johnson & Street, 2004). Content analysis reveals the types of knowledge and types of tasks and procedures required for high-quality instruction and practice. Becker (1986) describes the purpose of such knowledge taxonomies:

> Each knowledge structure identifies the kind of knowledge that can be taught with similar strategies, and identifies how different pieces of knowledge share samenesses to provide the basis for powerful generality, rather than isolated bits and pieces. These goals require logical analysis of knowledge itself, rather than of thinking processes. (p. 176)

At least four different systems for content analysis have been developed. Bloom (1956) developed an extensive taxonomy of cognitive knowledge objectives based upon six main categories: knowledge, comprehension, application, analysis, synthesis, and evaluation. Bloom's taxonomy prompts users to include component skills for each objective. Gagné (1985) and Gagné, Briggs, and Wagner (1992) specified eight types of learning or tasks that a certain component skill may require: signal learning, stimulus–response learning, chaining, verbal association, discrimination learning, rule learning, and problem solving. Engelmann and Carnine's (1991) taxonomy contains seven forms of cognitive knowledge: three basic forms (comparatives, noncomparatives, and nouns), two joining forms (logical transformations and correlated features), and two complex forms (fact systems and chains).

We prefer Tiemann and Markle's (1990) *kinds-of-learning* analysis because it is elegant and easily understood, but, more importantly, because it clearly differentiates between simple objectives (where what is taught is identical to what is assessed) and conceptual objectives (where examples used in instruction must be different from those used in assessment). Their content analysis sorts components into three *domains*, each of which is made up of three *kinds* of learning. Table 3.3 provides a 3 × 3 matrix that details the domains and kinds of learning described by Tiemann and Markle. The three domains are *psychomotor, simple cognitive,* and *complex cognitive.* Three kinds of learning make up the psychomotor domain:

- *Responses,* such as writing or typing letters.
- *Chains,* such as steps in operating a piece of scientific equipment.
- *Kinesthetic repertoires,* such as playing basketball or the piano.

TABLE 3.3. Tiemann and Markle's Kinds-of-Learning Matrix

Psychomotor	Simple cognitive	Complex cognitive
Kinesthetic repertoires	Verbal repertoires	Strategies
Chains	Sequences	Principle application
Responses	Associations	Concepts

Three kinds of learning make up the simple cognitive domain, the domain in which what is taught is identical to what is assessed:

- *Associations,* such as saying the sounds that letters make, reading numbers, saying the meaning of map symbols, or completing a page of math facts.
- *Sequences,* such as learning phone or account numbers, steps in keyboarding, or computational algorithms (such as column addition and long division).
- *Verbal repertoires,* composite skills such as retelling a story or giving a live report of a baseball game.

The last three kinds of learning reside in the complex cognitive domain, the domain in which examples used in instruction must be different from those used in assessment:

- *Concepts,* such as identifying the style of a painting, identifying the part of speech of a word in a sentence, or identifying a number's place value.
- *Principle application,* such as applying comprehension skills (e.g., finding the main idea, inferring the setting, making predictions); adding columns of numbers; regrouping numbers in subtraction; plotting a point on a grid by using Cartesian (*x*, *y*) coordinates; finding the hypotenuse of a triangle after being given the opposite and adjacent sides; or following spelling rules (e.g., "*i* before *e* except after *c*").
- *Strategies,* such as developing a recycling system for a classroom or writing an original script for a play.

We've included in Appendix 5 a list of tasks that will allow you to practice making discriminations among the kinds of learning in the simple and complex cognitive domains.[1] We recommend that you try the first five and then compare your answers to the answer key, then do another five, and so on.

Once we identify the kinds of learning involved in a set of skills, we use Tiemann and Markle's (1990) tasks and procedures to (1) analyze and (2) teach each component. For example, if a component skill is a principle, such as "writing persuasive paragraphs," we complete a principle analysis, analyzing the critical features of writing a paragraph that is persuasive. Terry Dodds (2005) has analyzed persuasive paragraph writing into 20 elements, including, among others:

[1] In this exercise, we've focused only on the last two domains, although some learners require instruction in the first domain as well. Tiemann and Markle (1990) provide examples of all the domains in their analysis.

- States opinion in the opening paragraph.
- Presents supporting details that include anecdotes, statistics, and expert opinion.
- Presents supporting ideas from a variety of sources.
- Persuades the reader in nonconfrontational language.

Tiemann and Markle (1990) also specify procedures for teaching each kind of learning identified during analysis. We highly recommend their excellent text, *Analyzing Instructional Content.*

Learning-Channel Analysis

Our third analytic tool is *learning-channel analysis,* which describes how a learner makes sensory contact with instruction (Eric Haughton, 1980; Johnson & Street, 2004). Stimuli may be *visual, auditory, tactile, olfactory,* or *gustatory;* these can be translated into everyday language as *see, hear, touch, smell,* or *taste.* Learning-channel analysis also describes the learner's response to stimuli. Responses may involve saying, writing, pointing, marking, and so on. For example, in sounding out words, the stimuli are visual and the response is vocal. In learning-channel parlance, this is described as "See/say words." Students may be required to hear/write words, as in taking dictation; see math facts/say answers; smell flowers/say their names; see word problems/write equations and solutions; hear words/mark correct meanings from a list; see passages/say predictions of what will happen next; and so on. A *learning-channel matrix* (see Figure 3.1)[2] resulted from brainstorming by Eric Haughton and Elizabeth Haughton, a husband-and-wife team working in Belleville, Ontario, Canada in the late 1960s and early 1970s. Elizabeth was a first-grade teacher and Eric, already steeped in PT, was a consultant to the school district. Elizabeth's classroom served as a type of laboratory classroom for Eric, and as they talked about the various ways that instructional stimuli could be presented and responses could be produced, the matrix emerged. Notice the wide range of "inputs" and "outputs" that a teacher can use to diversify instruction and practice.

Recap

To design instruction in such a way that it can be logically taught and effectively acquired involves at least five content analysis activities:

1. Identify teaching goals in a content area.
2. Complete a component–composite analysis of each goal.
3. Identify the kinds of learning inherent in each tool, component, and composite.
4. Identify examples and nonexamples for each part.
5. Prescribe learning channels for each tool, component, and composite.

[2]Note that the matrix includes "think" among the sensory inputs. Many precision teachers who had a behavioral orientation objected to the "think" input, arguing that one doesn't really know when someone's behavior is in response to what he or she is thinking. Consequently, they adopted the convention of using the word "free" in the learning channel to denote situations in which sensory input is not apparent. For example, when a learner says the alphabet without looking at it or hearing someone else say it, many precision teachers describe the pinpoint as "Free/say the alphabet."

Y | M | D

Topic ____________________

INPUT											
THINK (T)											
TOUCH (To)											
TASTE (Ta)											
SNIFF (Sn)											
SEE (Se)											
HEAR (H)											
FEEL (F)											
OUTPUT	AIM (A)	DO (Do)	DRAW (D)	EMOTE (E)	MARK (Mk)	MATCH (M)	SAY (S)	SELECT (St)	TAP (Tp)	THOUGHT (Tt)	WRITE (W)

______ Manager ______ Advisor ______ Manager ______ Behaver ______ Age ______ Label ______ Topic

FIGURE 3.1. Learning-channel matrix (designed by Eric Haughton in 1976). Reprinted with permission of Elizabeth Haughton.

In actual practice, these five activities are only roughly sequential; they involve lots of *recursivity*, in which a teacher moves back and forth among the five activities to perfect the eventual set of activities and assessments that learners will encounter.

FROM CONTENT ANALYSIS TO INSTRUCTIONAL OBJECTIVES

Once we understand the content, we are ready to specify the instruction and practice that needs to occur. Our next step is to define our *instructional objectives*. An instructional objective has three parts. It precisely states the conditions under which the learner will perform, the precise nature of the performance, and the criteria that need to be met in order to consider the instructional objective mastered. In PT, the criteria are stated as performance frequencies.

Setting Performance Frequency Aims

In Chapter 2, we have discussed the goals of fluency in terms of the MESsAGe acronym. Tables in the chapters on reading (Chapter 6), writing (Chapter 7), and mathematics (Chapter 8) provide lists of all the pinpoints you need, complete with frequency aims.

Aims for other pinpoints we may design can be derived from those in the tables. For example, an aim for a pinpoint for content teaching that requires both reading and writing can be derived from our reading and writing pinpoint aims.

Of course, these aims have not been verified with all learners. Each population may require some adjustments. The ultimate criterion is whether reaching the aim predicts MESsAGe. Fabrizio and Moors (2003) have developed a formal empirical method to determine whether a student's performance frequency would predict retention, endurance, stability, and application. Teachers ask students to practice until their performance frequency matches the performance frequency of other students who have demonstrated retention, endurance, stability, and application outcomes. Then they systematically check to verify that these students can indeed demonstrate endurance (by dropping the record floor from, say, 1 minute to 3 minutes), then stability (by introducing noise in the performance environment), then application (by introducing a new task in which the skill is required), and finally retention (by waiting a month, then probing to verify that the student can perform the skill at their previous performance frequency). To date, their excellent method has not taken generativity and adduction into account (Johnson, 2003).

Developing Precise Instructional Objectives

Let us examine four precise instructional objectives—a basic objective and an advanced objective in math, and a basic objective and an advanced objective in reading.

In a basic composite repertoire of fluent mental arithmetic, one of many objectives can be stated this way:

> When seeing a three-number fact family, the learner will say the two multiplication and division facts that can be derived from the family, every time, within 6 seconds.

Here's an example from the multiplication–division fact family: Present the student with the number family 7, 6, 42; from this, he or she derives these four facts—$7 \times 6 = 42$, $6 \times 7 = 42$, $42 \div 7 = 6$, and $42 \div 6 = 7$—within 6 seconds. Notice that the objective begins by stating the conditions under which the performance is to occur:

> When seeing a three-number fact family . . .

Then it states what the learner will do:

> . . . the learner will say the two multiplication and two division facts that can be derived from the family . . .

Last, the objective states the frequency criteria:

> . . . every time [meaning no errors] within 6 seconds.

One of many objectives in an advanced composite repertoire of quantitative reasoning and problem-solving skills can be stated this way:

> After reading a 15- to 50-word problem that requires a quantitative answer, the learner will write a three-term equation with one unknown that represents the problem to solve (e.g., $x - 10 = 3$), then correctly solve the equation and problem, every time, within 30 seconds. (Frequency aim = 6 correct in 3 minutes.)

Can you identify the three parts of the mathematics objective?

In a basic composite repertoire of fluent reading, one of many objectives can be stated this way:

> When seeing an unfamiliar multisyllabic word (e.g., *significantly, considerable*), the learner will apply a four-step sounding-out method, every time, within 2 seconds.

Here's an advanced strategic reading objective:

> While reading a selection, the learner will pause to write an application of one or more of 15 comprehension skills,[3] as appropriate to the text at that point, accurately and within 10 seconds. The learner will accurately repeat this process at least twice every 5 minutes, for at least 20 minutes.

This objective could just as well be practiced as a "say" task if a listener is available to listen and judge the performance. Can you parse both the multisyllabic and reading comprehension objectives into their three parts?

Instructional objectives are more precise than the typical curriculum *standards* and *benchmarks* that are stated in grade-level frameworks. Standards and benchmarks are usually gross statements of learning conditions and performance, and rarely specify performance standards. However, we applaud the standards movement in education, because it marks a significant advance toward the necessary levels of specificity defined by instructional objectives. Standards also remove the guesswork in deciding what to teach by making the goals in each subject and grade level clearer for learners, teachers, and parents. When precision teachers specify complete instructional objectives from grade-level standards and individualized education program (IEP) objectives, they make it even more likely that teaching and learning will occur effectively and efficiently.

From Instructional Objectives to Pinpoints

Once instructional objectives are stated, the teacher teaches the learner how to accomplish the performance specified by the objective. After instruction, learners engage in practice to frequency aims. Practice *pinpoints* (Lindsley, 1971, 1972, 1990) are derived from the objectives. A pinpoint states the learning channel, the performance, and the frequency aim. Here are pinpoints for the four objectives described above.

1. See math facts/write answers, 80–100 answers/minute.
2. See word problems/write equations and answers, 6 correct/3 minutes.

---

[3]Examples of comprehension skills include making predictions, drawing conclusions, stating main ideas, identifying cause–effect relations, and making inferences about a character or the setting.

3. See multisyllabic words/say words, 70–90 words/minute.
4. See passages/write comprehension questions and answers; 2 every 5 minutes, for 20 minutes.

Basic and Complex Pinpoints

Most precision teachers write their pinpoints in shorthand, stating the full learning channel first (e.g., see/write, see/say) and then the performance and aim. For example, "See math facts/write answers" becomes "See/write math facts" or "See/write math fact answers." Or "See multisyllabic words/say words" becomes "See/say multisyllabic words." The shorthand for these two pinpoints does not obscure their meaning. However, many objectives, particularly complex ones, cannot be written in shorthand because shorthand obscures the meaning of the objectives. For example, we cannot state the complex math pinpoint in our second example above as "See/write word problems": this would indicate that the learner's performance is copying word problems! Likewise, we cannot state the complex reading objective in our fourth example above as "See/write comprehension questions and answers"; this also indicates that the learner should engage in a copying task. When the referent for the first part of the learning channel is very different (i.e., reading) from the referent for the second part of the learning channel (i.e., writing equations and solving them, writing comprehension questions and answering them), then we should avoid shorthand.

Additional Learning Channels for Practice

The Haughtons' learning-channel matrix not only helps us specify the primary, real-world learning channel of an instructional objective and pinpoint, but also helps us specify a variety of additional learning channels to use in practicing the objective. For example, when sounding out multisyllabic words ("See/say multisyllabic words"), the learner could also "See word • hear pronunciation/say correct or error,"[4] or "See word/select correct pronunciation from a tape of four options," among other pinpoints. When practicing math facts, the learner could also "See/mark correctly answered math facts," and so on.

In fact, the Haughtons originally used the learning-channel matrix as a worksheet for creating a variety of practice activities that build the kind of depth about a topic that is characteristic of topical experts. Having a variety of ways to practice an objective not only adds depth to frequency building, but also reduces the monotony and tedium of practice. Students in Eric Haughton's college classes would fill in as many cells in a matrix for a given objective as possible. Figure 3.2 shows an example of a completed learning-channel matrix for teaching about vegetables.

Celeration Aims

In PT, building performance frequency is not enough. It is also important that learners reach frequency aims in a timely manner. Will a learner reach an aim tomorrow? Next

[4]The dot betweeen learning channels indicates "plus," "and," or "in addition."

80 | 10 | 03 (Y | M | D) Topic Vegetables

INPUT

THINK (T)		Pretend to be a veg. —mime	Favorite vegetable	Likes and dislikes veg.—preparation	Favorite foods	Vegetable to pick	Shapes, colors, textures	Likes and dislikes; textures, colors		Imagine odors, shapes, textures	
TOUCH (To)	Texture likes and dislikes		Texture	Likes and dislikes	Textures	Textures	Names of veg.	Nature origin mature smooth or rough			
TASTE (Ta)	Likes and dislikes —cooked —raw		Veg.	Likes and dislikes	Flavors	Cooked or raw	Favorite dish— names of veg.	Likes and dislikes		How to improve taste —spices	Sweet sour spicy
SNIFF (Sn)			Veg.	Likes and dislikes	Natures of veg.	Sample to whole	Names of odors Likes and dislikes	Favorite odor	Veg.		
SEE (Se)		Pretend to be a veg. —mime	Shapes, colors; country or grocery store	Likes and dislikes	Shapes, colors, plant and crop	Mature or immature veg.	Names, colors, shapes	Food prep. snacks fresh food	Shapes, textures	Plan groups for snack time	Names
HEAR (H)	Specified vegetable	Act like veg.	Specified vegetable		Nutritious vegetables	Color, shape, size	Names, vitamins	Nutritious vitamins Roughage	Veg.		Names
FEEL (F)		Pretend to feel like a veg.	Emotions	Likes and dislikes			Emotional description	Favorite food		Imagine eating vegetable ☺ ☹	Descriptive words
	AIM (A)	DO (Do)	DRAW (D)	EMOTE (E)	MARK (Mk)	MATCH (M)	SAY (S)	SELECT (St)	TAP (Tp)	THOUGHT (Tt)	WRITE (W)

OUTPUT

Jane Doe	John Smith	ECE I-II Students	Preschool Students	3–5 yrs	Reg. Preschool	
Manager	Advisor	Manager	Behaver	Age	Label	Topic

FIGURE 3.2. A completed learning-channel matrix on the topic of vegetables. Reprinted with permission of Elizabeth Haughton.

week? Next month? Next year? The celeration line drawn on the chart indicates the date by which the learner is expected to reach a frequency aim. Precision teachers provide interventions during practice not only to help students achieve accuracy and fluency, but also to meet celeration aims. If a learner's chart does not show performance growth that keeps the learner on his or her celeration line, the teacher or a peer might provide more cheerleading, tap a beat to a performance that is just a bit faster than the student's current rate, read just a bit faster than the learner is reading and ask the student to keep up ("duet reading"), and so on, depending upon the pinpoint. Table 3.4 summarizes the steps in designing pinpoints from instructional objectives.

Sequencing a Set of Pinpoints

Once we have a set of pinpoints, we cumulatively sequence them as a series of *slices*. Slices are the fine divisions of a pinpoint into its components. For example, grammar can be divided into a series of slices including nouns, verbs, adjectives placed before nouns, and adverbs, among others. Phonics can be divided into a series of slices such as consonant–vowel–consonant (CVC) words, CVCe words, *oi* and *oy* words, *ch* words, and so on.

Learners first practice pinpoint slice 1 to its frequency aim; then pinpoint slice 2; then a combination of slices 1 and 2; then slice 3; then a combination of slices 1, 2, and 3;

TABLE 3.4. Recipe for Making Pinpoints from Instructional Objectives

Steps	Details
Select an instructional objective . . .	. . . that specifies conditions, performance, and criteria.
Sharpen the verb that specifies the performance.	For example, *identify* could mean talking, writing, typing, selecting from a set, and so on. Use the learning-channel matrix to guide you.
Specify the learning channels inherent in the conditions and performance statements.	• Primary + supplemental practice pinpoints • Basic pinpoint: learning channel, performance + conditions • Complex pinpoint: first part of learning channel + description of stimulus, then second part of learning channel + description of performance
Verify that the criteria are stated as frequency and celeration aims.	If not, make the appropriate changes.

and so on. For example, learners may practice solving one type of word problem (slice 1); then a second type (slice 2); then types 1 and 2 together; then type 3; then a combination of types 1, 2, and 3; then type 4; then types 1 through 4; then type 5; then types 1 through 5. If the sequence is long, we drop the earliest pinpoint in the sequence after four or five slices have been combined.

By juxtaposing previous pinpoints with subsequent ones in this manner, learners must make finer and finer discriminations as they proceed. In our word problem example, at first the learner is required to apply only one principle of word problem solving, then to apply a second principle, then to determine which of the two principles must be applied, and eventually which of five different word problem principles is required to solve each problem on the addition–subtraction practice slice.

The same sequencing method can be applied to teach a chain of behaviors. Several methods for *chaining* are described in the literature (Gilbert, 1962a, 1962b). A particularly effective one for teaching chains is a process called *backward chaining* (Mayer, Sulzer-Azaroff, & Wallace, 2011). First the learner is required to engage in the last step, then the last two steps, then the last three steps, and so on. In this manner, the learner must discriminate among a larger set of options at each point. For example, when practicing long division, on slice 1 the learner encounters a long-division problem that is already solved except for the final subtraction operation needed to determine a remainder. In slice 2, the learner must (1) multiply the last digit in the quotient times the divisor, and (2) then subtract to find the remainder. In slice 3, the learner must (1) bring down the next number in the dividend, (2) then multiply the last digit in the quotient times the divisor, (3) then subtract to find the remainder, and so on. Each successive step requires a discrimination among a larger set of options. In the long-division example, a learner who reaches the third slice must begin asking him- or herself: "Do I divide now? Do I multiply now? Do I subtract now? Do I bring down now?"

Selecting and Designing Tasks for Practicing a Pinpoint

Designers of PT practice sets *calibrate* them to ensure that each task requires a similar amount of time and effort; thus each count of "1" is equal to every other count of "1."

Designers also ensure that practice sheets contain more items than students are likely to be able to complete during a timing, so that the measurement instrument doesn't place an artificial *ceiling* on performance.

Discriminating before Generating

The beginning of a pinpoint sequence should include discrimination practice. In fact, *Discriminate before you generate* is one of our PT mantras. Motor skill practice should begin with examples and nonexamples of the criterion response. For example, in practicing handwriting, the learner should first encounter well-formed and poorly formed letters and "See/mark well-formed (or poorly formed) letters." Research shows that discriminating well- and poorly formed letters before writing practice greatly reduces the amount of physical guidance and practice required to write them, and improves the penmanship and legibility of poor writers (Markle, 1990). Next, practice can focus upon making gradual progress toward the frequency aim for writing correctly formed letters and words. Practice can then proceed to transcription exercises in which learners copy text until legibility and frequency criteria are met. When practicing how to operate a piece of equipment, beginning slices should require learners to identify correct and incorrect execution of each step, as well as correct and incorrect step sequences. Later slices should engage learners in producing the steps until they meet the frequency aim.

Likewise, practice for simple cognitive learning should begin with discriminating examples and nonexamples. For example, when learning the meaning of map symbols, learners should discriminate between correct and incorrect symbol meaning. "Does this symbol designate a state's capital?" "Does this one? How about this one?" Matching tasks require discrimination among multiple symbols and meanings. Sequence learning should also begin with practice in discriminating examples and nonexamples. For example, "Someone completed this multiplication problem. Did they do it correctly? How about this one?" Or "Someone completed this multiplication problem. Which step is completed incorrectly? How about this one?" and so on. Then learners can practice completing sequences or slice back to partial sequences if the full sequence is too challenging until they meet frequency aims. Verbal repertoires can be practiced in a similar manner, beginning with discrimination tasks, such as "Someone retold the story we just read this way. Did they leave anything out? Is everything in the correct order?" Then learners can build their rate on retelling passages until they reach the frequency criterion across a series of passages.

Concept learning should also engage the learner in discriminating examples and nonexamples first, followed by fixing nonexamples to make them examples. "Is this word in the sentence an example of an adjective? Is this one?" and so on. Principle learning can be practiced like sequence learning. "Someone put commas in this paragraph. Did they do so correctly?" Or "Someone spelled *receive* like this: *r-e-c-i-e-v-e*. Did they spell it correctly?"

If your sequence of pinpoints omits discrimination exercises, add them! Of course, all the questions we have included in the examples above would not be repeated for each task. Tasks should be arranged to facilitate the fastest possible completion. Good instructions should be included up front, with a demonstration of how to complete the practice sheet.

Generativity Probes

A generativity probe is used to assess the learner's performance on new, untaught tasks for which all prerequisite components have been mastered. It provides a way for a teacher to determine when a learner has acquired a new skill without explicit instruction.[5] Generativity probes should *not* be included on practice sheets; rather, they should be included as exercises interspersed throughout instruction after all prerequisite skills have been taught and practiced to frequency aims. In this way, the teacher can engineer discovery learning efficiently and effectively (Layng, Twyman, & Stikeleather, 2004), and can also determine when it has been achieved.

Tryout and Revision

The final instructional design step—tryout and revision—is crucial: Tasks for frequency building should be empirically based: tried out with learners and revised on the basis of their performance. As instructional designers, we have had many humbling experiences with students who have questions and problems with tasks that we thought were very well designed. This step takes action on our belief that the learner is always right!

SUMMARY

Table 3.5 summarizes our instructional design steps—from goals, to component–composite analysis, to content analysis, to pinpointing. So far we have described generic procedures for analyzing any instructional content. Studying our examples and references will allow you to use PT effectively with any goal in any course. In Chapters 6, 7, and 8, we analyze the three core academic subjects—reading, writing, and mathematics. The prescriptions we provide for the "three Rs" will also help you manage reading, writing, and math expectations as you teach social studies, science, and literature classes.

[5] In Tiemann and Markle's (1990) content analysis model, *strategizing* in the complex cognitive domain is equivalent to *generativity*.

TABLE 3.5. Instructional Design Steps

Step no.	Step description	Details
1	Select a content domain.	
2	State goals or "areas of focus" to practice.	
3	Complete a component–composite analysis of each goal and focus area.	Be sure to include: • tool skills • components • composites
4	For each component and tool skill, complete a content analysis.	Apply Tiemann and Markle's kinds-of-learning matrix.
5	Write instructional objectives for each component and tool.	Be sure to include: • conditions • performance • criteria (both frequency and celeration aims)
6	Determine the primary and supplemental learning channels you will use during practice.	Apply the Haughtons' learning-channel matrix.
7	Write pinpoint(s) for each objective.	Be sure to include: • learning channel • performance • criteria (both frequency and celeration aims)
8	Sequence the pinpoints.	
9	Select or design the tasks you will use to practice each pinpoint, based on their content analyses.	Examples and nonexamples for teaching each kind. Steps in a sequence for teaching behavior chains, sequences, and algorithms, with examples and nonexamples. Checklists of aspects of verbal (oral and written) and motor repertoires + strategies for mastering each aspect. Exercises to check for and give opportunities for generativity.
10	Design clear instructions for practicing each pinpoint.	
11	Make revisions based upon student performance data.	

CHAPTER 4

Blending Precision Teaching Technology with the Response-to-Intervention Framework

MR. TSENG'S DILEMMA

Mr. Tseng is the third-grade teacher at Sandy Lake Elementary School in Jasper, Michigan.* He has been teaching for 10 years and has become increasingly concerned about the number of his students who seem to be floating through the curriculum without learning it at all, or learning it until a high-stakes test is given but never truly mastering it. These aren't just the students who start out behind their peers; the same can be said for students who are in the middle of the pack and even for some of his "best" students. He's discouraged when he hears the fourth-grade teachers talking about all of the parts of the third-grade curriculum they spend "half the year reteaching!" Although they never say anything about him to his face, he gets the feeling that they blame him more than they do the kids. In a way, he blames himself, but he recognizes that it's not for lack of trying. He incorporates the latest and most evidence-based and learner-verified curriculum; he incorporates project-based inquiry to engage students. He's been employing the RTI approach for several years now. Still, he knows that by the beginning of the next school year, many of his students won't remember the skills that they and he have worked so hard on. It's the same way when students come into third grade; he spends a great deal of time solidifying skills they were "supposed to have learned" in second grade.

That's why learning about the benefits of PT at a workshop has Mr. Tseng so excited. He likes the systematic and efficient PT practice strategies. But most of all, he gets the MESsAGe! He's beginning to see his students differently. There's Manuel, who remembers most of what he has learned but can't seem to apply it. There's Teresa, who can read at about 200 wpm with few if any errors for the first minute, but who needs to build her endurance so she can read an entire 1,000-word passage at that same speed and accuracy. Maxim can do math facts with the best students in the class so long as there is no distraction, but his accuracy fails when other students in the room are making noise around him. And Mr. Tseng is absolutely sure that Rachel, Nathan, and Jerome can make tremendous curriculum leaps once he assesses their ability to recruit existing skills to learn new component and composite skills. He's pretty sure he knows now what to do to get them where they need to be.

He's also intrigued by the notion that PT can improve a teacher's ability to predict how long it'll take for *individual* students to acquire new skills. He's always known there were differences, but the ability to predict would allow him to plan instruction and practice accordingly. One of the first things he's going to do this fall is to change his assessment protocols, so that he can see not only *what* students know, but also *how quickly* they can learn a new skill.

Mr. Tseng knows there will be a steep learning curve to put this new assessment and practice protocol in place, but he's motivated. He wants his students to be successful . . . and he also wants those fourth-grade teachers to see him in a different light.

*The teacher, students, school, and locale in this story are fictitious. The story is an amalgam of those we've heard and seen during our 30-plus years of working in schools.

We are persuaded by the evidence that the instructional technology of PT ideally complements the aims of the RTI framework. Our goal in this chapter is to explain this evidence. We will:

- Describe the increased interest among educators in fluency in key academic tool and component skills.
- Identify ways in which PT technology can enhance the effectiveness of the RTI framework.
- Provide examples of the ways in which the learning pictures that emerge from the data recorded on a Standard Celeration Chart inform interventions.
- Discuss the critical importance of providing practice in the correct curricular elements.
- Provide examples of prototypic PT practice sets.
- Show how speedier resolutions accompany a change from the quarterly or even biweekly data-based decision making that characterizes many RTI implementations to the daily decision making that characterizes PT implementations.

FOCUS ON FLUENCY

Interest in performance fluency—particularly fluency related to literacy and numeracy—has blossomed in recent years. For example, the 2001 report of the National Institute for Literacy (Armbruster, Lehr, & Osborn, 2001) lists fluency instruction as one of five key elements of good reading instruction. The report offers the following discussion of fluency:

> Fluency is the ability to read a text accurately and quickly. When fluent readers read silently, they recognize words automatically. They group words quickly to help them gain meaning from what they read. Fluent readers read aloud effortlessly and with expression. Their

> reading sounds natural, as if they are speaking. Readers who have not yet developed fluency read slowly, word by word. Their oral reading is choppy and plodding.
>
> Fluency is important because it provides a bridge between word recognition and comprehension. Because fluent readers do not have to concentrate on decoding the words, they can focus their attention on what the text means. They can make connections among the ideas in the text and between the text and their background knowledge. In other words, fluent readers recognize words and comprehend at the same time. Less fluent readers, however, must focus their attention on figuring out the words, leaving them little attention for understanding the text. (p. 19)

Similarly, the final report of the National Mathematics Advisory Panel (NMAP, 2008) recommends fluency with whole numbers and fractions as important preparation for the study of algebra. Specifically in regard to fluency with whole numbers, the NMAP advises:

> By the end of Grade 5 or 6, children should have a robust sense of number. This sense of number must include an understanding of place value and the ability to compose and decompose whole numbers. It must clearly include a grasp of the meaning of the basic operations of addition, subtraction, multiplication, and division. It must also include use of the commutative, associative, and distributive properties; computational facility; and the knowledge of how to apply the operations to problem solving. Computational facility requires the automatic recall of addition and related subtraction facts, and of multiplication and related division facts. It also requires fluency with the standard algorithms for addition, subtraction, multiplication, and division. Fluent use of the algorithms not only depends on the automatic recall of number facts but also reinforces it. (pp. 17–18)

Later in the same report, the NMAP notes that "to prepare students for Algebra, the curriculum must simultaneously develop conceptual understanding, computational fluency, and problem-solving skills. These three aspects of learning are mutually reinforcing and should not be seen as competing for class time" (p. 19).

The terms *automaticity* and *fluency* appear in this passage to have the same meaning. However, Armbuster et al. (2001) differentiate between these terms. They suggest that fluency should be reserved for more complex repertoires, whereas automaticity refers to the learner's capacity with foundational elements:

> Although the terms automaticity and fluency often are used interchangeably, they are not the same thing. Automaticity is the fast, effortless word recognition that comes with a great deal of reading practice. In the early stages of learning to read, readers may be accurate but slow and inefficient at recognizing words. Continued reading practice helps word recognition become more automatic, rapid, and effortless. Automaticity refers only to accurate, speedy word recognition, not to reading with expression. Therefore, automaticity (or automatic word recognition) is necessary, but not sufficient, for fluency. (p. 21)

Both reports also note that both reading comprehension and mathematics computational facility depend on automatic or fluent performance of tool skills.

The RTI framework embraces a similar perspective. In the two curricular areas where RTI is most commonly applied—reading and mathematics—virtually all of the progress-monitoring tools have a frequency aim. That is, number correct per unit of time is the metric used to evaluate performance. CBM (see Chapter 1), a commonly employed progress-monitoring tool, provides a good example. CBM chooses metrics that predict performance on high-stakes macro-level assessment, using speed as well as accuracy as a critical component of the prediction. Hosp et al. (2007) say about different measures of reading mastery that each assessment provides a different score, but all scores are based on the number of items correct in a set amount of time, reflecting the student's accuracy and fluency on the task. Stanley Deno (2003) concurs:

> All CBM scores are obtained by counting the number of correct and incorrect responses in a fixed time period. In reading, for example, the most commonly used measure requires a student to read aloud from a text for 1 minute and have an observer count the number of correctly and incorrectly pronounced words. (p. 185)

Deno also notes the evidence that performance on rate-based measures predicts success on high-stakes assessment:

> Students reading at least 40 words correctly in 1 minute by the end of first grade are on a trajectory to succeed in learning to read, and students reading more than 110 words correctly in 1 minute by the beginning of third grade are most likely to pass their state assessments in Oregon. . . . Eighth grade students who can read at least 145 words from local newspaper passages correctly in 1 minute are almost certain to pass the Minnesota Basic Skills Test in reading. . . . (p. 189)

Despite mounting evidence about the importance of fluent repertoires, neither CBM nor the RTI framework offers teachers guidance about how to facilitate their acquisition. Furthermore, the terms *fluency* and *frequency* are often used interchangeably, with little expressed interest in the other by-products of performance that constitute fluency. Third, much of the literature on building frequency or fluency doesn't take into account methods that achieve the best performance trajectories or celerations.

A MATCH MADE IN HEAVEN

PT is ideally suited to be a partner in the RTI movement, for several reasons: its development of effective practice strategies, its use of rate as the measure of performance, its interest in other by-products of fluency as well as frequency, and its emphasis on changes in rate over time (celerations) as an important indicator of learning. Current performance levels and learning trajectories are fundamental to the purpose and current use of RTI in classrooms and schools. In addition, PT's effective and efficient practice strategies provide the "how-to" that the RTI framework doesn't address. Last, its provision of strategies to assess the other important by-products of high-frequency performance that characterize everyday definitions of mastery (see the section on "getting the MESsAGe" in Chapter 2) make it a particularly useful companion. In the remainder of this chapter, we first describe a number of ways that PT can benefit the RTI framework. We then briefly review the history of the use of PT in the K–12 system. Finally, we relate PT to six key elements of the RTI framework: screening, Tier 1, Tier 2, Tier 3, progress monitoring, and data-based decision making.

PT Benefits RTI as a Screening and Placement Tool

The ease with which learning celerations can be depicted in standardized charts in the PT technology facilitates placement decisions. Although rate of performance at a given point in time is a useful measure, celerations, which track changes in rate over time, are much more helpful in determining *learning ability or tendency.* Typical RTI assessments measure snapshots of performance in a given moment. However, snapshots often misrepresent the true current level of performance. PT can be used to assess performance over 3–5 days until performance stabilizes, revealing a more accurate measure of present performance. It's for this reason that a Seattle-based neuropsychologist placed her clients at Morningside Academy for several days during her assessment process: to determine both her clients' true performance levels and their growth or learning potential.

Let's examine a prototypic example of the types of cases that have raised placement concerns and that have, in part, fueled the interest in RTI. José is the child of an immigrant family. His primary language is not English, and his family is a non-English-speaking monolingual family. It is likely that in the early grades or shortly after the family immigrated to the United States, José's rate of correct responding on tasks that require reading or speaking English words was considerably below that of same-age peers. However, using that information alone to classify José as in need of special education may disadvantage him. A better measure of his need for special services might be the speed with which he is able to acquire reading and speaking-related skills. The celeration feature of PT provides exactly that kind of information in an efficient way. It reveals José's learning trajectory by looking across a number of tasks on which he is building rate, to estimate how quickly he can acquire new skills. Regardless of his entering competency on critical skills, should José prove to be a speedy learner, this provides additional evidence that the placement team can and should consider in a placement decision.

Although the initial screening instruments that are applied to all children must necessarily be time-efficient, secondary screening of learners whose performance is below that of same-age peers may allow the district to avoid unnecessary special education placement. For learners whose initial screening suggests that they are lagging behind, districts can use the celeration feature of the Standard Celeration Chart to assess their probable learning trajectories and the type and level of instruction that will be required for them to catch up to and benefit from the core curriculum. For example, a paraprofessional might provide José with minimal instruction in a skill on which he showed a deficiency during screening, and then conduct several timings over several days to judge his growth trajectory. If José shows rapid acquisition, the paraprofessional may decide to maintain him in the Tier 1 classroom for the majority of the reading period, but to assign him and other learners with similar growth trajectories to a learner-verified Tier 2 intervention that is known to improve the reading skills of second-language learners for a portion of the reading period. As José masters skills in the specialized program, he may continue to do one or more daily timings on skills in the core curriculum as a way to determine when full-time reentry into Tier 1 is defensible. This empirical approach takes much of the guesswork out of placement decisions and benefits both teachers and learners.

PT Benefits RTI through Fine-Grained Assessment of Skill Acquisition

Some learners lag behind peers for reasons that aren't entirely obvious. A "smart" child may struggle in reading because he or she lacks tool skills that other learners have acquired but that are not directly assessed in the core curriculum. For such learners, PT can be used to diagnose elements of the deficits, provide interventions, and then assess benefits to the learner's performance on tool and component skills that *are* included in the core curriculum. For example, a traditional assessment in grade 6 reading may include reading a list of multisyllable nonsense words but may not assess the learner's fluency on a list of single-syllable nonsense words. Similarly, a traditional assessment in grade 6 math might ask a learner to add fractions with unknown denominators but may not include math facts assessment directly. In both cases, if the learner does not have facility with the lower-level skill, efforts to teach the higher-level one may fail. Because PT assessments can be done quickly, the focus can be on teaching the skills that are missing which, in turn, provides the support these smart learners need to catch up to grade level.

PT Benefits RTI by Providing Efficient Interventions

Many learners struggle in the core curriculum not because of an accuracy problem, but because of a frequency problem. For example, Macy may struggle with problems involving decimals because she isn't up to speed with place values less than 1 (10ths, 100ths, 1,000ths, etc.). She can name the place value correctly, but only after she thinks about it. PT program slices provide opportunities for practice and speedy movement toward fluency. Since this isn't an uncommon problem in the intermediate grades, several learners may benefit from a quick Tier 2 intervention that would get them back on track to benefit from the Tier 1 curriculum.

PT Benefits RTI by Providing Comprehensive, Predetermined Pinpoints for Tool and Component Skills

PT has benefited from expert instructional designers (see, e.g., Markle, 1990; Tiemann & Markle, 1990) over the last half century who have analyzed key academic tasks and identified the tool or component skills that underpin success. Precision teachers have turned these pinpoints into banks of practice slices related to tool and component skills that align, most commonly, with reading, mathematics, and writing curricula. Furthermore, as we have discussed in Chapter 2, they have identified aims that predict that the entire set of by-products of frequency—maintenance, endurance, stability, application, and generativity—will emerge. This saves substantial time and guesswork for teachers, whose days are already stretched to oversee the progress of more than 30 students in some classrooms.

Precision-targeted skill-building slices are typically not provided among the suite of options available from publishers of core curricula. Although virtually all publishers provide practice materials, these materials often lack the calibration that lends itself to efficient practice. Furthermore, only rarely have publishers incorporated the level of analysis needed to uncover the entire range of tool and component skills that, when built to fluency, result in improved performance on the components or composites of which each skill is a part. Access to both the analyses and the finely calibrated practice sets can benefit both teachers and learners, and, when used as prescribed, can result in the kind of performance growth that districts and parents desire.

PT Benefits RTI through Visual Analysis and Problem Solving with the Standard Celeration Chart

Another important feature of a fully adopted PT model is the Standard Celeration Chart. As we have discussed in Chapter 2, the chart is a ratio or multiply–divide chart instead of an equal-interval or add–subtract chart. This means, among other things, that it reveals learning trajectory or growth as more data points are plotted on the chart. This feature allows users to project the trajectory forward in time to estimate when a skill will reach rates that have been associated with fluency. Let's say a teacher knows that for learners to stay on track with the math curriculum, they need to have developed automaticity with multiplication and division facts by the end of the year. However, several learners' December learning trajectories suggest that they won't reach that goal. For those learners, the teacher can provide additional practice opportunities to change the slope of the trajectory and get them back on track.

PT Benefits RTI through Decision Rules That Accompany Standardized Learning Pictures

Among the other advantages of the Standard Celeration Chart, its standardization results in *learning pictures*—visual representations of the relation of correct and error celerations—that are easy to "read." These learning pictures assist teachers in the data-based decision making that is a key feature of RTI. The chart provides incontrovertible evidence to both a teacher and a learner about the learner's progress, and lets both know when the learner is ready to move on to a different skill because the desired aim has been achieved or to move out of an intervention entirely.

The chart may also reveal when the number of errors is so high that the best course of action is to build either accuracy or rate on a subset of items in the current practice set or even on a prerequisite skill. Sometimes learning pictures suggest that additional instruction is required to prepare for successful practice, or that *tips and quips* may be sufficient to get the learner on the right trajectory. Tips and quips (Johnson & Street, 2004) are quick reminders to the learner to apply a rule or to attend to particular characteristics of the problem. Often used in the pacing or individual-turns pieces in direct instruction boardwork, they also can improve responding during practice.

Figure 4.1 provides five examples that illustrate how the learning picture provided by the graph informs the teacher about the best course of action. Here's a story to accompany each of the five.

> *Example 1:* This is Jasper's learning picture. Jasper's corrects are increasing and his errors are decreasing, just as they should with appropriate practice and feedback. In fact, his performance looks so good that the teacher may choose to make no

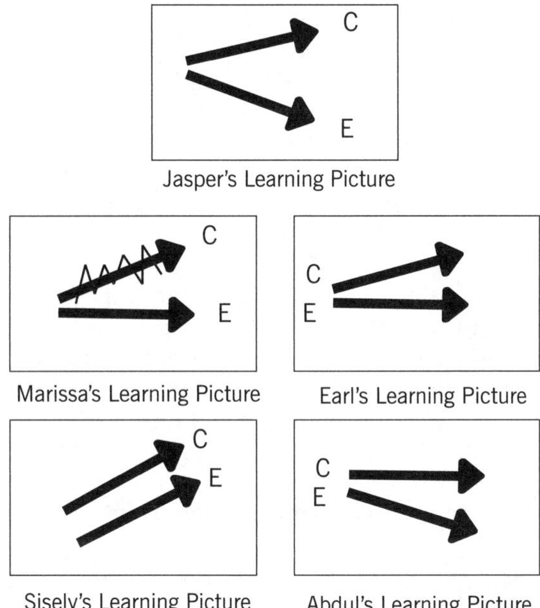

FIGURE 4.1. Five prototypic Standard Celeration Chart learning pictures. Adapted from Haring, N. G., Liberty, K. A., and White, O. R. (1980). Rules for data-based strategy decisions in instructional programs: Current research and instructional implications. In W. Sailor, B. Wilcox, and L. Brown (Eds.), *Methods of instruction with severely handicapped students* (pp. 159–192). Baltimore: Brookes. Copyright 1980 by Paul H. Brookes Publishing Co., Inc. Adapted with permission. Pseudonyms of learners have been added to correspond to stories in the text.

changes. Alternatively, she may decide that his progress warrants intervening to produce an even steeper celeration. Overall, though, this is the ideal learning picture.

Example 2: Marissa's corrects are increasing and her errors are holding steady, but her performance is highly variable from day to day. This pattern suggests that the teacher needs to identify circumstances that account for the variability. For instance, Marissa may need to be seated with her back to other students who may be distracting her until she improves her focus on the task at hand.

Example 3: Earl's corrects aren't increasing, but his errors are. This suggests that he is becoming increasingly confused about the task. A good solution might be to ensure that he is making the proper discrimination, in keeping with the PT adage *Discriminate before you generate.* For example, if the task is to say the place value of a number in a five-number figure, providing a mini-lesson on each place value name and giving Earl think time before he signals a response might be called for. When Earl's corrects stabilize, the teacher would then pace an increase in speed, ensuring that the error rate doesn't creep back up.

Example 4: Sisely's corrects are increasing at a good celeration, but her errors are also increasing. This may indicate that she is moving so quickly that she isn't attending to important instructional cues. For example, in a mixed addition–subtraction practice set, Sisely may need to be reminded to focus more on the addition or subtraction sign before responding. In other words, Sisely may need to be encouraged to slow down a bit and get her errors under control, and then build rate from there. The mantra that precision teachers use in such cases is this: *Fluency is not about a race, it's about a pace.*

Example 5: Abdul's learning picture reveals that although his corrects per minute are increasing and his errors are remaining quite low, the celeration or rate of increase is also very low. In this case, the teacher might use brief sprints of 15 seconds until Abdul's frequency for that period is a little more than one-fourth of the frequency that would put him on the right growth trajectory, and then build back up to the 1-minute timing from there. Alternatively, the teacher may note that he covers the next item while responding to the previous item, and may suggest a way he can follow along without losing the important "looking ahead" advantage.

Table 4.1 summarizes the most common learning pictures and recommends modifications to instruction or practice that may resolve those pictures where change is recommended. Of course, the test of any modification is a learner's progress. Should the next data point on the chart following an instructional or practice modification reveal that the learner's performance isn't improving or is heading in the wrong direction, the teacher should look even more carefully for potential sources of error or poor celeration.

PT Benefits RTI through Enhanced Support for Frequent, Time-Based Measurement

PT brings progress monitoring on key skills or its tools or components from a weekly, monthly, or (most typically) quarterly basis into the classroom's daily routine. Just as the RTI framework's addition of the meta-level assessment (CBM or CBA) reduced the wait time from annual (macro-level) assessment for a reliable indicator of performance growth, PT provides an even finer-grained opportunity to assess each student's learning trajectory. Most importantly, it provides information that enables teachers to make midcourse corrections even earlier than they are currently able to do with meta-level assessment. Just as the RTI process of quarterly assessment and interventions results in improved learning compared to annual assessment and intervention, daily assessment and decision making speed up progress even more. If a primary goal of RTI is to arrange circumstances that set the stage for the large majority of learners to benefit from the evidence-based core curriculum, then PT technology is well positioned to assist in meeting the goal.

PT Benefits RTI by Addressing the Roots of Problems

PT practice typically focuses on *tool* and *component* skill learning, which has been correlated with improvements on *composite* skills, giving it the added bonus of addressing the root of a struggling learner's problem. Let's look at some examples.

TABLE 4.1. Suggested Interventions for Six Types of Learning Pictures on a Standard Celeration Chart

Characteristics of the learning picture	Name for the intervention	Types of intervention most likely to work
Corrects are increasing at a reasonable celeration, and errors are decreasing or stable.	No change	• Leave it alone!
Correct rates are not getting better or are increasing more slowly than error rates (White & Haring, 1980).	Slice back (White & Haring, 1980)	• Select a practice set that isolates the part of the current skill on which the learner is *not* making errors, and build rate to aim on these parts before adding complexity (White & Haring, 1980). • Select a practice set that isolates the skill within the practice set on which errors are made; use tips and quips to remind the learner of important discriminations or associations; and build rate to meet the frequency aim on this skill before returning to the original practice set. • In both scenarios above, it may be helpful to introduce 10- to 15-second sprints until the learner shows improved performance (accurate and fluent). Then build up to 1-minute timings before returning to the component or composite skill.
Corrects are staying the same or going down and are lower than the error rate (White & Haring, 1980).	Step back (White & Haring, 1980)	• Move back to a slightly more elementary skill that is a prerequisite for the current material (White & Haring, 1980). • Step back to instruction in order to firm up responses. For example, provide more explicit direction in multiple modes; move back to a model/demonstrate if errors occur at the "lead" phase or back to "lead" if errors occur at the "test" phase; rethink types of prompts; modify materials; etc.
Errors are low, stable, or decreasing, and corrects are higher than errors but increasing slowly.	Sprint	• Introduce 10- to 15-second sprints to give the learner the feeling of going faster, and then build back up to 1-minute timings. • Increase positive consequences for improved rate. • Observe the learner to determine ceilings he or she may be placing on performance. Suggest ways in which item-to-item movement can be improved.
Corrects are decreasing or very unstable, and errors are decreasing or remaining level; or corrects are less than chance; or corrects decelerate after a promising start.	Monitor distractions and reinforcers	• Remove distractions at least until improvements appear, and then reintroduce appropriate levels of distraction. • Ensure that reinforcers are appropriate in quality and schedule, and contract for points related to improvement and stability. • Ensure that poor performance isn't resulting in greater payoff than appropriate performance.
Corrects and errors are both flat, or errors are increasing and corrects are decreasing or flat.	Provide guided practice and pace performance	• Review both antecedent and consequent variables. If the learner is not making correct responses during independent turns in instruction, he or she may need more guided practice. • If the learner is going faster than his or her prompts might be expected to drop out, thus producing a high error rate, you may wish to pace the learner's performance. • If the learner's performance is jerky, you may wish to do 10-second sprints with prompts to move smoothly from item to item until the performance evens out.

Example 1: Johnna is struggling with sound–symbol associations, the basis of decoding. Rather than automatically assigning more practice on that skill, a precision teacher might assess Johnna's phonological coding to determine whether her problem arises from weaknesses at the auditory level—sound discrimination. Should that prove to be the case, Johnna would be provided the opportunity to practice phonological coding. Depending on the severity of the deficit, practice on sound–symbol association might be interrupted during the phonological coding practice, or the teacher might decide to continue the sound–symbol work and look for changes in accuracy and fluency that correspond to improvements in phonological coding.

Example 2: Herschel is struggling with oral reading fluency and, despite repeated practice on passages, shows minimal improvement. Again, rather than practicing that skill in which errors are not only frustrating Herschel but also interfering with his comprehension, a precision teacher would assign practice on the word parts that an analysis revealed were creating the problem. So, for example, if Herschel's errors were related to discrimination of short versus long vowels, practice sessions would focus on that skill.

Example 3: Miranda's progress in mathematics stalls when she reaches long division. It would not be uncommon for her teacher to assume that she doesn't understand the long-division process. A precision teacher might instead focus on tool or component skills that are sufficiently weak to interfere with Miranda's proficiency with the long-division algorithm. The teacher may determine that Miranda needs greater fluency on add–subtract or multiply–divide number families, in order to succeed in the "divide–multiply–subtract–bring down" algorithm that characterizes long division. Alternatively, the teacher may determine that Miranda needs more practice in estimating.

Example 4: Darby's compositions are choppy and lack the kind of flow her teacher prefers. The teacher's first action is to provide additional opportunities to practice compositional writing, but the additional practice doesn't improve Darby's skills. Upon further investigation, the teacher discovers that Darby doesn't know how to use connecting words to combine several short thoughts into a unified whole. The teacher decides to assign Darby to practice sentence-combining exercises, and tracks improvements in her compositions during the time that this intervention is in place.

Example 5: Let's say that Sergio's reading rate is quite slow. Further investigation reveals that the disruption arises because he hasn't mastered the final-*e* rule. The teacher continues to pursue the case in order to institute a plan that will solve the problem in the least amount of time. Sergio might benefit from a direct instruction lesson that focuses on discriminating the presence or absence of the final *e* or on assigning the correct sound (long or short) to its presence or absence. Or if the assessment suggests that Sergio can correctly read the final-*e* words but does so very deliberately or slowly, the intervention might be limited to building rate on the skill.

These are just a few examples that support this PT adage: *The problem that a learner presents is not necessarily the problem to solve.* In each of these cases, a tool or component skill on which mastery of the composite skill hinges is the problem, even though it appears that the deficit is in a composite skill. In general, the more thorough the task analysis on which the core curriculum is built, the more adequate the instructional procedures will be. In addition, the greater the degree to which learners achieve frequency aims on tools and component skills, the more likely the majority of them will be able to progress through the curriculum without interruption.

Experienced teachers may recognize the roots of learners' problems, but they may not have easy access to calibrated and well-sequenced practice sets to address these. Simply put, the practice sets and standardized routines involved in the PT technology are preventive and allow for quicker and more enduring fixes.

HISTORY OF PRECISION TEACHING IN THE K–12 SYSTEM

PT evolved out of the need to provide additional support for struggling learners. As a result, it came to be associated with remedial programs, including Title I programs, academic tutoring, language therapy, and special education. The PT technology now is better developed and has been used more frequently in the K–5 system than in middle school, high school, or college instruction.

Many current applications of PT occur in 1:1 "clinical" interactions between a single teacher and a single learner. Learners may be meeting with an academic or behavioral therapist for academic tutoring or language therapy. Children with developmental disabilities and autism may also receive 1:1 PT. In a 1:1 arrangement, progress in both instruction and practice can be charted. It is relatively easy to keep data while teaching one person.

In classrooms and with groups, PT is used for practicing skills and concepts that a teacher has taught to the whole group. Each student then practices with a timer and works with at least one other peer in correcting and charting performance. It is not practical for teachers to provide 1:1 instruction with each member of a class, so other teaching methods must be employed. PT can reasonably be aligned with virtually any instructional method that specifies and calibrates learner outcomes. In fact, many core curricula and specialized interventions that are evidence-based and learner-verified already employ a form of frequency building in their activities. For example, after students achieve accuracy on elemental or basic skills, authors and publishers often recommend picking up the pace to ensure that the performance is not only accurate, but sharp. In a small group or with the entire class, this pacing is a preparatory step toward building frequencies with PT that will meet real-world requirements.

That PT has only rarely been associated with general education is due in part to its inclusion in preservice programs and professional development activities for special educators, and its exclusion from similar programs for general educators. However, there are exceptions that point to its utility in general education. According to Carl Binder (1988),

> Perhaps the most widely cited demonstration of this technology was the Precision Teaching Project in the Great Falls, Montana school district, accepted by the Office of Education Joint Dissemination Review Panel as an exemplary educational model for both regular and special education. . . . Teachers engaged elementary school students in 20 to 30 minutes per day

> of timed practice, charting, and decision-making in a range of basic skills over a period of four years. The results were *improvements between 19 and 44 percentile points* on subtests of the Iowa Test of Basic Skills, as compared with children in control group classrooms elsewhere in the same school district. These are exceptionally large improvements with a comparatively small expenditure of time and effort. In addition, original copies of the materials used for these practice and measurement sessions were available at very low cost from the Precision Teaching Project for unlimited duplication by teachers. (p. 13; emphasis in original)

A replication of the original Great Falls study was conducted in 1996–1997 at Chief Joseph School in Great Falls, Montana. As Figure 4.2 reveals, it produced growth almost identical to that described by Binder (1988).

Morningside Academy in Seattle, Washington, and the Roger Bacon Academy in Leland and Whiteville, North Carolina, are also notable PT implementations in general education. Both have employed PT successfully with students who are progressing through the curriculum at typical or even accelerated rates. Although many students first enrolling at Morningside Academy are behind same-age peers in reading, mathematics, and writing, only about 40% of them arrive with a special education diagnosis. Morningside attributes its outstanding outcomes in large part to the focus on PT practice technology (Johnson & Street, 2004). Roger Bacon Academy, which enrolls 900 students at its Leland site and 500 at its Whiteville site, conducts reading fluency trials 3 days per week in every K–5 classroom, and math facts timings occur daily (A. Calkin, personal communication, May 16, 2011).

MasterMind Prep, an online tutoring and test prep service that prepares students to master academic skills for school, college, and life, also employs PT in its work with

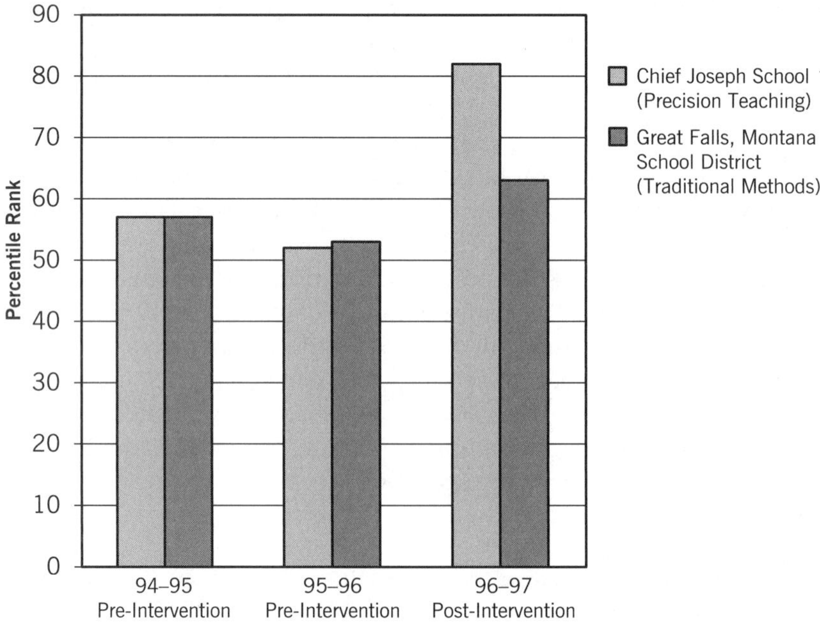

FIGURE 4.2. Percentile rank data from the Great Falls, Montana, PT replication in 1996–1997.

students in general education who want to improve their performance and in its SAT-Prep classes. MasterMind Prep says that PT

> uses a student's own performance data (some call it "the learner knows best") to set specific baseline skill levels and goals and to accelerate skill fluency, which is defined as accuracy plus speed. [As] in medicine ([e.g.,] measuring a heartbeat), Precision Teaching provides numerical performance fluency standards, frequent practice and a consistent method of recording, analyzing and making decisions based on student performance data. . . . Students chart progress that compares current with past performance and shows trend lines toward individual fluency goals and errors. ("Precision Teaching," n.d.)

In his 1985 doctoral dissertation, Binder described a series of classroom studies that revealed improved performance levels and learning rates as a result of adding brief, timed practice periods to the class day. Commenting on this evidence in his 1988 article in *Youth Policy,* he concluded that "explicitly timed practice, independent of any other instructional intervention, may be among the most cost-effective educational methods available" (p. 13).

RTI provides an opportunity to bring the benefits of PT to all students, regardless of their placement. PT holds promise for improving the number of students who thrive in Tier 1 settings, for speeding up the progress of students who require Tier 2 intervention, and for providing specialized skills training for students who require the individual instruction characterizing Tier 3.

FROM SCREENING TO DATA-BASED DECISION MAKING

PT has the potential to enhance the effectiveness of RTI in measuring and ensuring student progress, particularly in six key areas:

- Screening—to identify students at risk.
- Tier 1—as a systematic whole-class method to build core skills or supplement core skills instruction.
- Tier 2—to speed progress of learners who require instruction in small-group interventions.
- Tier 3—to benefit learners whose skill deficits are extreme or sufficiently unique that they require highly specialized individualized intervention.
- Progress monitoring—to assess growth and to project performance on annual standardized tests.
- Data-based decision making—to assist teachers in prescribing changes in programs or placements.

Screening

As we have noted in the earlier example with José, rate of performance at a given point in time is only one indicator that a learner is progressing well or failing to progress. Here's another example: Imagine that Anna has been diagnosed with developmental delays, and her parents have spared no expense to provide educational support. During screening, Anna's rate on specific skills—oral reading or math facts—may be at grade level, but a tool that looks at anticipated growth in a novel skill without special intervention may reveal the need for extra support. Recognizing the importance of keeping screening brief, improved diagnosis and prescription results when an "assessment classroom" approach is used to determine not only current rate of performance, but also typical growth trajectory with and without additional support.

PT and the Standard Celeration Chart can provide a fine-grained analysis of a learner's ability to thrive, and can reduce frustration and stigmatizing if educators provide appropriate Tier 1 support from the beginning instead of waiting for poor performance to trigger a review. For example, knowing that José is behind his classmates but is a fast learner, the placement team may plan for him to use some of his seatwork time to build vocabulary and rate on conventions of the English phonetic code. In Anna's case, the team could arrange for a teacher aide or even Anna's parents to work on building rate on tools and components that will allow her to match the progress of the rest of the class.

The chart can also be used to confirm placements. If, for example, José's case were to reveal that he is not only behind his same-age peers but also has a relatively slow learning trajectory, the team might begin the year by having José work in small-group instruction with other students whose screening reveals similar deficits, or might even decide that intensive individualized instruction holds the best promise to bring his skills to a level that he could thrive in the Tier 1 environment. Similarly, in Anna's case, the chart would reveal whether the provision of additional support would make it possible for her to keep pace with her Tier 1 classroom peers, and could thus be used either to confirm or to rethink her placement.

The advantage of estimating learning trajectory during screening is that interventions—whole-class, small-group, or individualized—can prevent performance failures down the road and reduce or even eliminate the emotional impact that can accompany them. PT can be used to confirm placements based on both learning status and trajectory.

Tier I

PT holds particular promise for learners who are in Tier 1, because of the speed with which it can assist them in developing fluency with tool and component skills, which will free them to focus on composite skills in the curriculum. In virtually any curriculum and particularly in K–5 classrooms, teachers recognize the importance of practice, and most core curricular materials in these grades provide opportunities for practice. However, the kinds of practice sets that are available and the way they are employed may not produce the most effective results and may even increase the chances that able students will require Tier 2 services. The well-known football coach of the Green Bay Packers, Vince Lombardi, was quoted as saying, "Practice doesn't make perfect; only perfect practice makes perfect." We agree, and offer the following critique of traditional (mostly imperfect) practice.

Only occasionally is practice timed, and when it is, the time available to complete the assignment often exceeds the time it would take an expert to do the work. This extra time allows learners to achieve correct responses by depending on prompts to complete the assignment. For example, they may count on their fingers or draw marks on the page to complete a math facts page. Or they may recall that *a* says "æ" as in *apple,* as a way to correctly read words with the short-*a* sound. Although such prompts may be useful during initial acquisition, they interfere with fluent performance during composite activities, such as reading with prosody or using math facts in math computation. However, when students reach expert-level performance rates on the tools and components, the likelihood that they'll be able to concentrate more fully on composite skills is greatly enhanced. Figure 4.3 provides a prototypic example of a publisher-provided seatwork or homework assignment in mathematics. It is not uncommon for teachers to set aside up to 25 minutes for an exercise of this sort, which should easily be accomplished in 1 minute by fluent performers. This not only creates an opportunity for off-task behavior; it also loses classroom time that could be spent on instruction or more focused practice.

Much of the practice that is prescribed by publishers is not sufficiently calibrated to allow rate-based comparisons from assignment to assignment. In Figure 4.3, for

Adding Three-Column and Two-Column Numbers with and without Regrouping

In this exercise, you'll be adding two- and three-column numbers just like these. Remember to regroup if you need to.

423 + 42 465	1 1 176 + 97 273

Find the total for each problem.

253 + 63	728 + 43	478 + 21	369 + 50	514 + 71
462 + 17	928 + 33	174 + 67	823 + 46	681 + 19

Write the answer on the line.

623 + 79 = _____ 843 + 86 = _____ 265 + 34 = _____ 517 + 81 = _____

Write in the missing numbers in these problems.

242 + 29 2_1	93_ + 47 982	783 + 1_ 795	377 + 65 _42

Find the answers to these problems. Use the space below to solve.

Marty had saved $465 to buy a guitar. He worked for his dad for one weekend and earned $38 more. How much does Marty have altogether?

Serena needed 23 more flowers to complete her project. She already had 277. How many did she need altogether?

FIGURE 4.3. Prototypic mathematics seatwork practice exercise.

example, learners move between different types of problems in which they add three- and two-digit numbers with and without regrouping. This makes it challenging for the learners to get into the flow of the task and interrupts overall performance rate. The teacher is left with accuracy as the only available measure of mastery. As we've noted earlier, however, accurate performance and fluent performance aren't the same thing. The kind of practice illustrated in Figure 4.3 may be appropriate at the end of a lesson in which the focus is responding correctly to different formats for adding three- and two-digit numbers with and without regrouping. However, it's not a good exercise for building frequency on the individual elements or on their combination.

PT practice sets and routines are arranged to make practice efficient and effective. Using these efficiencies, a Tier 1 classroom teacher could select practice sets for key curricular elements and establish a period of time in each curricular area during which all students would complete daily or three-times-weekly timings. In reading, for example, the ability to read nonsense words at prescribed rates predicts overall reading ability (Fien et al., 2008), and once readers have mastered the sounds of letters, the ability to read multisyllable words benefits oral reading passage fluency. Therefore, frequency-building exercises in reading might include basic decoding of single-syllable nonsense words in grade 1 (Figure 4.4) or multisyllable word reading in grade 2 (Figure 4.5). Reading comprehension is aided not only by the ability to read at conversational rates, but also by fluency with the vocabulary included in the passage (Tucci & Johnson, 2012). The practice cards in Figure 4.6 exemplify one way learners can build rate on vocabulary.

Good writing, as we have mentioned earlier, depends on a number of skills that can be practiced in isolation. One such example is sentence combining (Figure 4.7). Examples in math might include math facts (Figure 4.8) and simple computations (Figure 4.9).

Although some teachers do not subscribe to the tenet that rate or frequency is a necessary component of fluency, most would agree that practice to automaticity is important. PT provides a time-sensitive way to encourage a great deal of practice in a short period of time and to build the kind of automaticity that facilitates performance on more complex skills. Furthermore, the similarity between timed daily practice and timed meta-level assessment (e.g., CBM probes) reduces the learner's apprehension about the timed components of high-stakes assessment.

Another weakness of traditional practice is that there commonly is only one version of a practice set. This either assumes that the learner will meet criterion in one practice, or doesn't account for the possibility that learners will memorize the order of answers. Strange as it may seem, students who are struggling in a content area may find it easier to memorize the order in which answers appear than to learn the discriminations necessary to respond to an individual problem. Most PT practice sets provide several versions of each curriculum slice. Morningside Press's *Morningside Phonics Fluency: Basic Elements* (Johnson, Casson, Street, Kevo, & Melroe, 2005) provides four versions of each practice sheet. Multiple versions are also provided in *Morningside Mathematics Fluency* (Johnson, 2005, 2008a; Johnson & Casson, 2005a, 2005b) and in *Teaching Computation Skills: A Diagnostic and Prescriptive Instructional Sequence*[1] (Johnson & Melroe, 2006a,

[1]This program is made up of two volumes for addition and subtraction, two volumes for multiplication and division, three volumes for fractions, and two volumes for decimals.

CCVC				BASIC ELEMENTS					Slice 16	
brip	flit	plox	skib	smix	shiv	thux	shan	grez	prab	10
drot	fron	snil	smot	wrub	wres	plat	whap	glin	glup	20
gran	skot	brub	fleb	thim	swem	drod	scog	slub	drus	30
wheg	snup	spip	whin	frug	blos	frag	chot	blap	crod	40
wrub	grez	tros	wrab	creb	prem	clav	scog	shum	plat	50
snup	spip	glin	swem	prut	sced	fleb	gran	trub	sten	60
flit	frug	slub	shan	drod	frag	whap	brip	trix	chot	70
snil	brub	skot	slan	shiv	drus	swip	glup	crod	thux	80
blos	plox	wres	skib	spof	whin	smot	prab	smix	thed	90
cran	drot	fron	plen	clom	blap	thim	chux	stad	wheg	100
Aim: 100 - 80 Corrects per Minute									**Version 3 of 4**	

FIGURE 4.4. Frequency-building practice sheet for single-syllable nonsense word decoding. From Johnson, Casson, Street, Kevo, and Melroe (2005). Copyright 2005 by Morningside Press. Reprinted with permission.

Word Workout Fluency		lessons 14-15 Version 1		-al, -ous, -ent/-ant, -ence/-ance, -ency/-ancy ization, fication, already a word		
perpendicular	Mexican	Alaskan	aromatization	victimize	hypnotize	6
certification	seminar	capatalist	cellular	sanitization	rectangular	12
ratification	personalize	ratification	spectacular	metropolitan	modification	18
cosmopolitan	qualification	catamaran	modernization	republican	certification	24
qualification	molecular	immunization	equalize	cosmopolitan	globular	30
artisan	popular	cosmopolitan	nullification	spectacular	globular	36
vocalization	cosmopolitan	geneticist	cardigan	monopolization	mannerism	42
putification	victimize	secular	energize	samarian	cynicism	48
colonization	catagorization	pollenize	patronize	fortification	hypnotize	54
sanitization	popularize	mystification	veteran	sensitization	ratification	60
aromatization	nationalist	clarification	fantasize	summarization	sanitize	66
seminar	cardigan	apologize	economist	normalize	dramatization	72
consumerism	simplficaton	fertilize	terrorist	monopolization	exemplar	78
catamaran	pessimism	qualification	muscular	consumerism	qualification	84
generalize	monopolist	qualification	hypnotize	fertilize	energize	90

FIGURE 4.5. Frequency-building practice sheet for multisyllable words. Unpublished sheets created by Morningside Press to accompany Lewkowicz (1994). Reprinted with permission of Morningside Press.

2006b, 2009, 2011). Many other publishers of PT practice sets also provide multiple versions of each practice sheet.

Because protocols for practice and charting performance are routinized, both teachers and students can complete this work easily and often in less time than curriculum-based practice sets require. They also provide the added bonus of allowing teachers to project performance on meta- and macro-level assessments and to intervene as soon as needed. For example, if several learners are not meeting rate aims that predict success on meta- and macro-level assessments, an analysis of errors may suggest additional instruction or specific practice on a curriculum slice. Because these interventions can occur as problems emerge in real time, they have the advantage of correcting errors before they become entrenched or before they frustrate learners.

FRONT		BACK	
FRONT	Insatiable	BACK	Unable to be satisfied
FRONT	Predominant	BACK	Having superior strength or influence
FRONT	Sublime	BACK	Majestic, grand
FRONT	Laborious	BACK	Difficult; demanding great effort and hard work
FRONT	Nefarious	BACK	Very wicked, vicious
FRONT	Clamor	BACK	Loud noise, uproar, shouting

FIGURE 4.6. Sample SAFMEDS (an acronym for *Say All Fast, a Minute Each Day, Shuffled*) cards for vocabulary practice. See also Tucci and Johnson (2012).

Name_____________________ Date _______	**Slice 13**	**Aim: 320-360** letters *written* in three minutes

Chapter 8: Combining Three or More Sentences with the Same Subject (Continued)

Following the patterns you learned in Chapter 8, combine these sentences using commas and the word AND. Repeat words when you think it makes a sentence sound or communicate better. Write your answers on loose-leaf paper.

9. Every child can tell of his ominous presence.
   Every child can tell of his ruthless temper.
   Every child can tell of the fate of his wives.
   Every child can tell of his own fate.

10. The woman felt her heart ache with sorrow.
    The woman cried bitterly.
    The woman could not believe what they had done.

11. The grave gentleman led the way to the coach.
    The grave gentleman opened the door.
    The grave gentleman helped the children in.
    The grave gentleman quietly shut the door behind them.

12. One afternoon, Master No-book skipped school.
    One afternoon, Master No-book sprawled on the sofa.
    One afternoon, Master No-book ate potato chips.
    One afternoon, Master No-book played Nintendo all day.

13. The stranger was a man of the world.
    The stranger was kind and gentle.
    The stranger was easily trusted.

14. Sandra and Jamie sat on the swings.
    Sandra and Jamie gathered up speed.
    Sandra and Jamie spun themselves around.

15. The King of the Golden River uttered his final speech.
    The King of the Golden River turned away.
    The King of the Golden River walked into the center of the flames.

FIGURE 4.7. Frequency-building practice sheets created by Morningside Press for sentence combining. Reprinted with permission of Morningside Press.

___________ Name

Morningside Math Facts Fluency
Add-Subtract
ALL FACTS

Review 1 - 16
Missing Numbers

0 9 ___	5 5 ___	___ 9 13	___ 2 11
3 ___ 12	___ 5 10	3 ___ 6	3 2 ___
9 ___ 14	9 5 ___	4 ___ 10	5 ___ 7
5 ___ 7	7 8 ___	8 4 ___	4 ___ 11
___ 9 18	8 ___ 13	6 ___ 9	___ 4 7
8 2 ___	___ 4 9	___ 9 18	___ 4 7
9 ___ 17	___ 7 10	___ 5 11	4 ___ 6
9 ___ 13	___ 7 13	2 ___ 2	3 3 ___
6 ___ 12	___ 9 14	2 5 ___	2 ___ 10
___ 3 12	8 ___ 10	6 ___ 8	8 ___ 16
7 8 ___	___ 4 11	6 2 ___	___ 9 18
5 ___ 9	7 6 ___	2 7 ___	8 4 ___
___ 2 3	___ 2 9	7 ___ 14	7 ___ 9
___ 9 17	3 ___ 8	5 ___ 12	8 ___ 12
6 ___ 13	4 4 ___	8 6 ___	2 5 ___
8 3 ___	___ 9 14	7 7 ___	___ 4 8
___ 7 14	3 6 ___	1 5 ___	9 ___ 16
8 ___ 17	___ 8 17	___ 5 9	9 3 ___
7 4 ___	3 8 ___	___ 5 7	9 9 ___
8 ___ 13	6 ___ 13	___ 8 17	4 ___ 9
3 2 ___	0 0 ___	___ 5 11	___ 2 4
3 4 ___	___ 7 14	___ 8 12	9 9 ___
7 5 ___	6 5 ___	___ 2 11	3 ___ 9
___ 10 11	3 3 ___	6 6 ___	6 ___ 15
5 5 ___	2 2 ___	6 2 ___	___ 3 6
25	*25*	*25*	*25*

FIGURE 4.8. Frequency-building practice sheet for all math facts (1–16). From Johnson (2008a). Copyright 2008 by Morningside Press. Reprinted with permission.

Morningside Math Fluency:
Computation with Whole Numbers
Subtraction

Version: **9** Facts: **1 – 16**

60,000 – 57,410	120,082 – 88,047	1,308 – 654	689 – 233	50,045 – 34,771	20/20
6,002 – 455	104,240 – 76,845	706 – 166	663 – 316	108,804 – 74,647	20/40
750 – 120	120,208 – 77,468	50,181 – 44,808	3,064 – 1,564	8,504 – 1,463	20/60
905 – 660	603 – 223	7,600 – 7,130	104,000 – 77,456	10,370 – 2,074	18/78
7,070 – 5,228	20,742 – 4,300	702 – 61	440 – 225	360 – 124	18/96

FIGURE 4.9. Frequency-building practice sheet for simple computation. From Johnson and Melroe (2006a). Copyright 2006 by Morningside Press. Reprinted with permission.

Tier 2

Including PT as an intervention in Tier 2 holds promise for producing speedier results and enabling a quicker return to full inclusion in Tier 1 activities. That, of course, is the primary purpose of Tier 2 interventions. Typically, schools are encouraged to avoid individualized instruction in favor of standard teaching and practice protocols in Tier 2. The assumption here is that the 10–15% of students who aren't progressing in the core curriculum reflect deficiencies in the instructional protocols; therefore, a standard intervention should result in improved learning for all students. Ideally, teachers would have at their disposal a number of mini-curricula that are capable of responding to the most common curricular weaknesses. These may include both additional instruction and well-calibrated practice.

Tier 2 interventions typically focus on building tool and component skills that are critical to success in the composite skills that predict improved performance on meta- and macro-level assessment. Two examples of skills that are often overlooked in math curricula or for which many publishers provide limited practice are "See/say or hear/write whole numbers" and "See/say place value." For some learners, the typical coverage results in limited mastery. Figures 4.10 and 4.11 are drawn from *Morningside Mathematics Fluency: Basic Number Skills* (Johnson, 2005) and represent the last in a series of increasingly challenging practice sets that build up to these terminal levels. Well-designed practice sets like these that focus on building frequency on the tool skill certainly improve performance on the skill itself, but they also lead to improvements on components and composites in which it is embedded. For example, students who struggle with place value or with hearing and writing whole numbers that include a zero may not only improve their performance on these two skills, but also reduce errors on problems they are to write as the teacher reads them.

Similarly, practice sets such as those exemplified in Figures 4.4–4.7 may prove too challenging for some learners, who may need a slower progression to apply rules (e.g., discriminating when a long or short vowel is appropriate) effectively. For another example, learners who struggle with the cumulative set of all add–subtract math facts reflected in Figure 4.8 may benefit from a few minutes of practice daily on component sets that include only a portion of the number families[2] (Figure 4.12). Depending on the number of students who fail to progress on the cumulative sheet (more than or less than 20% of all students in the class), the teacher might introduce subsets of the cumulative number family practice sets for all students in Tier 1 or might assign them as a Tier 2 intervention.

As we've indicated earlier, many students struggle with subsequent or composite skills because they still depend on prompts to ensure that they respond correctly. Practice gradually reduces the need for prompts and moves a task from accuracy to fluency. However, some students require additional instruction to make progress on a skill set or pinpoint. Another major benefit of the fine-grained task analysis and calibration of many PT practice sets for mathematics and reading is that they make any additional instruction on the skill to be practiced fairly straightforward.

---

[2]Morningside Academy uses a *number families* approach to teaching both add–subtract and multiply–divide facts, because it embeds math facts in the reciprocal properties of the two sets of operations, and also reduces the number of individual facts to be learned by 75%. Thus students learn the add–subtract number family 4, 3, 7, from which they can derive two addition and two subtraction facts: $4 + 3 = 7$; $3 + 4 = 7$; $7 - 3 = 4$; and $7 - 4 = 3$. Chapter 8 discusses number families in more detail.

Morningside Math Fluency: Tool Skills

See/Say, Hear/Write Numbers

Cumulative Whole Numbers with Zeroes

Version: **5**

Number of Digits: **9**

1.	**3,000,004**	26.	**70,008**	51.	**50,900,003**	76.	**104,812,600**
2.	**739,070,700**	27.	**600**	52.	**29,000**	77.	**420,620,500**
3.	**109**	28.	**219,000,700**	53.	**800**	78.	**6**
4.	**80,050**	29.	**203,100**	54.	**10,061,120**	79.	**8,004,028**
5.	**80**	30.	**90,000,400**	55.	**8,069,002**	80.	**570,807,000**
6.	**70,000**	31.	**510,050,740**	56.	**83,000**	81.	**903**
7.	**508,018**	32.	**2,068**	57.	**80**	82.	**5,400,958**
8.	**1,908**	33.	**50**	58.	**700**	83.	**820,292,060**
9.	**402,497,020**	34.	**2,070,033**	59.	**10**	84.	**109,200,010**
10.	**88,080**	35.	**1,000,038**	60.	**80**	85.	**20**
11.	**40,300,030**	36.	**60,200**	61.	**90,041,290**	86.	**7,000**
12.	**307**	37.	**700**	62.	**967**	87.	**882,605,300**
13.	**4,191**	38.	**70**	63.	**10,070,010**	88.	**800,050**
14.	**7,202,103**	39.	**900,050,090**	64.	**7,108**	89.	**80,030**
15.	**4**	40.	**6,004,057**	65.	**6**	90.	**500**
16.	**35**	41.	**73,030,600**	66.	**1**	91.	**5,007**
17.	**300,612**	42.	**862,404**	67.	**207,806,000**	92.	**6,000,070**
18.	**68,700**	43.	**360,000**	68.	**5,030**	93.	**800,000,060**
19.	**76**	44.	**70,000**	69.	**896,001,050**	94.	**5,009**
20.	**410**	45.	**80,400**	70.	**916**	95.	**20**
21.	**400,008,000**	46.	**14**	71.	**200**	96.	**78,800,700**
22.	**465,100**	47.	**5**	72.	**5,905**	97.	**1,395,130**
23.	**5,000,042**	48.	**29**	73.	**614,002,000**	98.	**6,771,060**
24.	**2**	49.	**20**	74.	**4,005**	99.	**10,000**
25.	**60,000**	50.	**50,006,880**	75.	**500,104**	100.	**109,008,000**
	124 : 5.0		131 : 5.2		121 : 4.8		154 : 6.2

(Total Digits : Average Digits per Entry)

FIGURE 4.10. Frequency-building practice sheet for "See/say or hear/write whole numbers" (cumulative whole numbers with zeroes). From Johnson (2005). Copyright 2005 by Morningside Press. Reprinted with permission.

Morningside Math Fluency: Tool Skills

Sheet Number: 4	Digits in Whole: 9
Place Value & Rounding	Digits in Fraction: 0

1. **1** 35,073,767	16. 20 **6** ,980,096	31. **4** 89,917,592
2. 2 **8** 8,480,375	17. 309,98 **9** ,486	32. 163,503, **0** 44
3. 746,91 **0** ,967	18. 868, **5** 71,982	33. 3 **5** 8,730,041
4. 416,8 **9** 5,582	19. 5 **8** 1,281,457	34. 52 **1** ,579,920
5. 8 **5** 7,376,422	20. 551,3 **6** 7,462	35. 820,99 **6** ,720
6. 895,602, **2** 55	21. 530,6 **0** 4,315	36. 414,537,2 **7** 7
7. 389,0 **4** 4,500	22. 375, **0** 84,125	37. 4 **7** 3,845,735
8. 156, **5** 49,602	23. 397,3 **8** 9,051	38. 171,6 **4** 5,283
9. 996,597, **2** 71	24. 712,709,56 **7**	39. 478,74 **2** ,647
10. 1 **5** 3,147,694	25. 509,65 **2** ,408	40. 34 **1** ,194,840
11. 221,7 **3** 3,294	26. 851,4 **3** 8,986	41. 38 **6** ,691,424
12. 744, **2** 65,795	27. **7** 68,582,107	42. 385,073, **7** 77
13. **5** 20,966,124	28. 5 **8** 5,947,658	43. 925,71 **3** ,120
14. 9 **8** 7,765,599	29. **5** 22,891,568	44. **5** 30,410,622
15. 2 **3** 6,438,971	30. 14 **1** ,385,964	45. 5 **2** 1,133,537

FIGURE 4.11. Frequency-building practice sheet for "See/say place value." From Johnson (2005). Copyright 2005 by Morningside Press. Reprinted with permission.

___ Name	Morningside Math Facts Fluency Add-Subtract		Cum 1 - 5 Missing Number
0 1 (All digits), 2 2 4, 2 3 5, 2 4 6, 2 5 7, 2 6 8, 2 7 9, 2 8 10			
2 7 ___	___ 6 8	___ 2 10	7 ___ 9
8 2 ___	5 2 ___	2 ___ 9	3 2 ___
0 0 ___	6 2 ___	___ 2 4	3 2 ___
8 ___ 10	2 ___ 6	___ 7 9	2 8 ___
___ 6 8	___ 2 9	8 2 ___	7 2 ___
2 ___ 5	2 7 ___	2 ___ 5	3 ___ 5
8 2 ___	5 2 ___	___ 7 9	1 6 ___
___ 2 9	2 2 ___	2 ___ 4	2 ___ 4
___ 2 7	2 ___ 8	2 ___ 4	6 2 ___
3 2 ___	2 8 ___	___ 7 9	2 8 ___
1 2 ___	2 ___ 4	8 ___ 10	___ 2 9
2 ___ 4	2 4 ___	5 ___ 7	2 ___ 4
2 ___ 6	6 ___ 8	4 2 ___	2 ___ 6
3 2 ___	0 1 ___	___ 2 9	2 5 ___
2 2 ___	7 ___ 9	4 ___ 6	2 7 ___
6 ___ 8	___ 2 9	___ 8 10	2 ___ 8
___ 2 9	2 ___ 4	2 ___ 7	2 ___ 4
___ 2 10	___ 2 8	2 5 ___	2 ___ 8
___ 2 9	6 2 ___	2 4 ___	2 ___ 4
7 2 ___	___ 6 8	3 2 ___	4 2 ___
4 1 ___	___ 8 10	2 8 ___	4 ___ 6
2 6 ___	2 ___ 5	2 2 ___	2 5 ___
8 ___ 10	___ 2 8	2 2 ___	2 ___ 7
6 ___ 8	___ 7 9	6 ___ 8	8 ___ 8
7 ___ 9	___ 8 10	___ 5 7	___ 2 10
25	*25*	*25*	*25*

FIGURE 4.12. Frequency-building practice sheet for a subset of math facts. From Johnson (2008a). Copyright 2008 by Morningside Press. Reprinted with permission.

This is particularly true for teachers who have access to two outstanding guides for teaching these content areas: *Designing Effective Mathematics Instruction: A Direct Instruction Approach* (Stein, Kinder, Silbert, & Carnine, 2006) and *Direct Instruction Reading* (Carnine, Silbert, Kame'enui, & Tarver, 2003). Each provides more and less structured scripts that communicate in unambiguous terms how a learner is to respond and the conditions under which different responses are appropriate. Figure 4.13 provides an example of a script for reading numbers from the Stein et al. (2006) text. Note that this script has both a structured and an unstructured board presentation. These scripts are designed for use with small groups of learners who respond chorally to a teacher's instructions. Once learners have responded correctly to several examples, the teacher may provide some additional independent practice opportunities and then have learners work in pairs to practice using PT practice sets like those illustrated in Figure 4.10. We provide guidelines for peer coaching in Chapter 5.

Tier 3

PT is well positioned to improve the performance of Tier 3 learners as well. If a teacher employs the evidence-based Tier 1 curriculum and Tier 2 interventions with fidelity, fewer than 10% of students in a classroom should require individualized instruction to make progress in the curriculum. Although instruction in Tier 3 is based on a careful analysis of an individual learner's skill and process deficits, learners may or may not work alone. If two learners present a similar learning challenge, the same instructional protocol may be appropriate for both, and working as a pair may have some advantages. However, as we note in Chapter 5, peer coaching may not be appropriate if neither learner is well positioned to assess, provide feedback on, or recommend interventions for a peer's performance. Those whose learning trajectories show particularly slow celeration may require individualized support or individualized contracts to meet their performance goals.

Students in Tier 3 may vary considerably in the instructional, practice, and management tasks and protocols that they will require to make adequate progress relative to their current performance. Some may be sufficiently behind their peers that they need to acquire a fairly large repertoire of academic skills to be able to work with their classmates. Others may have achieved 100% accuracy on skills being taught in the Tier 1 curriculum, but may be struggling with rate building in all curricular areas. Some may require a schedule or type of reinforcement to maintain and accelerate their progress that is not available in Tier 1 and Tier 2 programs. Still others may present behavior management challenges that have slowed their progress. However, even in these situations, practice is an essential ingredient. PT technology can facilitate performance gains on a wide array of academic goals and remove many of the occasions for misbehavior.

For many Tier 3 students, it is often necessary to build tool skills that are not within the scope of the typical general education classroom. Some learners that are placed in Tier 3 will spend the majority of their time working on preacademic tasks, for which PT provides practice activities that correspond to evidence-based teaching programs. In most cases, these will be learners whose overall learning trajectories are well below those of the typical learner. However, other learners who will require individualized Tier 3 instruction may have skill deficits because they have not received the kind of naturalistic instruction on skills that are prerequisite to reading or math. For example,

FORMAT 5.9 Reading Numbers 100–999

TEACHER	STUDENTS
PART A: STRUCTURED BOARD PRESENTATION	
1. *(Write the following chart on the board.)*	
hundreds / tens / ones — 5 / 4 / 8	
(Point to appropriate column as you say the following.)	
This is the hundreds column.	
This is the tens column.	
This is the ones column.	
Tell me the names of these columns.	
(Point to the columns, starting with hundreds; repeat until students are firm.)	hundreds, tens, ones
2. The first thing we do when we read a number is identify the column the number starts in. *(Point to 5 in 548.)*	
What column does this number start in?	hundreds
How many hundreds do we have?	5
What do five hundreds equal?	500
3. *(Point to 4.)* What column is this?	tens
How many tens do we have?	4
What do four tens equal?	40
4. *(Point to 8.)* What column is this?	ones
How many ones do we have?	8
What do we say?	8
5. Let's read the whole number. When I touch a numeral, you tell me what it says.	
(Point to 5, pause a second, touch 5.)	500
(Point to 4, pause a second, touch 4.)	40
(Point to 8, pause a second, touch 8.)	8
6. Say the whole number.	548
7. *(Repeat steps 2–6 with 697, 351, 874, 932, all written in place value charts.)*	
Note: When presenting examples with a 1 in the tens column, present the following steps instead of steps 3, 4, and 5 in the format. The following example shows how to teach the number 514.	
8. What column is this?	tens
How many tens do we have?	1

(cont.)

FIGURE 4.13. Direct instruction script for reading numbers 100–999. From Stein, M., Kinder, D., Silbert, J., and Carnine, D. W. (2006). *Designing effective mathematics instruction: A direct instruction approach* (4th ed.). Upper Saddle River, NJ: Prentice Hall. Printed and electronically reproduced by permission of Pearson Education, Inc., Upper Saddle River, New Jersey.

TEACHER	STUDENTS
9. How many ones do we have?	4
We have one 10 and four ones, so what do we say?	14
10. Let's read the whole number. *(Point to 5.)* What do we say for this?	500
(Points to 14.) What do we say for these?	14

PART B: LESS STRUCTURED BOARD PRESENTATION

1. *(Write the following chart on the board.)*

hundreds	tens	ones
4	4	6

2. Now we are going to read the numbers without saying the parts first.
   This time when I point, you are going to tell me the whole number.
   (Point to 446 and then pause 2–3 seconds.)
3. *(Repeat step 1 with 249, 713, 321, 81, 720, 740.)*
4. *(Give individual turns to several students.)*

FIGURE 4.13. *(cont.)*

prior to working on "See/say sounds or words," teachers may need to build frequency in phonological coding—a skill that the majority of learners have at the time they enter kindergarten—for children whose life experiences haven't provided the instruction. For a good number of them, intensive individualized instruction may bring them into line with their peers very quickly, and they may be able to rejoin Tier 2 or Tier 1 curricular or program activities. Once again, the teacher should keep a watchful eye on learning celeration: Learners who acquire the skill quickly are likely not to have encountered it before in any systematic way. On the other hand, those whose celerations are low or for whom progress stalls may continue to require intensive individualized instruction on each newly encountered academic skill.

Progress Monitoring

The Daily per minute Standard Celeration Chart is the ideal tool for progress monitoring, because it displays not only current performance levels but also shows growth trajectories or celerations. Let's say, for example, that Figure 4.14 provides a picture of Abeer's performance on "See/say nonsense words," a skill that predicts oral reading fluency. The aim for this skill is 100 words per minute (wpm), and Abeer is currently at 80 wpm. However, the chart also reveals a fairly steep learning curve or celeration. Her rate grew from 40 to 80 wpm in the last week, a celeration of ×2. In other words, her rate doubled in the last week. By extending Abeer's celeration line, the teacher can project that Abeer will get to the prescribed rate of 100 wpm with another 2 days of practice. She is also tracking Abeer's oral reading rate and sees that they parallel each other. That

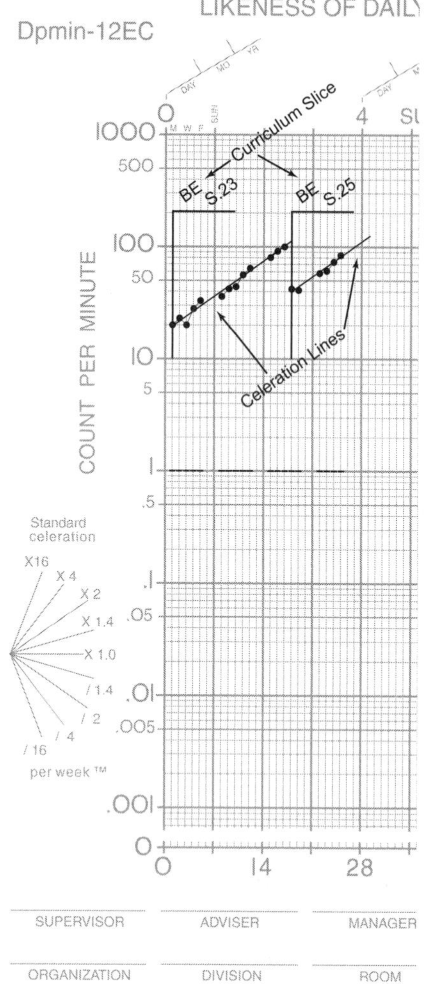

FIGURE 4.14. A likeness of a Daily per minute Standard Celeration Chart showing data and celeration lines for Abeer on "See/say nonsense words." Used with permission of the Behavior Research Company.

is, as her rate of reading nonsense words increases, her celeration for oral reading rate is also doubling.

The chart can also reveal when low celerations are specific to one or a few areas of the curriculum or are generic to all areas. Let's say, for example, that Grace's celerations in reading are at ×1.25, but that in math her "See/say place values" rate is doubling every week (a ×2 celeration) while her errors remain low. This scenario suggests that Grace can work quickly; that is, building rate on a see/say task itself is not a challenge for her.[3] However, the two pictures suggest that additional interventions in reading may improve her progress.

[3]It's important to make judgments about overall fluency potential within each learning channel. Had the math worksheet required a written response (e.g., "See/write missing elements from number families"), it wouldn't have necessarily revealed frequency-building potential for "See/say words" (Fabrizio & Moors, 2003).

Data-Based Decision Making

An advantage of combining PT technology with the RTI framework is that it provides the opportunity for more frequent performance feedback and, as needed, interventions. As we have noted in Chapter 1, Ysseldyke (2006) has presented preliminary evidence suggesting that data from students' daily performance predicted their performance on annual high-stakes state tests. Similarly, teachers at Morningside Academy have a long history of tracking daily celerations on the Standard Celeration Chart and accurately projecting performance on meta-level assessments. When daily performance suggests that learners are below the trajectory required to meet the meta-level assessment benchmarks, teachers intervene immediately. Even for our expert precision teachers, the first intervention isn't always successful. But because they are monitoring and making decisions daily, the probability that they'll solve the problem is greatly increased. Furthermore, when performance on meta-level assessments such as the SRI (see Chapter 1) project lower-than-anticipated performance on annual tests, the first line of defense is to intervene to improve daily celerations. The benefit of using PT technology to gauge learning progress is that when daily practice sets are similar to the meta-level assessments, teachers can intervene each day to improve corrects over errors and can take actions that have a good track record of increasing celerations. The end result is smoother progress toward improved end-of-year performance.

SUMMARY

In this chapter, we have:

- Described educators' growing interest in fluency in important academic tool and component skills.
- Identified ways in which PT can increase the effectiveness of RTI.
- Provided examples of the ways in which the data-based learning pictures that emerge from recordings on a Standard Celeration Chart inform interventions.
- Discussed the major importance of providing practice in the correct curricular elements.
- Provided examples of prototypic PT practice sets.
- Showed how faster resolutions accompany a change from quarterly or even biweekly data-based decision making (which characterizes many RTI implementations) to daily decision making (which characterizes PT implementations).

In Chapter 5, we describe how to implement the five steps of the pure case of PT, and we describe the complementary roles of teachers and peer coaches in achieving efficiencies in implementation. In fact, teachers who combine the Timings Chart and peer coaching approach we describe there with the Daily per minute Standard Celeration Chart avoid many of the faulty learning pictures that are depicted in Table 4.1!

CHAPTER 5

Precision Teaching Technology in Practice

MS. MOORE USES 10 MINUTES A DAY FOR PRACTICE

Ms. Moore* is a fourth-grade teacher in a Tier 1 classroom in a public elementary school in the Midwest. This school has adopted PT practice technologies to firm up core tool skills for Tier 1 students and to build skills for Tier 2 students who require additional small-group instruction and practice. Let's drop in on Ms. Moore's room at the beginning of the year. Today we find her teaching reading. She wants to ensure that students maintain their optimal reading rates, even though their passages are becoming increasingly challenging, with many more multisyllable words and more complex ideas. On the first day of the first unit, she conducts a quick direct-instruction-type lesson by writing new words on the whiteboard and having students respond chorally to each on her signal. She does any necessary error corrections and continues until students are responding accurately. Using individual turns, she then ensures that each learner can see/say each word. She repeats this process on the first day of each new unit. However, on the remaining days for each unit (typically 5), she devotes 10 minutes of the 90-minute reading block to building or maintaining reading fluency. About half of her students need only to maintain their current reading rate of 180–220 wpm, but the other half are still working toward that goal. She has taken several passages from the units in the core reading program and added word counts at the end of each line; she has also made folders for each student with the passages, a timings chart, and a daily chart.

Because these students have used PT practice the preceding year, they are already primed to do peer coaching. Ms. Moore has assigned the students to peer pairs based on their performance on the test given at the end of the previous year; both members of each pair are approximately equal in skill level.

When the 10-minute time period begins, Ms. Moore says, "It's time now for your individual practice. Take out your fluency folders, and move quickly to sit next to your partner. You have 1 minute to get settled." She gives them a point on their daily "support" card if they are ready within the minute, and then says, "Both readers in a pair should prepare their timings charts by identifying today's goal from the daily chart."

She circulates the room, praising students for their speed and accuracy in identifying and recording their daily goal. When students are ready, she says, "Raise your hand if you are going to read first. . . . Good. . . . Ready? Please begin." She starts the timer, which has been set for 1 minute, and "listens in" on several pairs—especially if the reader in a pair has had trouble meeting daily goals in two daily timings. Even though the room is active and noisy, it's clear that students are focused on their own reading. Once the timer rings, Ms. Moore says, "Please count the total number of words, subtract any errors your listener has noted, and record your performance. Please work quickly." The readers record their first performance and draw a line to their daily goal. When each learner in a pair has completed two timings, Ms. Moore has them record their best performance on their daily chart. She then gives them 1 minute to return to their seat and begin practice on definitions of vocabulary words. As students work, Ms. Moore is listening to them read.

At the end of the first week, Ms. Moore scans the charts and divides them into three groups: students who are maintaining and/or exceeding the 180–220 wpm rate; those who haven't yet achieved the criterion but who have celerations of ×1.25; and those who haven't yet achieved the criterion and whose charts show no celeration at all. Of her 30 students, half are in the first group and 6 more are in the second group. However, 6 of the 9 who remain are slowing considerably when they encounter multisyllabic words, and their rates aren't moving up at all. Three more are struggling to read single-syllable words.

Ms. Moore decides to continue the daily timings for the first and second groups. However, she believes that the 9 remaining students need a more intensive approach. To address the 6 who are struggling with multisyllable words, she adopts the REWARDS program, an evidence-based and learner-verified program that teaches "See/say multisyllable words" by using a systematic approach that includes learning pronunciations and meanings of affixes. Beginning with the next unit, she pulls those readers aside, and they devote 30 minutes of the 90-minute reading block to REWARDS. In addition to the exercises in the book, she devotes 10 of the 30 minutes to building fluency on "See/say multisyllable words." They also continue rate building on passages with the other students in the class.

For the 3 students who appear to have more systemic problems, Ms. Moore consults with Ms. Mabry, the school psychologist. Ms. Mabry agrees to assess these three students' reading and suggest the best way to remedy their deficiencies.

*The teacher, students, and locale in this story are fictitious. The story is an amalgam of those we've heard and seen during our 30-plus years of working in schools.

Think back to the five steps of PT that we have described in Chapter 2 and summarized in Figure 2.8. First, the teacher defines a learning objective or pinpoint of what the learner is to accomplish. Second, the teacher arranges materials and procedures for learning and practicing the pinpoint. Third, the teacher and the learner time the student's performance and count its frequency. Fourth, the learner and the teacher chart the learner's performance on a Standard Celeration Chart. And fifth, the teacher and learner review performance trends on the chart and make decisions about the necessity of and possible interventions to improve its growth. The PT motto is *Pinpoint, time, record and chart, decide, and—as needed—try, try again.*

As we have noted in Chapter 2, as long as the five steps of the pure case of PT are present, the system can be adapted in various ways to accommodate a classroom full of learners, a small group of learners, or an individual learner. Ogden Lindsley (1992) has described PT practice sessions this way:

> The only adult in the classroom seems to be loitering. She is not standing in the front lecturing, or sitting at the teacher's desk reading to the class, or grading papers. She is moving about the classroom from student to student, answering a question with a whisper here, offering a quiet suggestion there, helping with a chart decision here, and giving a pat and a smile of appreciation there. . . . The students are busy at their desks, in teams of two, timing each other's practice. . . . The students are noisy, shouting correct answers as fast as they can at 200 words a minute, several shouting at once at neighboring desks. It sounds more like an adult cocktail party or a school recess, than a school classroom. . . . The "precision teacher" performs like a coach, an advisor, and an on-line instructional designer. She arranges materials and methods for the students to teach themselves, including self-counting, timing, charting, and one-on-one direction and support. (p. 51).

Although some aspects of the PT classroom have changed since Lindsley wrote this description, the part that remains is the sense of a busy and productive classroom in which learners are coached to take control of their own mastery, behave in goal-directed ways, and demonstrate learning efficiency that is remarkable.

In this chapter, we begin with a description of how PT technology currently is implemented in the Morningside Model of Generative Instruction at Morningside Academy.[1] We also describe the important role of peer coaching and provide guidelines for its appropriate implementation. We follow with a discussion of how teachers can use these procedures to best advantage in Tier 1 classrooms and as primary components of Tier 2 interventions. We also discuss the important role PT technology can play in achieving improvements for Tier 3 learners. Last, we explain why we are committed to *daily* practice of important tool skills.

IMPLEMENTATION OF PRECISION TEACHING TECHNOLOGY AT MORNINGSIDE ACADEMY

Approximately 40% of class time at Morningside Academy is devoted to practicing critical tool, component, and composite skills. Practice follows instruction that is designed to move learners toward accurate performance and is directly tied to learning objectives that have been the targets of instruction. Although it is beyond the scope of the current book to discuss instructional technology in depth, see Johnson and Street (2004) for a detailed discussion of the critical features of good instruction.

Morningside's PT practice sessions are more structured than many other practice protocols, but they are not (strictly speaking) regimented. Learners and teachers play separate but complementary roles, the outcome of which is well-orchestrated and efficient practice that builds frequency and aids fluency development for targeted skills. Learners may practice the same or different skills during each session. Some learners

[1]See the Preface for more information about Morningside Academy.

meet their daily aims on the first timing, while others require multiple opportunities. When timings call for an oral response, the classroom is awash in sound. Even so, learners—including those who have been diagnosed with attention-deficit/hyperactivity disorder (ADHD) or other disorders that include among their symptoms difficulty in attending or concentrating on a single task—quickly accommodate to the noise level and develop skills necessary to focus only on their own work.

Morningside teachers select worksheets and flashcards from a vast library of materials, and develop new materials as new pinpoints are added to the curriculum. The worksheets and flashcards give learners the opportunity to practice the concepts and skills they have learned during instruction. Learners repeatedly practice completing tasks in a series of short timings, often 1 minute in length. Each skill has a *frequency aim*, stating the number of tasks that should be completed in a timing period to demonstrate fluency. For examples, learners practice math facts until they can write 80–100[2] answers a minute with no errors, solve 8–6 math word problems in 3 minutes with no errors, add and subtract fractions at a rate of 100–80 steps in 5 minutes with no errors, orally read 220–180 wpm in passages with 0–2 errors, find the main idea of 75-word paragraphs at a rate of 8–6 main ideas in 5 minutes with no errors, and write persuasive paragraphs in proper format at 20 words per minute for at least 20 minutes. Depending on the pinpoint, learners may practice over successive days, weeks, or even months until they meet the frequency aim.

Teachers also set 5-day minimum celeration aims for practice. For example, a ×2 (say "times 2") celeration aim requires learners to double their performance frequency each week until they meet the frequency aim. If on Monday a learner can write 40 math fact answers a minute, the learner should be answering 80 math facts a minute by the end of the week. A ×1.5 celeration aim requires a learner who is answering 40 math facts a minute on Wednesday to be writing 60 math fact answers a minute by the end of the following Tuesday. The slope of the celeration line indicates how quickly or timely the learner is to achieve a frequency aim. In most cases, Morningside's celeration aim is ×2. Teachers and learners draw celeration lines on the learners' charts, projecting a doubling of growth every 7 days from the initial plotted frequency, to indicate ×2 growth. Learners then practice to increase their daily frequency at a pace that keeps them on or above these minimum celeration lines.

The PT technology was initially conceptualized to be implemented by a teacher or aide who observed and gave feedback on each learner's performance—and, in the early days of Morningside Academy, that's exactly how it worked. One teacher, sitting in a horseshoe-like seating arrangement on a chair with casters, would "roll" among learners and observe their performance. Often the teacher would set one timer for all learners, and everyone would practice at the same time on the same or different pinpoints. When the timing ended, the teacher would comment on each learner's performance,

---

[2]Many of the practice sets from Morningside Press describe this aim as 100–80 wpm rather than 80–100 wpm. As Eric Haughton observed, the purpose of this transposition is to focus the learner on the higher end of the aim range rather than the lower end; it communicates that although the by-products of frequency may accrue at 80 wpm, striving for the higher end will more clearly achieve the kind of mastery that ensures maintenance, endurance, stability, application, and generativity. From here onward in this book, we state frequency aims from high to low.

noting errors and providing prompts. He or she would then either chart the learners' data (for younger learners) or confirm when older learners charted their own.

It quickly became apparent that using a single teacher to coach all learners was an inefficient use of time. In addition, the amount of time needed to assess and provide feedback varied among students. As a result, Morningside began to experiment with other protocols. The result, which Morningside has used with outstanding results for over 20 years, is *peer coaching*. Peer coaching has been the vehicle through which Morningside has achieved Vince Lombardi's notion of "perfect practice."

PEER COACHING

A coach provides important feedback about a learner's performance and helps to ensure that practice sessions are effective. Without a coach, learners may practice and firm up errors that the teacher will need to correct later—an outcome that will slow progress in achieving frequency aims. Practice is not effective just because there is a lot of it; only when learners receive targeted feedback on their performance are they able to improve its accuracy and frequency. The feedback and evaluation that are hallmarks of coaching avoid this problem. However, it is often impractical for a teacher to serve as a coach for each learner, and precision teachers have found that several benefits accrue from preparing learners to serve as peer coaches for each other:

- Teachers are able to spend more time on problem solving.
- Learners learn more, because feedback is frequent and powerful.
- Learners often learn better and faster from their peers.
- Learners learn the importance of self-evaluation.
- Learners learn self-management and self-monitoring skills.
- Learners learn from "teaching" (coaching) others.
- Learners learn social and cooperative learning skills.
- The teacher's job is easier, because the classroom is filled with effective "teachers" (peer coaches).

Peer coaching has enormous implications for learners' success. In a classroom of 20 or more learners, the teacher cannot possibly provide specific cheerleading and coaching to each learner during and between timings. The experience at Morningside Academy indicates that, at most, only about a third of learners make progress in a timely manner without coaching between timings; for the majority of them, progress simply stalls. Furthermore, both teachers and learners become very discouraged when the learners' frequencies don't improve and their charts "flat-line." This outcome reasonably leads teachers to doubt the effectiveness of PT technology and becomes the reason why some teachers abandon it. Peer coaching frees teachers' time for problem solving and allows them to ensure that all learners are making necessary progress.

In the sections that follow, we discuss the teacher's and learner's roles in the peer coaching paradigm, outline goals and strategies for teaching learners to be effective peer coaches, and describe a procedure known as *chart sharing* that helps to maintain the practice regimen.

The Teacher's Role

Even though learners serve as peer coaches during practice, the teacher plays a substantial role in setting up practice sessions and ensuring their efficacy. First and foremost, the teacher teaches learners how to be good coaches, monitors their performance during peer coaching episodes, and models when learners get off track.

A teacher's first duties occur *before the session begins*. He or she is, first of all, responsible for designing[3] or selecting practice sheets and other materials. Materials should not place a ceiling on learners' performance by limiting the number of opportunities to respond. A good rule of thumb is that there should be more items on a given practice sheet than the frequency aim that is established for it. This rule alone means that many curriculum-based practice sheets need to be modified or enhanced if they are to serve well in the PT regimen.

The teacher should also determine the length of practice timings. Although the standard timing for most practice sets is 1 minute, shorter (*sprints*) or longer (*endurance trials*) timings may be appropriate, depending on a learner's performance. For example, a learner who is overly sensitive to the timer may benefit from a 10-second or 15-second timing as a warm-up for the 1-minute timing. Or a learner who has mastered math facts and uses them correctly in word problems for 1 minute may need a 5-minute or 10-minute timing to build endurance that mimics real-world requirements for applying facts. Or readers who read silently for 5 minutes without a decrement in comprehension may be asked to read for 10 minutes at a comparable speed, all the while maintaining their comprehension.

Next, the teacher should determine the frequency aim and the *celeration aim*—a projection of the optimum number of days it should take to get to the terminal frequency aim. Chapters 6, 7, and 8 provide frequency and celeration aims[4] for reading, writing, and mathematics currently set by Morningside Academy.

The teacher also plays an important role *during the practice session*. First, the teacher assigns learners to pairs. Student pairs should be approximately equal in skill levels. Therefore, the teacher should pair high-performing peers with high- and middle-performing peers and pair middle-level students with high- or low-performing peers. She should avoid pairing high- and low-performing peers, because low-performing peers will not be able to coach high performers. Similarly, pairing two low-performing peers together is not advised, because neither is likely to be helpful to the other.

Second, the teacher confirms that each learner's celeration lines and aims have been established appropriately on the daily chart. He or she also looks to see if the daily goal box has been transferred to the timings chart. Third, the teacher confirms that learners have written the start time for the practice session at the top of the timings chart, and provides feedback on the timeliness with which learners begin their first timing. Once first timings are completed, the teacher circulates and checks to be sure learners have recorded the results of the first timing and drawn a celeration line from the first

---

[3]Although teachers are sometimes called on to design a few specialized practice sheets, development of entire practice sets is time-consuming and challenging work. That's why we recommend obtaining materials such as those developed by Morningside Press or other companies.

[4]These aims are based on more than 30 years of experience at Morningside Academy and at schools and agencies where the Morningside Model has been implemented.

timing to the goal box. If a learner's celeration line is less than ×2, the teacher observes subsequent timings by that learner to ensure that he or she is making adequate progress toward his or her daily goal or to intervene with additional support as needed. The learner who is practicing on a given round continues until the daily (intermediate) goal is reached, and the teacher provides praise or suggests interventions as needed. The teacher also observes and gives feedback on the interactions between members of each pair. For example, during early practice sessions, she may need to remind the member who is in the role of "observer/coach" to provide constructive feedback on errors or to be more forthcoming in praising his or her peer.

The teacher also plays a major role when learners have two consecutive timings that are below the celeration lines on their timings chart. He or she encourages such learners to identify possible sources of errors or stalled celeration, but is also available to provide support and assistance. Should an intervention be required, the teacher ensures that it is appropriately recorded as a phase change on the timings chart.

When learners reach their intermediate aim, they call on the teacher to verify their fluency by watching or listening in on the next timing. It is possible and often necessary for the teacher to observe a timing for more than one learner at a time, although doing so takes practice, particularly on practice sets that require oral responses. The teacher's last step during the practice session is to ensure that each student correctly transfers the day's best timing from the timings chart to the daily chart.

Following the day's practice session(s), the teacher reviews each learner's daily charts and identifies learner pairs that will require attention the next day. If the teacher has not done so during the practice session, he or she can use this time to verify that in situations where the timing produced a permanent product, data are recorded properly, and that corrects and errors are accurately transferred from the timings chart to the daily chart. The teacher also assesses the working relationship within each assigned pair and notes any skills that need to be strengthened. Sometimes he or she may change assignments. This is also a good time to review charts with colleagues. In fact, schoolwide chart shares have played a significant role in many schools in maintaining the practice and charting regimen. We discuss chart sharing later in this chapter.

The Learner's Role

Once paired, learners decide who will be the first performer.[5] Then the peer pair inspects the first performer's Daily per minute Standard Celeration Chart to determine the approximate frequency that will keep this performer on his or her minimum celeration line for that day. We call this the *intermediate* aim. Since the celeration line is continually sloping upward, the frequency that keeps a learner's daily performance on that line is continually increasing as each day passes. For example, suppose that yesterday Jason achieved 40 math facts correct per minute, which kept him on his minimum

[5]When both learners are practicing think/write or see/write timings, both may perform at the same time, setting just one timer. Following the timing, peers take turns looking at each other's work, one at a time. For example, if the timing is for "Think/write the missing element in a number family," both of the performers scan several problems of each family for accuracy. They stay with the first performer's paper until the timing has been charted and each has verified it for accuracy. They also assign short bursts of practice on elements with errors between timings if the data indicate that doing so is needed.

celeration line. Today when he inspects his chart, he determines that he needs to reach a frequency in the upper 40s (he picks 48) to remain on that celeration line. Figure 5.1 shows a Daily per minute Standard Celeration Chart with daily data, a frequency aim, and an arrow pointing to an intermediate frequency aim for a given day.

After determining the frequency that will keep his performance on his celeration line, Jason then plots that frequency as a daily, intermediate aim on a different, second chart—a Standard Celeration *Timings* Chart. He plots his intermediate aim on the 10th vertical timing line. Then he records his start time near the top left of the timings chart, completes his first timing, and plots it on the first timing line. Next he draws a celeration line on his timings chart, projecting from his first timing frequency to his intermediate frequency aim. If this intermediate celeration line is steeper than ×2, he may require constant coaching to reach the daily aim. Learners whose intermediate celeration line is very steep should sit in close proximity to where the teacher is most often located, so that the teacher can provide support, suggestions, and feedback. If the slope of the celeration line is less than ×2, the daily aim may be achieved quickly, with minimal effort.

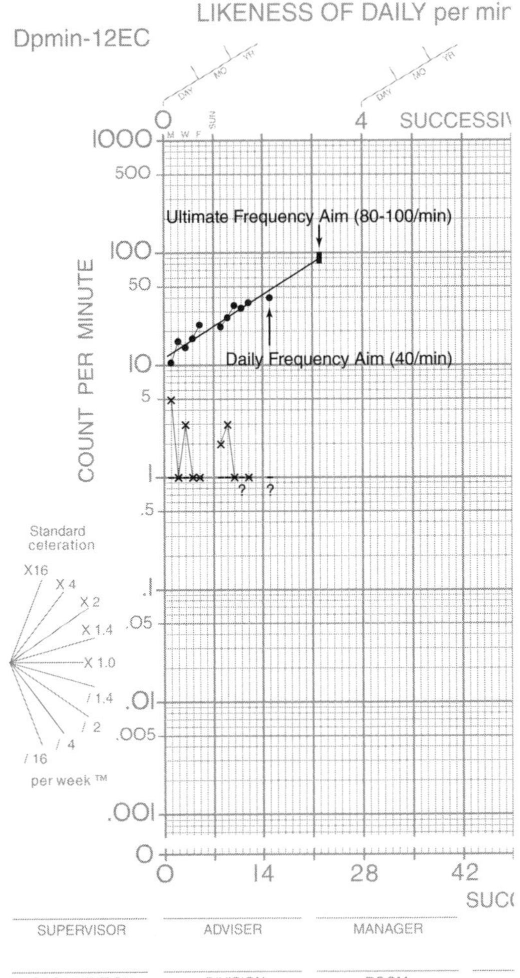

FIGURE 5.1. A likeness of a Daily per minute Standard Celeration Chart showing data, celeration line, and aim. Used with permission of the Behavior Research Company.

Next Jason completes and charts as many timings as it takes to reach his daily aim—in his case, 48 facts per minute. His peer coach, Mandy, provides feedback at the end of *each* timing. When his frequency falls below the celeration line on his *timings* chart or when his error rate is too high, he asks Mandy for recommendations about how to improve his performance. However, if Mandy doesn't have any suggestions, or if her suggestions aren't effective and a second data point falls below the celeration line, the partners ask the teacher for help to make more accelerated progress.

When Jason reaches the intermediate frequency aim specified on his *timings* chart, he records his stop time near the top left of the timings chart. Then the pair calls the teacher to verify that Jason has met his aim. Depending on the teacher's judgment about the accuracy of the timing and charting, the teacher may accept the data or may provide a "verification" timing. Once the frequency has been verified, Jason plots it on his *daily* chart. The pair then switches performer–coach roles, and Mandy repeats the process. For each learning objective or pinpoint, learners typically complete 5–7 timings per day in order to meet their daily aims and thus remain on the ×2 minimum celeration line on

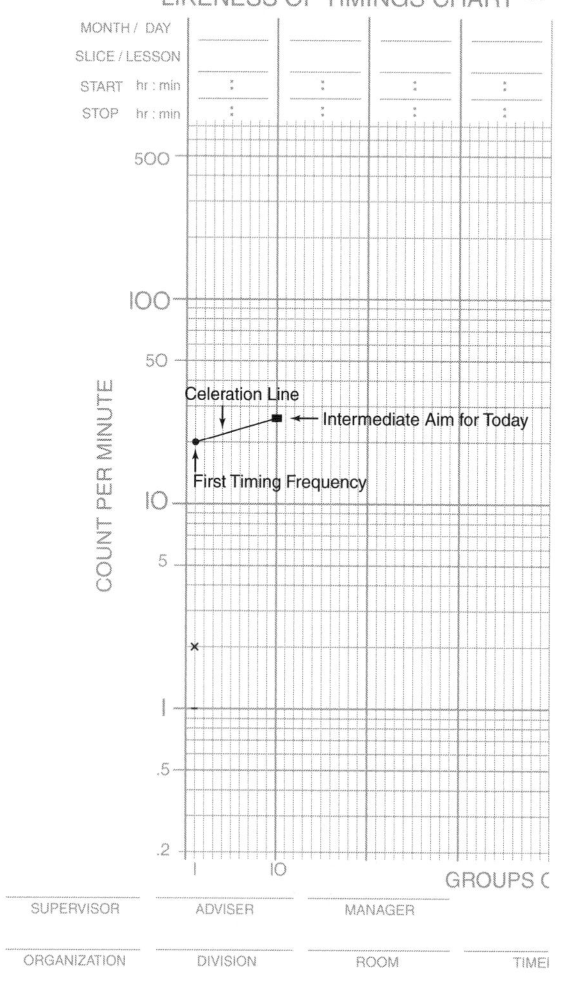

FIGURE 5.2. A likeness of a Standard Celeration Timings Chart with initial frequency, intermediate aim, and celeration line. Used with permission of the Behavior Research Company.

their daily charts. Figure 5.2 shows a timings chart with an initial frequency plotted, and a celeration line drawn from that dot to the intermediate frequency aim for a given day.

Learners inspect their charts in pairs, with one learner observing and cheerleading the other to do better on each successive timing. Between timings, the peer observer provides coaching to the performer. For example, when Jason is doing math facts timings, Mandy has a copy of the same math facts worksheet that Jason is using. During the timing, Mandy observes Jason and marks each math fact answered incorrectly on a copy of the practice sheet Jason is using. Mandy also marks each math fact that Jason hesitated before answering. When the timing is complete, Mandy smiles, says words of encouragement, gives a high-five clap, or in other ways provides positive "strokes" to Jason. Mandy then shows Jason his errors and hesitations, and asks him to practice just those error and hesitation math facts before starting the next timing. When Mandy discovers a new intervention that proves helpful, she should describe the intervention on the back of Jason's chart. You may be surprised at how effective peer-designed interventions can be!

The students' roles are quite critical throughout the learning process, both because of the help they provide each other in the peer coaching scenario and in the feedback they provide to instructional designers. On some occasions, students have told us that our frequency or celeration aims are too low. Sometimes, though not always, they are talking about what they can achieve rather than what is necessary to "get the MESsAGe." In any event, we've learned to take students' feedback seriously and have on occasion changed our aims when evidence suggests that they are right.

Figure 5.3 provides a convenient coaching form that supervisors can use to determine whether teachers and learners are fulfilling their respective roles. Table 5.1 summarizes the steps in Morningside Academy's PT practice sessions. See also Figure 2.6.

Peer Coaching Levels

Some students take to peer coaching more readily than others and develop helping skills that set them above their peers. Teachers may wish to develop guidelines that encourage students to progress through peer coaching levels. For instance, Level 1 peer coaches would be those who have learned how to carefully observe their peers' work and correctly identify errors. Level 2 peer coaches might be those who meet the Level 1 criterion and also have demonstrated accuracy and fluency with respect to plotting their own and their peers' data. Level 3 might be reserved for peer coaches who meet the Level 2 criterion and, in addition, demonstrate effective problem solving; that is, they can prescribe interventions that improve rate or celeration of performance. Additional levels might be established between Levels 1 and 2 and between Levels 2 and 3. For example, the teacher might want to recognize peer coaches who have mastered the art of giving feedback. Most important, however, is to develop a system that rewards students as they perfect the challenging skills that constitute peer coaching. Teachers can establish their own systems for recognizing students as they move through the levels; for example, some may wish to issue certificates, while others may wish to post names in a public place. In all cases, peer coaching works best when the teacher has a clear understanding of each peer coach's level of mastery and uses that information in making assignments and in deciding which students need additional support in the role.

Step	What	Teacher's role	Learner's role
1	Partners move to assigned practice location.	Teacher determines pairings. 0 1 2 3	Partners determine who goes first. 0 1 2 3
2	Daily chart is inspected to determine daily goal (intermediate aim) for day.	Teacher scans for daily goal, celeration line, and aim. 0 1 2 3	Partners verify each others' charts. 0 1 2 3
3	Goal box on timings chart (intermediate aim) is marked.	Teacher circulates and checks. 0 1 2 3	Partners check and request help. 0 1 2 3
4	Start time is written at top, and the first timing begins.	Teacher circulates and monitors. 0 1 2 3	One partner observes and one performs. 0 1 2 3
5	The celeration line from the first timing to the goal box is drawn.	Teacher circulates and monitors. 0 1 2 3	Partners work together and check. 0 1 2 3
6	The celeration line is inspected.	Teacher looks for celeration lines that are more than ×2. 0 1 2 3	Partners work together and check. 0 1 2 3
7	Learners whose celeration line is more than ×2 are observed because they may need more support.	Teacher monitors and determines interventions. 0 1 2 3	Partners move quickly and quietly. 0 1 2 3
8	Partners do as many timings as needed until daily (intermediate) goal is reached.	Teacher gives praise and makes intervention suggestions. 0 1 2 3	Partners coach each other and record stop time. 0 1 2 3
9	Observer acts as a peer coach during and between timings.	Teacher monitors pairs' work and interactions. 0 1 2 3	• Peer coach identifies errors and hesitations. • Coach cheerleads. • Coach leads a mini-practice session between timings. 0 1 2 3
10	Teacher makes a change when two consecutive data points are below celeration line on timings chart.	Teacher identifies pair(s) needing interventions and analyzes data. 0 1 2 3	Partners refer to handout or get help from teacher. 0 1 2 3
11	Intervention is recorded on timings chart with the use of a phase change line.	Teacher checks to see whether intervention is successful. 0 1 2 3	Partner observes and gives feedback. 0 1 2 3
12	Timings are verified when performance reaches daily (intermediate) goal.	Teacher observes multiple learners at one time. 0 1 2 3	Partners are responsible for getting teacher's attention. 0 1 2 3
13	Performance is plotted on daily chart.	Teacher plots if learners are not accurate. 0 1 2 3	Partners check each other's charts for accuracy. 0 1 2 3
14	Partners switch roles and start over.		

FIGURE 5.3. Morningside Academy's supervision form for peer coaching.

TABLE 5.1. Morningside Academy's Steps before, during, and after Classroom Implementation of a PT Practice Session

Prior to implementation

- Teacher designs or selects practice sheets or flashcards with no ceilings.
- Teacher specifies length of practice timings.
- Teacher specifies frequency aim.
- Teacher specifies 5-day minimum celeration aim.

During implementation

- Teacher pairs learners for practice and coaching, but does not pair high with low performers. Partners determine who will practice and coach first.
- Partners inspect performer's daily chart to determine today's *intermediate* frequency that will maintain minimum celeration to the *ultimate* frequency aim.
- Performer plots intermediate aim on timing 10 line of timings chart.
- Performer writes start time near top left of timings chart, completes first timing, and plots on first timing line.
- Performer draws a celeration line from first data point to intermediate frequency aim.
- Performer determines the celeration value of the celeration line.
- Partners sit near teacher for frequent coaching if performer's intermediate celeration aim is greater than ×2.
- Partners complete successive timings until performer reaches intermediate frequency aim. Performer records stop time near top left of timings chart.
- Performer gets peer coaching between each timing. If peer pair is using practice sheets, peer coach follows along on a copy, marking errors and hesitations. If peer pair is using flashcards, coach sorts cards into three piles: corrects, hesitations, and errors. Coach provides cheerleading for correct responses, and practice for errors and hesitations.
- Partners get teacher coaching after each timing that drops below intermediate celeration line drawn on the timings chart.
- When first learner reaches his or her intermediate frequency aim, teacher verifies that he or she has reached the aim.
- Performer plots today's highest performance on daily chart.
- Peers switch performer–coach roles and repeat steps for second learner.

After implementation

- Teacher reviews all timings and daily charts, and prepares remedial instruction for learners who did not reach their daily intermediate frequency aim.

Preparing Students for Peer Coaching

There are at least eight peer coaching skills that require explicit instruction. Following is a description of each.

1. *Organizational skills.* Students need to be able to get out all materials and start working immediately. The goal is to begin a session within 2 minutes of a transition. This means that the classroom must be organized in such a way that everything students need to get started is easily accessible. In the early stages of implementation, teachers may set a stopwatch when the transition begins, rewarding learners who are ready to go within the 2-minute window and providing direction for those who aren't.

2. *Tracking and marking skills.* Peer coaches need to be able to follow along and not lose their focus or place. This may require following along with a finger. Coaches also must be able to mark errors lightly and correctly on their own copy of the exercise with an easily erased pencil.

3. *Endurance skills.* Students need to maintain focus and work as long as needed for both partners to reach their intermediate goals. Teacher praise and encouragement is critical. Students may need to be reminded that "it's about a pace, not about a race." Students should accomplish their intermediate aims with fluid, purposeful movement.

4. *Charting skills.* Students need to know how to count corrects and errors accurately. They must also be able to identify what is being counted during a particular timing, differentiate between the timings chart and the daily chart, identify the daily (intermediate) aim from the daily chart and draw a goal box on the timings chart, draw the celeration line from the results of the first timing to the goal box/intermediate aim, chart performance quickly and accurately on the timings chart, and transfer the day's best timing to the daily chart.

5. *Error analysis skills.* Peer coaches need to discriminate when they can provide a suggestion that would be helpful to their performing peer and when they need to get help from the teacher. To do this, they need some facility in seeing error patterns. For example:

- On a "See/write math facts" timing, a coach may notice that all of the performing peer's errors occurred on one number family, and may recommend a short burst of practice on that family ("Say the number family four times").
- On a "See/write numbers" timing, the coach may notice that one or two numbers are causing trouble, and may recommend a short burst of practice on that number.
- On a "See/say words" timing, the coach may notice that the learner always confuses two words, and may go through the practice sheet pointing out just those two words and asking the learner to say the rule and practice saying the word.

Coaches must also practice recording their "interventions" on the chart.

6. *Feedback skills.* Peer coaches require skill building in giving feedback in a calm and supportive manner and in the spirit of cooperation.

- They should avoid making timings into competitions with their partners, instead emphasizing competition with the performers' last best timing.
- Errors should be corrected without criticism, and coaches should avoid words that might make the performers feel stupid.
- Coaches also should see themselves as cheerleaders for correct responding, and should provide specific praise to their partners for all improvements. For example, instead of saying, "Good work," the coach might say, "Wow, you didn't miss any of the 6, 7, 13 number family problems that time," or "Your errors went down and your corrects went up. That's awesome."
- Here are some other areas where feedback is appropriate:
  - Starting immediately and stopping with the timer.
  - Hesitations.
  - Mini-practice sessions that are used as interventions.

7. *Skills in accepting feedback.* Performers learn not to argue with their coaches' feedback. When disagreements arise, a coach and performer should ask the teacher for help.

8. *Self-reflection skills.* Coaches and performers should be encouraged to use their thinking skills to determine what possible mini-practice or interventions could be effective.

Teachers can employ a variety of strategies to ensure that these skills are successfully acquired.

CHART SHARES

One of the beauties of the Standard Celeration Chart is its uniformity across behaviors and learners. The same celerations always look the same, and as users become familiar with celeration trajectories, they can easily "see" when performance is soaring or stalling. This also sets the stage for sharing charts with others in a time-efficient manner.

Formal and informal chart-sharing sessions by learners, coaches, and teachers provide opportunities to celebrate charts where learners are on or above their celeration line and to recruit assistance in problem solving for those who aren't progressing as expected. Chart sharing also can broaden the abilities of all parties to be *intervention detectives.* Intervention detectives are those who sleuth out performance problems—for example, error rate is too high or celeration slope isn't steep enough—and recommend interventions to solve them. Expert and novice charters both encounter problems for which an easy solution isn't readily apparent, and brainstorming with others can be helpful in achieving an outcome that works to everyone's advantage. In addition, chart sharing appears to be a source of reinforcement for maintaining charts and continuing the PT protocol.

Here's how a chart share works. Each participant "signs in" to indicate that he or she has a chart to share. A timekeeper sets a stopwatch for an agreed-on length of time (typically 2 minutes), during which the participant can say as much about the chart as is needed to set the stage for suggestions or applause. As participants' familiarity with what improvements or stalls look like improves, the presenter can focus on interventions that worked or that have been tried unsuccessfully. As presenters and observers become more and more conversant with the chart, a presenter can show several charts within the allotted time. When the time ends, another participant takes the stage and presents his or her chart(s). When all "signed-in" participants have had an opportunity to present charts, and if the time set aside for the chart share hasn't ended, participants who have more charts to celebrate or discuss can take another turn.

PRECISION TEACHING INTERVENTIONS AT EACH TIER

Tier I (Whole-Class) Implementations

Through implementations of the Morningside Model of Generative Instruction at schools and agencies across the United States and Canada and beyond, Morningside consultants and coaches have had broad experience implementing PT technology in Tier 1 classrooms. In those implementations, we have discovered that virtually all students—even those who are at the top of the class—require some amount of frequency building to get the MESsAGe. (See Chapter 2.)

Mathematics provides an excellent object lesson. Many mathematics curricula use a spiraled approach in which a topic—let's say fractions—is introduced in 1 year for one or two units. Once the unit is concluded, the topic doesn't resurface until the next year. For children whose learning prowess is very strong, this doesn't present a problem. But for the majority, when fractions are reintroduced, teachers must spend an inordinate amount of time getting learners back to where they were at the end of the unit the previous year. Some students may require only brief reminders, but others may need substantial reteaching. It's easy to see the problem this presents: Time that was allocated to teach the new concepts related to fractions must now be spent on review. In addition, this situation often puts in motion the "blame game," in which the fifth-grade teacher blames the fourth-grade teacher for not teaching the content, and so on down the line. In fact, it's not uncommon for students to enter college with mathematics and reading skills that are well below state or institutional standards. For example, a study by the Community College Research Center of Teachers College at Columbia University revealed that half of the students in community colleges in the state of Virginia were enrolled in at least one developmental mathematics, writing, or reading class (Roksa, Jenkins, Jaggars, Zeidenberg, & Cho, 2009)

This is particularly sad, given that efficient and effective practice to prescribed frequencies considerably reduces the amount of reteaching that is required after periods without practice. At most, a few tips and quips plus two or three practices will restore the skill to its previous frequency levels and render it accessible for new applications. At Morningside Academy, even though our students spend nearly half of their time engaged in practice, the payoff is tremendous: They master typical grade-level curriculum at nearly twice the rate students achieve in the public schools.

This suggests that those working with Tier 1 learners should identify skills that are critical to progress in each content area but that appear to be forgotten over months of nonuse. Once these skills are identified, Tier 1 teachers and learners can benefit from efficient and effective practice to build frequency rates that predict the skills will be maintained across typical periods of down time.

Tier 2 (Small-Group) Interventions

PT practice is a particularly powerful way to achieve efficient and effective Tier 2 improvements. Tier 2 interventions are typically employed with small groups of students who have similar skill deficits. They may include instruction and practice or practice only. As we've noted in other chapters, the decision about the focus of the intervention is critical. Progress-monitoring data place learners in Tier 2, and although the ideal scenario has Tier 2 students working together in small groups, such learners will frequently come to Tier 2 with a variety of needs. Charted data on tool and component skills will reveal the specific needs of each learner. Some may need to build tool skills; others may need instruction and practice in component skills. Typically, Tier 2 students continue to participate in the core curriculum while they improve splinter skills. Therefore, it's important to improve tool and component skills first, because they will have the biggest payoff and will ease these students' participation in Tier 1 classroom activities.

Tier 3 (Individualized) Interventions

Two kinds of learners may qualify for a Tier 3 intervention: those who haven't been exposed to the curriculum and are therefore behind their same-age peers, and those who have been exposed to the curriculum but are progressing more slowly than same-age peers. PT is particularly well suited to providing support for both kinds of learners. When students are behind because they haven't been exposed to the curriculum, PT can be combined with well-designed instruction to help them catch up to their peers. For those who have been exposed but are progressing more slowly than their peers, well-designed instruction with PT practice can provide a more solid foundation for moving forward in the curriculum. For students who have not acquired the prerequisite skills necessary to engage in academic learning, PT can be used to assess their general learning rate, as well as to develop the tool skills that are prerequisites for academic or vocational skill development.

AN APPLE A DAY

Learners practice their pinpoints daily in order to reach frequency aims in a timely manner. Our experience tells us that when learners practice every other day or once a week, their celerations are flatter; they take many more practice sessions to reach their frequency aims, if at all. We also schedule PT sessions that are no longer than 30–40 minutes. After 40 minutes of timings and coaching, many learners begin to tire, and the work becomes tedious.

Sometimes learners achieve a frequency aim in a session or two. This occurs for at least two reasons. First, they may already be fluent and do not need the formal practice inherent in PT. For example, none of us probably ever engaged in frequency building in school, yet we have many fluent repertoires. Second, learners may also be good at cramming, and may not be able to perform the skill later. For example, we've noticed many learners who can quickly meet a frequency aim for definitions of vocabulary flashcards, but are unable to define the words after a significant period of no practice. To determine which of these two scenarios is in play and to prevent the "cramming and forgetting" phenomenon, teachers at Morningside have learners engage in at least one practice opportunity across at least 7 days to confirm their facility with a skill.

SUMMARY

In this chapter, we have described a typical PT practice session; discussed the importance of and strategies for implementing peer coaching; differentiated among the uses of PT for Tier 1, Tier 2, and Tier 3 classrooms; and explained why we believe daily timings result in the greatest student progress. Remember, using the Daily per minute Standard Celeration Chart with the Timings Chart and peer coaching approach we've described here avoids many of the faulty learning pictures that were described in Table 4.1! In the next three chapters, we describe instruction and practice routines for reading, writing, and mathematics, respectively, and point readers to sources for well-designed practice sets.

CHAPTER 6

Precision Teaching in Reading

Evaluation of reading programs has received a great deal of emphasis in the last decade. The U.S. Department of Education's National Reading Panel (2000) described five essential ingredients for reading programs in its Reading First mandate (*www.nichd.nih.gov/publications/nrp/upload/smallbook_pdf.pdf*): (1) phonemic awareness, (2) phonics, (3) (passage) fluency, (4) vocabulary, and (5) comprehension.

Our component–composite analysis of reading includes four composite repertoires: (1) prerequisites to reading, including a broad category known as phonemic awareness; visual perceptual behavior; language and listening skills; the alphabetic principle; and print conventions; (2) reading behavior, including decoding words and fluent passage reading; (3) understanding text, including comprehension skills; and (4) strategic, engaged reading, which blends the first three composites and includes self-monitoring of one's own reading performance. Our definitions and descriptions of each component and the methods we suggest for practicing each are closely aligned with the large body of research devoted to reading content analysis and effective reading instruction.

PREREQUISITES FOR READING BEHAVIOR

Phonemic Awareness: Auditory Perceptual Behavior

Phonemic awareness is a broad category of prereading behaviors that encompasses fluency in manipulating phonemes, the smallest meaningful units of sound in a language. Research has repeatedly confirmed that phonemic awareness is a powerful predictor of success in learning to read, more powerful than tests of general intelligence, reading readiness, and listening comprehension (Adams, 1990a, 1990b, 1998; Begeny et al., 2012; Stanovich, 1993). Indeed, phonemic awareness is the chief repertoire that separates "normal" from "disabled" readers (Share & Stanovich, 1995). Adams (1990b) notes that the discovery of the important role of phonemic awareness in learning to read was a pivotal breakthrough in reading pedagogy.

In our behavior analysis, phonemic awareness is further and better described as auditory perceptual behavior.[1] Auditory perceptual behaviors include segmenting sounds in words, blending sounds into words, and discriminating between one sound and another.

The auditory perceptual behaviors that are required for reading include reproducing, discriminating, and manipulating the sounds in a language. Auditory perceptual behavior can be deconstructed into a variety of different pinpoints, each of which can be practiced to fluency. Below we describe suggested pinpoints with aims for practicing each component of auditory perceptual behavior: blending, segmenting, auditory discrimination, and rhyming. Of course, experienced teachers may think of other possible pinpoints to supplement these.

1. *Blending* ("Hear separate, segmented sounds of a word/say [blend] whole word fast"). The teacher or peer coach says the sound segments of a word (e.g., *b-a-n-d,* with a 1- to 2-second pause between each successive sound. The teacher or coach then signals, and the students say a blended word in unison. Practice continues until students respond correctly to 25–20 segmented words per minute. Since phonological coding practice targets auditory behavior, teachers should never supplement their auditory teaching with text, writing, or pictures. These supplements should be reserved for teaching visual perceptual behavior.

2. *Segmenting* ("Hear whole [blended] word/do • say segment into sounds"). The teacher or peer coach says a word (e.g., *band*). The teacher or coach then signals, and the students say the sound segments of the word (*b-a-n-d*) in unison. Practice continues until students respond correctly to 25–20 segmented words per minute.

3. *Auditory discrimination* ("Hear word plus sound/say with sound missing"). The teacher or peer coach says a word (e.g., *street*), then says, "Now say it again, but don't say *st*." The teacher or coach then signals, and the students say *reet*. Practice continues until students say 25–20 words without the sound correctly per minute.

4. *Auditory discrimination* ("Hear two words that are different in only one sound/say missing sound in second word"). The teacher or peer coach says two words, with one sound from the first word omitted in the second word (e.g., *black/back*). Then the teacher or coach signals, and the students say the sound *l* in unison. Practice continues until students say 25–20 missing sounds correctly per minute.

5. *Rhyming* ("Hear two words/say rhyme or not," "hear two sentences/say rhyme or not"). The teacher or peer coach says two words or sentences, then signals, and students say "Rhyme" or "Not" in unison. Practice continues until students respond correctly to 25–20 pairs of words, and approximately 12–10 sentences per minute.

[1]In a pragmatic view, shared by behaviorists (e.g., Skinner, 1974), behavioristic philosophers (e.g., Dewey, 1896, 1981), and several notable cognitive scientists (e.g., Gibson, 1966; Chemero, 2009), perception and cognition are understandable only in terms of action in the environment. Perception is directly observable behavior, in interaction with and subject to environmental influences. Mental representation in the mind has no place in these accounts.

Elizabeth Haughton and a colleague (Haughton & Freeman, 1999a, 1999b) have written an excellent program to teach auditory perceptual behavior. Its two volumes are called *Phonological Coding: Phonemic Awareness and Phonological Coding: Word and Syllable Awareness.* This program includes a placement test, practice sheets, and frequency aims.

Visual Perceptual Behavior

Fluent reading involves many component skills, including a generalized repertoire of rapidly and automatically naming objects, written letters, or symbols in a sequence. Some students need explicit practice in what is called *rapid automatic naming* (RAN) to learn the basic generalized visual perceptual repertoire of rapidly naming successive objects or symbols. Preliminary research suggests that reading fluency is facilitated by providing RAN practice in saying the names of letters in rows on a practice sheet or in saying the names of objects in a series of pictures (Mannis & Freeman, 2002; Neuhaus, Foorman, Francis, & Carlson, 2001). RAN practice continues until students can say 80–60 names correctly per minute.

Elizabeth Haughton (2002) has written an excellent program called *Rapid Automatic Naming: RAN* to build this prerequisite skill. The program includes a placement test and practice sheets with frequency aims for building RAN with objects, letters, and numbers.

Word recognition components of reading require the learner to coordinate both auditory and visual perceptual behaviors. Specifically, readers see a letter or letter combination, listen to the sound it makes, and produce the sound while seeing it. Figure 6.1 illustrates our component analysis of word recognition. Some learners experience difficulty learning these decoding skills. In the last two decades, researchers have made breakthroughs in teaching reading (Adams, 1990a, 1990b, 1998; Rosner, 1993). They have

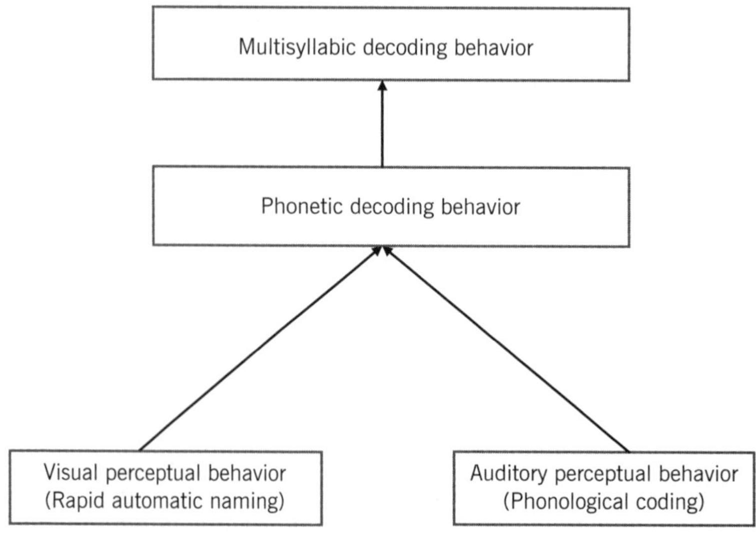

FIGURE 6.1. Morningside Academy's analysis of a word recognition repertoire.

provided evidence of the need to identify and teach the auditory and the visual skills separately and have also provided guidance about how to teach them.

Language and Listening

For successful learning of reading behaviors, a learner's language repertoires should at least match the language repertoires required to understand and describe the "meaning" of the materials the teacher is using to teach reading. Language repertoires also underlie the ease with which word mechanics are mastered. It is easier to chain sounds that lead to a known word, and then to build its frequency to make it a sight word. Sounding out unknown words is quite an arbitrary process and requires prolonged memorization to bring it to fluency, such as when we memorize nonsense words, irregular abbreviations, or statistical formulas that contain parts we do not understand.

Teachers also use language to teach new concepts and skills. If a teacher says, "Break a word into segments that each contain a vowel sandwiched by consonants," a learner who does not know the meaning of *break, vowel, consonant, segment,* and *sandwiched* will not learn the rule. In fact, Engelmann and Osborn have written two programs, *Language for Learning* (2008a) and *Language for Thinking* (2008b), to teach the basic language of instruction used in the primary grades.

The decontextualized language used in books is also foreign to learners whose language background is mostly oral and contextualized. In *contextualized* language, gestures and voice tones "fill in" or replace words and clarify vague pronoun references. For example, when using contextualized language, a learner can point at a person or group of people while saying "him," "her," "them," and so on. Users of context-based language will also point at pictures and objects to facilitate a dialogue without having to express the referents in words. Contextualized language requires a shared experience to be effective. When contextualized language is used out of its context, it cannot be understood by anyone who was not present. For example, if Marcos bothered Katie on the playground by pulling her hair, a child who witnessed the event may say, "He done this to her here." A teacher who was not present will not understand the statement. Written language is not contextual; it is *"decontextual."* Text depends solely upon words and punctuation to reveal meaning.

Many children with reading comprehension problems have not learned decontextualized language; their language is context-bound. They may not have been read to very much, and their home language may be primarily imperative, such as "Go get that" and "Tell her to pick this up." Early in life, meaning is communicated collaboratively, in a social context, with mutual understandings. Learners must learn to communicate without context, gestures, and voice tones to become successful readers.

Fluency building in language may also be a challenge for people with certain types of disabilities. For example, Michael Fabrizio and Kent Johnson conducted a workshop entitled "Language Foundation Skills and Reading Comprehension Success for Learners with Autism Spectrum Disorders" for the Organization for Autism Research, in which Johnson presented the components of reading comprehension, while Fabrizio provided a running commentary on the language repertoires required for each component (Johnson & Fabrizio, 2006). Further analysis of the language skills required for reading is beyond the scope of this chapter.

Our analysis of prereading behavior also includes two other components: the alphabetic principle—that letters stand for sounds in words; and print conventions—identification of book covers, titles, words, pictures, and left-to-right progression from word to word and page to page. Further analysis of these skills is also beyond the scope of this chapter.

READING BEHAVIOR

Our component–composite analysis of reading identifies three composite repertoires of an expert reader: word fluency, passage fluency, and understanding text. Let us describe each in turn.

Word Fluency

The word fluency composite repertoire is the gateway to expert reading. In our analysis, this composite can be broken down into seven component decoding and reading skills, listed in Table 6.1. These are the tool skills for mastery of the next component repertoire, passage fluency. For each of these components, learners practice reading lists containing newly taught sounds, word parts, or words in a series of 1-minute timings. The first three of these components are as follows:

- Saying letter sounds and letter combination sounds.
- Chaining sounds to say a one- to three-syllable word.
- Saying one- to three-syllable words on sight without decoding.

These are relevant to shorter word mastery, and are typically learned in preschool and the primary grades. The next four components are typically learned in grade 4 and higher:

TABLE 6.1. Seven Components of the Word Fluency Composite Repertoire

Step	Step description
1	Saying letter sounds and letter combination sounds
2	Chaining sounds to say a one- to three-syllable word
3	Saying one- to three-syllable words on sight without decoding
4	Saying word part sounds
5	Chaining sounds and word parts to say a whole multisyllabic word (four or more syllables)
6	Accenting the correct word parts while sounding out multisyllabic words
7	Saying multisyllabic words on sight without decoding

- Saying word part sounds.
- Chaining sounds and word parts to say a whole multisyllabic word (four or more syllables).
- Accenting the correct word parts while sounding out multisyllabic words.
- Saying multisyllabic words on sight without decoding.

Saying Letter Sounds and Letter Combination Sounds

The English language includes 44 letter and letter combination sounds. The list is presented in Figure 6.2. The frequency aim we have set for letter sounds is 90–70 sounds per minute.[2] Our celeration aim for building sounds is ×2.

Chaining Sounds to Say a One- to Three-Syllable Word

The second component involves saying each sound in succession, holding the sound until we say the next sound. When all the sounds have been chained together without any pauses between sounds, learners say the word fast, decide whether it sounds like a "real" word they know, and adjust pronunciation accordingly. Our frequency aim for sounding words out/saying words fast is 40–25 per minute. Our celeration aim is ×2.

Saying One- to Three-Syllable Words on Sight without Decoding

The third component involves saying words that incorporate all 44 letter and letter combination sounds without sounding out the words; this is essentially a memorizing activity. Our program, *Morningside Phonics Fluency: Basic Elements* (Johnson et al., 2005), includes practice sheets for 56 types of words, each type emphasizing certain sounds and sound combinations. Figure 6.3 presents the 56 kinds of word slices practiced in the program. Virtually all the words in *Basic Elements* are nonsense words, which prevents older learners from recalling words they have memorized and requires them to apply a decoding strategy. In fact, nonsense word fluency is an excellent predictor of overall reading proficiency in grade 2 (Fien et al., 2008). Our frequency aim for saying one- to three-syllable words is 100–80 per minute, with 0–2 errors. Our celeration aim is ×2.

Saying Word Part Sounds

When learners are sounding out longer words, it is helpful to chunk sounds into longer units, particularly at the beginnings and ends of words. If the number of sounds they attempt to chain is too large, they may forget the initial sounds they produced by the time they get to the end of the word! Archer, Gleason, and Vachon (2005a) provide a table of 18 beginning word parts or *prefixes*, and 39 ending word parts or *suffixes*. The frequency aim we have set for word part sounds is 90–70 per minute. Our celeration aim for building word part sounds is ×2.

---

[2]During instruction, it is important that early readers "stretch" or hold each sound for 2–3 seconds (i.e., about 40–25 sounds per minute). Once the skill is "firm," they can practice until they reach the frequency aim.

Consonants		Vowels	
Sound	Key word	Sound	Key word
/b/	*boy*	/a/	*hat*
/d/	*dog*	/e/	*bet*
/f/	*fan*	/i/	*sit*
/g/	*get*	/o/	*hot*
/h/	*hot*	/u/	*cut*
/l/	*log*	/a_e/	*cake*
/m/	*man*	/ee/	*seem*
/n/	*not*	/i_e/	*time*
/p/	*pan*	/o_e/	*home*
/qu/ (koo)	*quit*	/u_e/	*cute*
/r/	*red*	/aw/	*law*
/s/	*sit*	/ou/	*out*
/t/	*top*	/oi/	*oil*
/v/	*vet*	/oy/	*boy*
/w/	*won*	/oo/	*book*
/x/ (ks)	*fox*	/oo/	*soon*
/z/	*zip*	/ar/	*car*
/ch/	*chin*	/er/	*her*
/ng	*ring*	/or/	*for*
/sh/	*ship*	/ir/	*girl*
/th/	*thin*	/ur/	*fur*
/th/	*them*		
/zh/	*vision*		

FIGURE 6.2. Pronunciation key for the 44 letter and letter combination sounds in the English language.

Chaining Sounds and Word Parts to Say a Whole Multisyllabic Word; Accenting the Correct Word Parts While Sounding Out Multisyllabic Words

Accenting the appropriate word segment for words with four or more syllables requires imitating a model. Nancy Lewkowicz (1985) has identified four core rules and five supplementary rules for dividing and accenting multisyllabic words such as *pedestrian, allergic, hospitality,* and *metabolism.* In her decoding program (Lewkowicz, 1994), students learn how to identify the final suffix in a word, to progress backward from that suffix to identify successive CVC word parts, and to determine whether each vowel says its short sound or the abbreviated *schwa* sound. Different suffixes also determine which

Slice number	Skill	Elements
1	CV	*bi, gu, sa*
2	VC	*ad, et, ub*
3	VCe	*ade, eze, ote*
4	VC/VCe	*ac, ave, ib*
5	CVC	*bix, huf, muj*
6	CVCe	*buze, kise, paje*
7	CVC, CVCe	*bof, fibe, jeze*
8	Endings	*y, ed, tive*
9	CVC + Endings	*buppy, ginnest, lenner*
10	CVCe + Endings	*bener, geping, lopest*
11	CVC, CVCe + Endings	*biping, dotely, hemer*
12	CVC, CVCe ± Endings	*bively, gavest, kibe*
13	VCC	*ald, izz, omp*
14	CCV	*bru, pho, sca*
15	VCC, CCV	*azz, elp, fla*
16	CCVC	*brip, frug, sced*
17	CCVCe	*blefe, crode, grize*
18	CCVC, CCVCe	*brip, skot, whap*
19	CCVC, CCVCe ± Endings	*blossing, plox, swemless*
20	CCVC, CVCC, CCVCC	*glax, clonk, twelp*
21	CCVC, CVCC, CCVCC, CCVCe	*chib, chade, trime*
22	CCVC, CVCC, CCVCC, CCVCe + Endings	*phum, smoded, glize*
23	VCCC, CVCCC, CCCV	*cutch, junch, scre*
24	CCCVC, CCCVCC	*thrabb, thrilt, sprism*
25	CCVCCC	*dranch, scutch, wrinch*
26	Diagraphs: *ai, ay*	*caid, nays, zaik*
27	Diagraphs: *ea, ee, oa*	*yeen, noak, weaz*
28	Cumulative Diagraphs	*beeb, geap, noak*
29	Cumulative Diagraphs ± Blends	*bleeb, frait, keet*
30	Cumulative Diagraphs + Blends ± Endings	*bainful, dreag, laitive*
31	Diphthongs: *ou, ow*	*bowd, moun, zouf*
32	Diphthongs: *oi, oy*	*coyl, noib, zoyf*
33	Diphthongs: *au, aw*	*cawl, maun, zauf*

(cont.)

FIGURE 6.3. Practice slices in *Morningside Phonics Fluency: Basic Elements.*

Slice number	Skill	Elements
34	Cumulative Diphthongs: *easy*	*coit, fowd, houf*
35	Cumulative Diphthongs: *complex*	*mawd, drawld, frawp*
36	Cumulative Diphthongs + Blends ± Endings	*flauted, poithless, smaud*
37	*R*-Controlled Vowels: *er, ir, ur*	*lerth, kwirt, urch*
38	*R*-Controlled Vowels: *ar, or*	*arx, smarch, yarp*
39	Cumulative *r*-Controlled Vowels	*kerth, dreshar, jorb*
40	Hard and Soft *c*	*blic, narcel, sprice*
41	Hard and Soft *g*	*gustly, murging, fent*
42	Contractions: *'ve, 'll, 'd* (Real Words)	*they'll, you've, he'd*
43	Contractions: *'s, n't, 're* (Real Words)	*can't, he's, you're*
44	Cumulative Contractions (Real Words)	*doesn't, they'd, we've*
45	Prefixes	*adarl, comploit, exflect*
46	Suffixes	*centive, furnate, pedeless*
47	Prefixes and Suffixes	*abtraction, discorist, ingarding*
48	Three-, Four-, and Five-Syllable Words	*misbountal, unlaudent, abfectistly*
49	*wh/th* Words (Real Words)	*than, when, why*
50	*tion/sion* Words	*cosion, melation, zermotion*
51	*ure* Elements Mixed with Other Elements in Words	*bedder, faxture, starpest*
52	*ough* Words (Real Words)	*though, thought, through*
53	*tch/igh/wa* Words	*blatching, ighting, waddest*
54	*al/oul/ol* Words	*cralls, kould, nolling*
55	*al/tch/igh/wa/ol/oul* Words	*klights, rall, torchest*
56	Words with Bs, Ds, Ps	*babs, buppy, doddle*

FIGURE 6.3. *(cont.)*

CVC word parts to accent. You can visit Lewkowicz's Word Workshop website at *www.thewordworkshop.com.* Morningside Academy has been developing frequency-building worksheets to accompany Lewkowicz's outstanding program.

Saying Multisyllabic Words on Sight without Decoding

Our frequency aim for multisyllabic word practice is 85–65 wpm; our celeration aim is ×2. It is important to vary the order of words in a series of practice sheets by making several parallel versions of the same list. Each time learners read the same list, they remember more and more of the word order; in effect, the learning channel changes from see/say to think/say. Some learners recognize this when they ask with a sly grin, "Can I have the *take, spot, behind, coat* list?" When building word-reading fluency, learners should practice reading words and not recalling sequences of words from memory! We have more to say on this point in the next section.

Passage Fluency

Passage fluency requires instruction and practice in *prosody*—the rhythm and intonation of reading text. Passage fluency practice benefits from teachers' or peers' modeling of reading in a manner that sounds like speaking in a conversation. At Morningside Academy, we routinely stop a timing when a learner reads in a monotone or staccato, or sounds like a machine gun. As learners' reading skills progress, text becomes increasingly difficult and may require practice at each level of difficulty.

Learners should practice until their reading is comprehensible—that is, until it is clearly articulated and at a pace that allows a listener to remember the substance and sequence of ideas. If you are a kindergarten or first-grade teacher, you know what it is like to comprehend a beginner's reading. If not, try reading a magazine article at 40–50 wpm and retelling what you've read!

Typically we want readers to read at their speaking and listening frequencies, which vary by region. Speakers and listeners in many Latin and Asian countries practice understanding much quicker speech than rural New Englanders or Southerners in the United States. In general, the frequency aim lies somewhere between 150 and 250 wpm. Our frequency aim at Morningside is 220–180 wpm. We always begin with 1-minute timings. However, once learners achieve the frequency aim, they practice for increasingly long periods of time. These 2- to 5-minute timings ensure that they can read a whole chapter, maintaining the same frequency as they read in one minute.

When our students practice building passage fluency, they always answer a few literal comprehension questions after each timing, to guarantee that they don't speed through a passage at an incomprehensible rate. From the beginning, students need to learn to attend and think about their reading as they read. Mindless reading is a trap we all fall into on occasion, but it is not effective reading. It is always important to read with comprehension.

We also advise that learners read different texts for each timing. Reading the same passage over and over (a procedure known as *repeated reading*) may produce steep celerations, but these gains most often are not maintained when a new passage is encountered. Again, each time learners read the same passage, they remember more and more of the words and sentences; again, in effect, the learning channel changes from see/say to think/say. Some students who are looking for an easier exercise provide evidence that this is true when they ask, "Can I read that part [of a passage] over again?" or "Can I start here [the same place as last time]?" To guarantee that learners are practicing in the true reading channel, see/say, we need to provide a new text for each timing, to avoid inadvertent memorization.

John Begeny and his colleagues have developed a comprehensive reading fluency program for elementary and middle school learners called *Helping Early Literacy with Practice Strategies*, or *HELPS* (Begeny, 2009, 2011). It includes 100 sequenced lessons incorporating modeling, prompting, and feedback procedures, with accompanying reading passages.

The passages our students practice at the beginning of a school year and chart at the beginning of the Standard Celeration Chart are easier to read than the passages we present and chart at the end of the school year. To adjust for the increasing complexity across passages, our celeration aim is set at ×1.25, not ×2.

Passage Fluency Interventions

Some learners fail to increase their rates over successive timings and require interventions during practice. Teacher or peer modeling of passage reading is very helpful. Unison reading provides a more intensive level of intervention beyond modeling: A teacher or peer and a struggling reader simultaneously read a passage aloud. The teacher or peer gradually increases his or her frequency or rate (and, when the intervention calls for it, volume) so it is slightly faster (and/or louder) than the rate of the learner, while encouraging the learner to keep up the pace, slowing down as needed. Eventually the teacher/peer begins to lag behind the learner's rate (and lowers his or her voice), fading out over time.

Some learners do not breathe well during timings, and need modeling of breathing. Other learners read monotonically, like a machine gun. If breathing or monotony problems occur, the teacher or peer should immediately terminate the timing, provide modeling, and ask the learner to begin again.

Some learners read one word at a time, in staccato, as if they were reading a word list. These learners must learn to "see" more than one word at a time. We have found it helpful in these cases to take a king-sized, light-colored marker and mark chunks of relevant phrases in the passages. Once passages are marked, the teacher or peer model reads chunk by chunk instead of word by word.

MS. CALLEN'S TIER I READING CLASS

Let's visit Ms. Callen's fourth-grade reading class.* It's a Tier 1 class. The students have just finished a vocabulary lesson, and now it is time to practice reading passages fluently. Ms. Callen schedules 30 minutes of her 90-minute reading period for practice: 20 minutes for passage fluency, and 10 minutes for interventions to improve passage fluency performance. If no interventions are needed, students practice building vocabulary with flashcards in 2-minute timings. It is mid-September, and the class has been building its passage rates each day for a week.

Ms. Callen says, "Get your 'See/say passages' folder and sit with your partner while I pass out timers. You have 1 minute to get ready!" Each folder contains a daily chart stapled to the back cover, a packet of passages, and several timings charts stapled to an inside cover. The members of each pair have been carefully matched: High performers are paired with high performers, and medium or lower performers are paired with lower performers. Lower performers are not paired with each other. Ms. Callen hands each pair a timer as the partners sit in their designated seats next to each other.

"Let's quickly review how you know what frequency you need to meet today. Parker?"

Parker says, "Well, I look at my daily chart. It has a learning line drawn from my best rate last Thursday when we started, all the way up to the aim of 150. I found today's day line, Wednesday, and saw where it crosses the learning line. My aim for today is about 90."

"Very good, Parker!" Ms. Callen says. "Everyone, check your daily charts to see what rate you need to match or beat today. Make a goal box at that number on the last of Wednesday's timings lines on your timings chart. That's your aim for today."

Ms. Callen checks two pairs of students who incorrectly determined their rates yesterday. "Good, Michael; good, Lolo—you both found your frequency aim for today! And you two as well, Zoe and Imara!"

"OK, everyone, now decide who will go first. Set your timers for 1 minute, and look at me when you're ready." When everyone is ready, Ms. Callen says, "OK, please begin!"

As students read, their partners are marking errors on a "follow-along" copy of the passage. A buzz of performance prevails. A minute later, Ms. Callen says, "OK, now count the corrects and errors."

To help her students become more efficient in the counting process, Ms. Callen has hung a poster on her wall based upon the average number of words per line of passage. Each row indicates a number of lines read, from 1 to 30, and its cumulative total number of words. A minute later, she says, "Now take a minute or two to coach your partners' performance, and chart their rate of corrects and errors on the first of today's (Wednesday's) timing lines on their timings chart."

A buzz of learning now fills the room as students coach their partners by reviewing words incorrectly read, words self-corrected, and words read correctly but with prior moments of hesitation. The coaches also sprinkle praise for correctly read hard words throughout the process. Ms. Callen then says, "OK, everyone is working so well! Be sure to draw a learning line on your timings chart from your first timing to your aim for today. Let the readers continue to practice until they meet their aim, then switch and let the coaches do the practicing. Remember, every time a timing falls below the learning line, be sure to call me for extra coaching. Carry on!" At the end of the 20 minutes set aside for "See/say passages," the students mark their "personal best"† performance on their daily charts. (Remember, 10 minutes remain in the 30-minute practice block for practicing other reading activities, such as "See/say vocabulary words and definitions" and "See/say hard [or new] words.")

By the next week, no pairs need the prompts for how to practice that Ms. Callen has provided earlier. Each pair gathers materials and practices with little or no assistance. Ms. Callen is free to circulate and cheerlead successful practicers, help students who need extra coaching, and teach partners how to coach similar errors. Later in the class period, she calls a few pairs (one pair at a time) to a side table positioned so that she faces the class, to verify the rates they are charting. She verifies by conducting an additional timing and matching its rate to the charted frequency. Ms. Callen accepts frequencies within a range of their reported frequency, plus or minus 5 or so.

---

*Thanks to Molly Callen and her students for teaching and learning while Kent Johnson summarized this episode.

†The use of the term *personal best* in this context originated in Elizabeth Haughton's kindergarten classroom in the 1970s. Students originally described their progress to parents and siblings by saying, "I went up!", but their listeners did not understand. After Elizabeth taught the students to call the highest frequency they had achieved a "personal best," they began to communicate more clearly—for example, by exclaiming that they "made three personal bests in math today!" Elizabeth warns, however, that an exclusive focus on personal bests may slow learning if teachers and learners shoot for minimum improvement by setting "just one better" as the criterion for rewards. She gives reward tickets for each personal best that also maintains a ×2 celeration.

MS. SCHWARTZ CORRECTS STUDENTS' READING ERRORS

Now let's visit Ms. Schwartz's Tier 1 classroom.* This time we'll focus upon some of the kinds of errors students are making and possible interventions to eliminate them. A week has passed; students do not need any prompts for following the practice and charting procedures. Students have retrieved their materials and are sitting with their partners.

"OK, let's review some interventions you could use with your partners. Meimee?"

"You can ask your partner to break the word into parts."

"Right on, Meimee!" Ms. Schwartz starts a list on the board. "Oscar?"

"Only breathe between sentences," Oscar says.

Ms. Schwartz writes that one. "Maxwell?"

"Read words in chunks."

"Cool. Ainsley?"

"Sound out words you don't know, then say them the fast way."

"OK, everyone, carry on!"

Ms. Schwartz circulates the room observing pairs and providing extra coaching. She stops at Evan's desk. Evan has just completed a timing, and his frequency is below his celeration line. Finn, his coach, has pointed to each error word and asked him, "What word?" Evan struggles with the words in isolation even after Finn prompts him to sound out each word slowly and then say it fast, and suggests that he break each word into parts.

Ms. Schwartz's records indicate that she has helped Evan twice this week. She has also documented his error words.

"Evan, would you do a timing while I watch?" He agrees. After the timing is complete, she says, "You know what? Most of your errors are with words we've recently learned in class. How about if we set up another chart and practice just the new words before we do passage timings?"

Evan and Finn readily agree. Finn says, "I noticed that too, Ms. Schwartz! Look: *precarious, participate, register*—we learned those words this week!"

Ms. Schwartz then says, "OK, Evan, go get a new folder, a timings chart, and a daily chart. And in the top drawer of the 'Words' filing cabinet, you'll find word lists for every 10 lessons. Get the list from the folder for lessons 11–20." Evan adds "See/say new words" to his regimen. He draws an intervention line on his "See/say passages" chart. Succeeding days show a dramatic drop in passage errors.

*Thanks to Erin Schwartz and her students for teaching and learning while Kent Johnson summarized this episode.

MR. MENG'S TIER 2 READING INTERVENTION CLASS

Mr. Meng's reading class is down the hall from Ms. Callen's.* He works with 12 students in a Tier 2 reading intervention class. Some of these students leave Ms. Callen's reading class during her 30-minute practice block to work on prerequisite skills with Mr. Meng, while others come from other classrooms. Students who have similar deficits are paired. Mr. Meng's job is to provide a bit of instruction to each pair and monitor the pairs' practice. We'll focus on two pairs of students with different needs: Lucas and Eli, who practice phonological coding, and Valentina and Maya, who practice phonics with nonsense words. It is October: students are well grounded in practice and charting procedures.

"OK, get your practice folder and sit with your partner while I pass out timers," Mr. Meng says. "You have 1 minute to get ready!"

Mr. Meng cheerfully greets his students. He knows that it's hard for struggling learners to engage in such difficult work.

"Hey, Lucas and Eli. You're such hard workers. Give me high fives for that! . . . Today we're going to work on segmenting. Can you tell me what to do when you segment words? Lucas?"

"You say a word, and we break it into its sounds," Lucas drones.

"That's right, Lucas! Eli, can you give me an example?"

"If you say *band,* we'll say *b, a, n, d.*"

"Wow, correct, Eli," responds Mr. Meng. "OK, let's try some harder words. How about *pounding*?

"*Pou, n, d, ing,*" they chime in unison.

"Almost right," Mr. Meng says. "I heard you say *pou.* There are two sounds in *pou.* What are they?"

"*P* and *ou,*" they say regretfully.

"That's it!" Mr. Meng says. "*Pou* has two parts: *p* and *ou.* Feel the way you move your mouth when you say *p.* . . . Now feel the difference in the way you move your mouth when you say *ou.* . . . Let's try another one." Mr. Meng continues with single-syllable roots with common endings. The boys make more errors, but pretty soon they are errorless for several words. "OK, let's do some timings. I'll start with Lucas. When I say a word, you segment it. We'll do this as rapidly as we can for 1 minute. Are you ready?"

"Yeah," Lucas says. After 1 minute, Mr. Meng stops. "Wow, you got 18 in one minute!" exclaims Mr. Meng. "Chart that on today's line. Congratulations! Take a break while Eli takes his turn. Eli? . . . "

Next, Mr. Meng approaches Valentina and Maya. Both girls are great memorizers. There's no hope that they'll be able to memorize every word in the English language, but at this point in their reading career it seems easier to do that than to learn all those sounds and word parts! That's why Mr. Meng uses nonsense words: There's no chance they've been able to memorize those, because they've never seen "words" like *ip, vock,* and *blent.* They have been working on two-syllable nonsense words, at first struggling with each new combination of letter sounds, but eventually becoming quite fluent.

"Hi, Valentina; hi, Maya. How are you two doing today?"

"It's hard," says Maya, "but I finally broke 40 words in a minute!" she blurts happily. Valentina smiles and concurs. "Yeah, and I broke 50 today, Mr. Meng!"

"Great job, girls! Before I verify your hard work with timings, let's practice nonsense words that have three parts." Mr. Meng provides a series of three-syllable nonsense words. Valentina and Maya make several errors at first, but eventually reduce their errors.

"OK, great work, girls; now let's verify your two-part words with one timing each." After matching their rates with his, Mr. Meng says, "Very good. Tomorrow, we'll practice more three-part words before we do some timings. See you tomorrow!"

All of Mr. Meng's students return to their Tier 1 reading classes for further instruction, while Mr. Meng fields another Tier 2 group from other classes.

---

*Thanks to Paul Meng and his students for teaching and learning while Kent Johnson summarized this episode.

UNDERSTANDING TEXT

Our third composite repertoire for reading—understanding what was read—can be divided into four component repertoires:

- Vocabulary.
- Background knowledge.
- Recalling what was read.
- Comprehension skills.
  - 20–25 component comprehension and literature concepts and principles.

We describe each in turn.

Vocabulary

Understanding text is impossible without knowing the meaning of the words read. Our teachers regularly comb through reading, social studies, and science textbooks and articles that they will be assigning, and preteach suspected unknown vocabulary words before students read them in text. A simple probe of definitions and examples will reveal necessary vocabulary instruction. Vocabulary can also be taught in categories—for example, words related to carpentry, vegetables, opposites, or musical sounds—or through root word analysis.

Students can practice building vocabulary in many ways. Sometimes the definition of a word or phrase is important. Sometimes it is examples that are most relevant. Sometimes mastering synonyms is most critical. The design of vocabulary instruction is beyond the scope of the present chapter; however, an unpublished study conducted by classroom teacher Marianne Delgado at Morningside Academy supports work by Beck, McKeown, and Kucan (2002) in which they advocate for enriched instruction. In Delgado's study, students generated definitions of selected words either by applying four approaches to each word (context clues, connotation and mood, word forms, and generating sentences) or by using flashcards to memorize definitions. When they took a vocabulary retention test more than 6 months later, students could accurately define many more words that they learned by applying the four approaches than words they learned by using the flashcard approach. Archer, Gleason, and Isaacson (2008a, 2008b) and Kame'enui and Baumann (2012) also provide excellent recommendations. Currently, at Morningside, we have found that a combination of these authors' recommendations with frequency building results in the most favorable outcomes.

See/say and see/write tasks are most relevant to vocabulary fluency. Here are seven pinpoint examples to illustrate the possibilities.

1. See words/say (or write) definitions.
2. See words/say (or write) synonyms (one or more per word).
3. See words/say (or write) example(s).
4. See word + examples/say (or write) yes, example, or no, nonexample.
5. See examples and nonexamples of words/select examples (one or more per word).

6. See underlined words in sentences/say (or write) yes, used correctly, or no, used incorrectly.
7. See underlined words in sentences/say (or write) sharper words, or less mundane words.

Two formats for practicing these pinpoints have been explored by precision teachers: worksheets and flashcards. In the late 1970s, Lindsley coined the acronym SAFMEDS to describe a flashcard fluency process—an approach that Stephen Graf promoted and perfected throughout his lifetime (Graf, 1994). The SAFMEDS protocol requires flashcards and a card-flipping tool skill. SAFMEDS stands for *Say All Fast, a Minute Each Day, Shuffled*. In Morningside's version of SAFMEDS, students may say, write, or type the definition. Depending on a number of variables, such as the number of definitions included, the number of timings to meet a celeration aim may range from one to six or more. The practice should occur each day, and the flashcards should be shuffled before each timing, to prevent memorization. Tucci and Johnson (*www.tuccisolutions.com*; 2012) are creating a tablet software application called Fluency FlashCard to automate this process.

Our vocabulary frequency aims vary according to the number of words read, as well as the number of words spoken or written during a timing. We ask students to practice until they can say 150–100 words, and write or type about 35 words (with five letters per word). Our celeration aim is ×2.

Background Knowledge

The more facts, procedures, and critical analyses learners know about the topic of their reading, the better their understanding of the text will be. We encourage you to preteach the main or most important facts, procedures, and critical analyses about the topics your students will be reading. *Reading Mastery Signature Edition*, levels 3–5 (Engelmann, 2008); *Horizons: Reading to Learn* (Engelmann, Engelmann, Davis, & Hanner, 1998); and Archer, Gleason, and Vachon's *REWARDS Plus: Reading Strategies Applied to Social Studies Passages* (2004) and *REWARDS Plus: Reading Strategies Applied to Science Passages* (2005b) illustrate good formats for teaching background information before reading text. SAFMEDS or "See topic or subtopic/say or write facts and details" would be an ideal PT approach. See our description of retelling, below, for information about setting a frequency aim. The celeration aim should be at least ×2.

Retelling

In the past decade, many states have added retelling or recall tasks to their achievement tests. Students read a passage and retell its details, in sequence. What began as an assessment tool has become a method for teaching students to attend to the literal details of what they are reading, while they read.

Morningside has developed a PT approach to practicing passage recall and retelling, integrating PT methodology with refinements of constructivist activities described by Benson and Cummins (2000). Students read a passage, selection, or chapter in a small group, with participants taking turns reading several sentences each. They then pair up to design checklists of important points about the selection, in sequence; these include title, characters, setting, problems, main events, and resolution. Then they study the checklist, preparing to retell the text in a *duration timing*—a timing in which the teacher or a learner sets a timer that runs until each learner finishes retelling the text. During the timing, they take turns retelling the text, while another student marks the spoken points on the checklist. Students chart their practice with different passages until they can retell a story at a speaking rate of about 100 words in correct sequence, and a writing or typing rate of about 25–20 words (with five-letter words) in correct sequence. Our celeration aim is ×2.

Two programs feature peer-assisted practice and coaching opportunities for retelling fluency: *PALS Reading* (D. Fuchs & Fuchs, 1994, 2008; D. Fuchs, Fuchs, Mathes, & Simmons, 1997), and *HELPS*, which we have described earlier (Begeny, 2009).

In addition to the three components we have described—vocabulary, background knowledge, and retelling—the "understanding text" composite repertoire consists of two smaller composites: (1) comprehension skills and (2) strategic, engaged reading. Teachers have typically ignored PT when teaching comprehension. The following descriptions are meant to inspire precision teachers to specify practice procedures for comprehension.

Comprehension Skills

The smaller composite repertoire of comprehension skills includes 20–25 operations that a reader can perform on text content. Some reading programs divide the operations into reading comprehension and literature concepts. Table 6.2 presents a typical reading and literature comprehension skills inventory included in most reading programs.

In the curriculum program *Reading Success*, each of these skills is taught as a principle, with rules to apply to comprehend text (Dixon et al., 2008). After initial instruction, we introduce practice in applying the rules to reading selections. It takes 6–8 months of daily practice during group reading selection for students to achieve fluency in these skills. The teacher calls on individual students to apply skills throughout the reading

TABLE 6.2. Commonly Referenced Comprehension Skills and Literary Concepts

Typical comprehension skills inventory	Typical literature concepts inventory
• Compare and contrast • Identify causes and effects • State the main idea and supporting details • Draw a conclusion • Make a prediction and verify or refine it • Paraphrase • Summarize • State author's purpose • State author's point of view and biases • Visualize author's descriptions • Identify persuasive devices and propaganda • Identify inferences	• Identify story elements, including: • Plot and plot structure • Setting • Character • Theme • Identify literary devices, including: • Simile and metaphor • Irony • Mood • Personification • Foreshadowing • Flashback • Exaggeration and hyperbole

selection, giving any prompts needed and noting what help she provided for the student to correctly apply the skill. Students rarely need explicit timings to improve and eventually master these skills, so we don't specify a frequency aim or celeration aim for this composite. Some teachers report that multiple-choice practice with very short passages, in a 3- to 5-minute timing, is helpful for the few learners who fail to improve comprehension skill application during group selection reading. The *Specific Skills Series* (Science Research Associates [SRA]/McGraw-Hill, 2006) provides ideal material for these remedial comprehension skills timings.

STRATEGIC, ENGAGED READING

It's all very well to master comprehension skill principles, but these principles are of no consequence if they are not applied during authentic reading situations. At Morningside, students practice applying comprehension skills during group selection reading, as described above. Applying comprehension skills, *as needed,* is part of a "strategic, engaged reading" composite repertoire; it requires self-monitoring during reading. Components of self-monitoring (phrased from the learner's point of view) include the following:

- Asking questions about my reading.
- Answering the questions I've asked, after I read further.
- Clarifying the author's main ideas.
- Making connections between text and my experience/my history.
- Predicting upcoming events.
- Confirming my predictions.
- Summarizing text periodically to check for understanding.
- Visualizing authors' descriptions.
- Adjusting reading rate up or down, depending upon familiarity of content, vocabulary, decoding level, and so on.

Strategic, engaged reading is mastered over months and years, and develops with the practice, feedback, and coaching we have mentioned during our discussion of comprehension skills. We don't specify a frequency aim or celeration aim for this composite.

Figure 6.4 presents our curriculum ladder for the "understanding text" composite repertoire. Table 6.3 provides a list of pinpoints for applying PT to reading.

SUMMARY

This chapter has provided guidance on pinpoints for which frequency building has proven helpful in producing good readers. We have identified pinpoints and provided frequency aims and celerations in the areas of prerequisites for reading, reading behaviors, understanding text, and strategic engaged reading. In the next chapter, we describe pinpoints for writing.

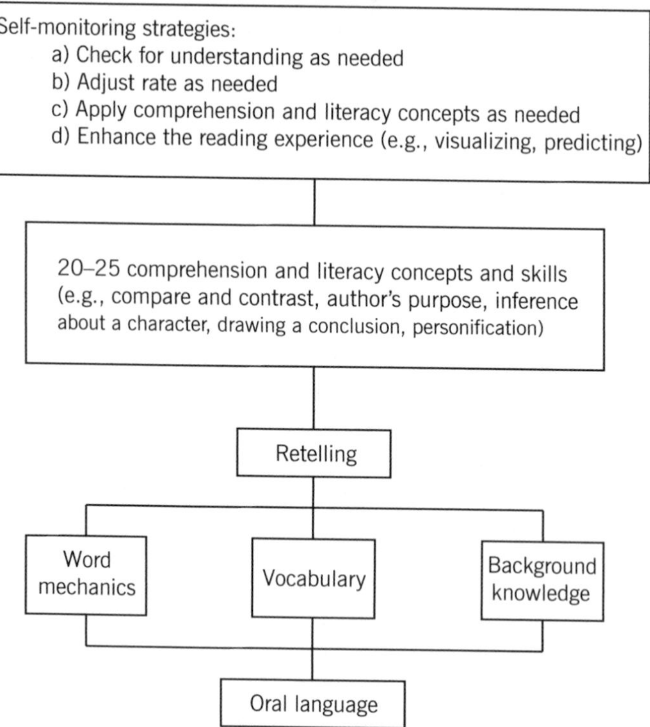

FIGURE 6.4. Morningside Academy's component–composite analysis for strategic, engaged reading.

TABLE 6.3. Practice Pinpoints for Reading

Pinpoint	Counting what	Frequency aim per minute	Celeration aim
1. Hear segmented word sounds/say (blend) whole word	Words	25–20	×2
2. Hear whole (blended) word/say separate segmented sounds	Sound segments	25–20	×2
3. Hear word + sound/say word with sound missing	Words	25–20	×2
4. Hear two words that differ in only one sound/say missing sound in second word	Sounds	25–20	×2
5. Hear two words/say "rhyme" or "not"	"Rhyme" or "not"	25–20	×2
6. Hear two sentences/say "rhyme" or "not"	"Rhyme" or "not"	12–10	×2
7. See/say letter or picture names (RAN)	Names	80–60	×2
8. See/say (stretch) sounds	Sounds	40–25	×2
9. See/say sounds	Sounds	90–70	×2
10. See/say word parts	Word parts	90–70	×2
11. See/say words with one to three syllables, on sight	Words	100–90	×2
12. See/say words with more than three syllables, on sight	Words	85–65	×2
13. See/say passages with expression (grades 1 and 2)	Words	90–70	×1.25
14. See/say passages with expression (grades 3 and 4)	Words	140–120	×1.25
15. See/say passages with expression (grade 5 and up)	Words	220–180	×1.25
16. See/say vocabulary (words, definitions, examples, yes–no correct usage, etc.)	Words spoken	150–100	×1.25
17. See/write vocabulary	Words written	40–30 (5 letters per word)	×2
18. Free/say (retell) story or passage previously read	Words spoken	100	×2
19. Free/write (summarize) story or passage	Words written	25–20	×2
20. See passage (75 words)/select main idea statement (SRA's Specific Skills Series)	Multiple-choice marks	10–8 in 10 minutes	×2

CHAPTER 7

Precision Teaching in Writing

MS. DELGADO'S TIER 1 LANGUAGE ARTS CLASS

Let's visit Ms. Delgado's fifth-grade language arts class.* It is a Tier 1 class. The students have just finished a lesson in logic and deduction. Each day Ms. Delgado schedules 25 minutes for practicing components of good grammar, punctuation, and sentence writing prior to composition work. She uses sentence combining to teach many of these components. Last Thursday and Friday she taught the students about prepositional phrases, and today they are ready to practice writing sentences that include them. "OK, get your sentence-combining folders and workbooks and sit with your partner while I pass out timers!" she says. "You have 1 minute to get ready." Each folder contains a daily chart stapled to the back cover, and several timings charts stapled to an inside cover. Students keep the week's sentence-combining work in their folders, moving them to their three-ring notebooks every Friday. They use Morningside Academy's sentence-combining workbook, which provides practice in over 50 different types of sentence combining related to grammar, punctuation, and sentence styles. Each member of a pair has been carefully matched: High performers are paired with high performers, and medium performers are paired with medium or lower performers. Low performers are not paired with each other. Ms. Delgado hands each pair a timer as the partners sit in their designated seats next to each other.

"Turn to slice 40 and get ready to read the title. Ready?" After she signals, the class says in unison, "Adding Prepositional Phrases."

Ms. Delgado then turns to Hannah. "Hannah, please read the directions."

Hannah says, "Combine the sentences by adding the prepositional phrases in the appropriate places. Write your answers on loose-leaf paper."

"OK, Erik, please read the first one," says Ms. Delgado.

Erik reads, "The small company received a donation. The company was from Seattle. The donation was through a grant. The grant was from a generous millionaire."

Ms. Delgado addresses the class: "Everyone, think about how to combine these sentences into one sentence that contains propositions. Try not to change any of the word forms used in the sentences. You have 1 minute." Students busily read to themselves, some murmuring out loud, others jotting notes about how they'll combine them. After 1 minute, Ms. Delgado says, "Liam, tell us what you came up with."

Liam clears his throat and says, "The small company from Seattle received a donation through a grant from a generous millionaire."

"Very good!," Ms. Delgado exclaims. "Now tell us the prepositional phrases you used."

Liam says, "Well, there's 'from Seattle,' and 'through a grant,' and 'from a generous millionaire.'"

"Excellent," Ms.Delgado says." Did anyone have a different combined sentence?"

Shaylyn raises her hand. "OK, tell us yours, Shaylyn," Ms. Delgado says.

Shaylyn says, "Well, I wrote a complete sentence by beginning with 'A generous millionaire,' but I see that Liam was able to get more prepositional phrases by starting with 'The small company,' and he also didn't need to change verb forms and make other changes to the words in the sentences. So I like his better."

Shaylyn then reads her sentence, which contains considerable word changes. "So we won't count that one as correct, and it seems you agree. Good analysis, Shaylyn. Anyone else?" No one else offers a variation.

Ms. Delgado says, "Indeed, this one is very straightforward—not like the few we saw Friday that had several possible versions. OK, let's do our first timing. You'll have 3 minutes to combine sets of sentences in slice 40. See how many you can do. Ready? . . . Please begin!"

Everyone works busily until the end of the timing. After the 3-minute beep, Ms. Delgado says, "OK, exchange papers and check your partner's work with this answer key." She distributes the key. Lively discussions ensue as students listen to variations from the key and give a thumbs-up or thumbs-down about whether the student has a good case to present to Ms. Delgado and the rest of the class. After about 2 minutes, Ms. Delgado leads a discussion of variations. Another 3 minutes later, she says, "OK, our ultimate aim is 3 combined sentences in 3 minutes. How many completed 1 that time?" Almost all the students raise their hands. "How about 2?" This time only a third of the students raise their hands. One lone student has met the aim of 3 combined sentences. "OK, everyone, now count up your corrects and errors. Remember, if you wrote a variation that we all agreed is acceptable, then count it as correct; otherwise, count it as an error. Then fill out a timings chart, record your frequencies, and get ready for another timing."

Ms. Delgado leads three timings, discussions of variations, and charting; each timing process takes about 8 minutes. After three timings, Ms. Delgado says, "Now record your personal best† on your daily chart, and draw a celeration aim from your personal best to the ultimate frequency aim of three combined sentences by the Thursday day line." (Today is Monday.) Then the class moves on to a persuasive paragraph exercise. After school, Ms. Delgado will review the charts and be ready to do some checking and coaching during the timings tomorrow with students who made more than one error.

---

*Thanks to Marianne Delgado and her students for teaching and learning while Kent Johnson summarized this episode.

†The use of the term *personal best* in this context originated in Elizabeth Haughton's kindergarten classroom in the 1970s. Students originally described their progress to parents and siblings by saying, "I went up!", but their listeners did not understand. After Elizabeth taught the students to call the highest frequency they had achieved a "personal best," they began to communicate more clearly—for example, by exclaiming that they "made three personal bests in math today!" Elizabeth warns, however, that an exclusive focus on personal bests may slow learning if teachers and learners shoot for minimum improvement by setting "just one better" as the criterion for rewards. She gives reward tickets for each personal best that also maintains a ×2 celeration.

Our content analysis of writing reveals one composite repertoire (composing paragraphs, essays, and reports); seven component skills related to composing sentences (parts of speech, grammar, word usage, capitalization, punctuation, writing with sharp vs. mundane words, and spelling); and two tool skills (handwriting and typing). These skills form a rough hierarchy, illustrated in Figure 7.1. We discuss tool skills first, build to sentence composing, and end with the composite repertoire.

TOOL SKILLS IN WRITING

Composing requires handwriting or typing, the basic tool skills in writing. Many learners write or type at frequencies that are well below their thinking rates. This makes writing a very tedious process, and one to be avoided. Thoughts are lost and sentence quality suffers as a learner's thinking rate repeatedly pauses to allow production rate to catch up. When learners are able to write or type at their thinking rate, their writing quality greatly improves. At Morningside Academy, we build the students' writing and typing rates through transcription and dictation practice.

Transcription—"See/Write Letters or Words"

During transcription practice, learners copy text. They may copy by writing the text or by typing it. In this chapter we focus on written transcription, because it presents

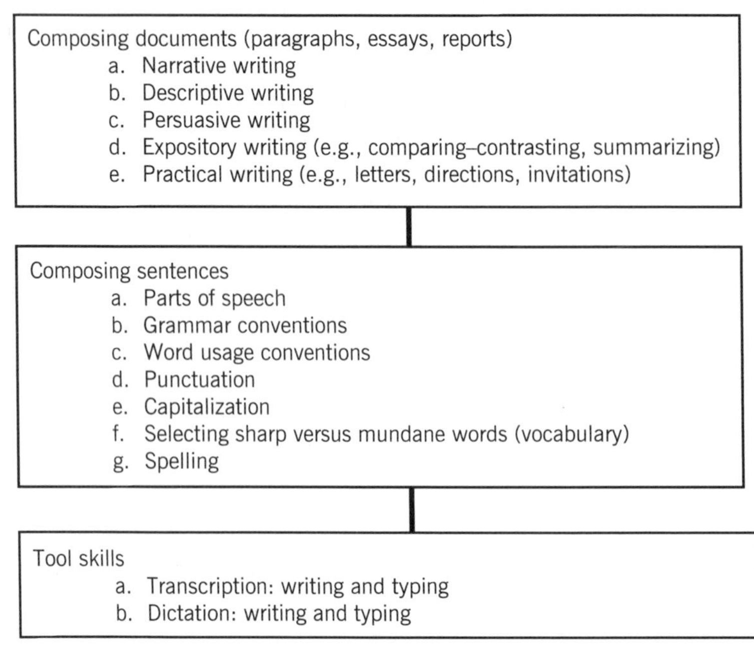

FIGURE 7.1. Hierarchy of skills for the writing composite.

certain problems that we have learned how to solve; typing is more straightforward, but it involves the same general procedures as writing.

When writing, students remove extraneous objects from their writing area and copy text from books or handouts onto slanted paper placed directly on the surface of their tables or desks. Later they may transcribe from blackboards or overhead transparencies as a beginning step in learning to take notes. It is important to select text that is slightly below the students' decoding and comprehension skills, so that they do not spend transcription time decoding and comprehending what they are copying.

Learning to copy fluently requires instruction and practice in inspecting sets of words with their associated punctuation, temporarily memorizing and writing them, and repeating that process for a specified timing period. Learners gradually build up the number of words and punctuation in each set, checking for accuracy once each bout of "look and write" is completed.

In our transcription fluency protocol, learners practice in pairs, writing simultaneously for 1 minute. When the timing is finished, the learners exchange transcriptions and make a slash through any illegible letter or punctuation mark. Errors may also include inappropriate spacing and capitalization (also marked with slashes), and of course any missing letters, words, and punctuation. Then they return transcriptions to each other and take turns giving feedback. Finally, they count the number of correct and incorrect letters and punctuation marks written, and chart the results on timings charts.

Our students need lots of practice and feedback in writing legibly, with words, letters, and punctuation marks appropriately spaced. Many also need practice in detecting illegible letters and marks. We make copies of each student's transcription performance and ask him or her to make slashes through illegible letters on the original while we make slashes on the copy. Then we compare slashes and give feedback. The student continues to practice until his or her slashes agree with ours at least 90% of the time.

The ultimate frequency aim for adult transcription is 180–160 letters and punctuation marks written per minute. Elementary students and students with motor skill deficits may not achieve this aim until they are adolescents or adults. Gradually rising intermediate aims can be established across grade levels until students achieve the adults' aim, beginning with 50 letters and marks written per minute in the primary grades, 100 in the intermediate grades, and 150–130 in middle school.[1]

When we first began building transcription frequency, we were startled to find that many students would suddenly begin making extraordinary progress in learning to compose sentences and paragraphs when they were able to write or type more than 100 letters or punctuation marks per minute (about 15 wpm, with 3–5 letters per word for primary grades and 5–7 letters per word for intermediate and middle school grades). A linguistics professional has told us that this writing rate matches the average rate of words people think to write. When writing speed is in synchrony with word-thinking speed, thoughts flow to paper more fluidly, without disruptions (Y. Jones, personal communication, 1988).

---

[1] In order to meet our sentence-writing frequency aim of 20–15 wpm, including "think time," writing tool skill frequency must be 125–90 letters per minute, or 25–18 words averaging 5 letters each per minute.

As with all of our practice pinpoints, daily frequency aims for timings charts are determined by inspecting learners' daily charts and noting what approximate frequency they need to achieve to stay on their celeration lines. Because the transcription pinpoint involves motor skills—difficult behaviors for teachers and peers to coach—we set our celeration aim at ×1.25.

Counting individual letters and punctuation marks after each timing is a tedious process that can be sidestepped by counting the average number of letters per word in passages, and basing the frequency aim upon number of words written. For example, if the average number of letters per word is 7, the word-based frequency aim would be calculated as follows: 180 ÷ 7 = 25, 160 ÷ 7 = 23. The aim would thus be 25–23 words written per minute. If words vary widely in number of letters, more uniform text should be selected, such as those "decodable reading books" published in basal reading series (see, e.g., Afflerbach et al., 2008, 2011).

Many learners achieve our frequency aims by following these steps, but some require more intensive coaching and interventions. Sometimes a certain letter needs to be repeatedly practiced in short timings or "sprints" lasting 10–30 seconds, in between formal 1-minute timings or as warm-up exercises before formal timings begin. Sometimes inspection of multiple transcriptions reveals patterns of letters and punctuation marks that need to be practiced in sprints. Sometimes teachers or peers need to watch a learner complete a transcription timing in order to determine which letters or marks are written slowly and need isolated practice.

It is important to make transcription corrections with humor and sensitivity, particularly for students with motor skill deficits. Many students will react defensively about the illegibility of their writing, and many older learners will say that transcription is "baby work." You can make jokes about what their illegible forms look like—for example, "What do you think that *p* looks like? A piece of curly hair?" Or show students their illegible forms "out of context" and ask them what letter or word they wrote. What appears legible in context often is not when context is removed. And always give "strokes" for increasing legibility—for example, "Wow, none of your 9s look like 4s any more!" Have fun with this work!

In grade 4, our students begin typing their transcriptions—a "See/type letters or words" pinpoint. We gradually increase the frequency requirement in each grade until they achieve an aim of over 45 wpm by middle school. Our celeration aim for typing is the same as for handwriting: ×1.25. Many students who have visual–motor integration problems blossom as writers when they switch from handwriting to typing. Illegible writing at some point becomes aesthetically displeasing to see, and thus may discourage further writing. The vertical position of typing interfaces also contrasts with the horizontal surfaces used for handwriting, which may help control a learner's attention. We use a program called *Master Key* (available at *http://macinmind.com*). *Master Key* features timed drills and mastery goals, accuracy- and fluency-building exercises, Internet support for schools, and formatting for class reports. It is a school-ready product.

Dictation—"Hear/Write Letters or Words"

Another writing tool we have found useful to build is taking dictation. During a dictation timing, a teacher or peer reads text, while the writer writes what the reader says.

This pinpoint is a particularly important prerequisite skill for students' developing facility as note takers. We begin dictation timings in middle school. Taking dictation requires choreography between speaker and listener. In the early stages, it is important for the reader to watch the writer write and adjust his or her speaking rate accordingly. Poor synchrony between the reader and writer will invalidate a dictation timing by putting a ceiling on frequency of words written. Good choreography is usually achieved in 6–10 practice timings. Gradually the reader will speak in lengthier phrases, until these approximate a lecturing style. The learner will be able to take notes without missing points and without feeling rushed or unable to comprehend the speaker. Our frequency aim for taking dictation is 130–110 letters written per minute, and can be adjusted for word length as described earlier. Our celeration aim is ×1.25.

In middle school, our students begin taking dictation by typing—a "Hear/type letters or words" pinpoint. Our frequency aim is 45 wpm, with a celeration aim of ×1.25.

COMPOSING SENTENCES

Sentence writing requires fluency in applying parts of speech, grammar and usage conventions, punctuation, capitalization, writing with sharp (vs. mundane) vocabulary, and spelling. Fluent sentence writing is the gateway to composing essays and reports. Arthur Whimbey and Myra Linden (2001) have developed a technology for teaching sentence writing called *prototype construction,* which is fully adaptable to frequency building with PT. The method teaches learners the general case of sentence writing by teaching the three basic parts of a kernel sentence—subjects, verbs, and objects. Prototype construction exercises then systematically teach the writer to add parts of speech to kernel sentences (e.g., adding adjectives to nouns, adverbs to verbs, and adverbs to adjectives). Prototype construction exercises also teach writers to add phrases and clauses to kernel sentences, such as adverbial phrases and prepositional phrases. The Whimbey and Linden (2001) book clearly outlines how to proceed without the grammarian background that so many teachers think is needed to teach writing components.

A key technique in prototype construction technology is *sentence combining.* In sentence combining, learners put two or more sentences together to make one sentence. Each sentence-combining pattern focuses upon a particular part of speech or grammatical convention. For example, to teach the learner to discriminate among the conjunctions *and, but, so,* and *for,* the learner encounters sentences like these.

> My neighbor said she wanted to go to Europe in the worst way.
>
> I let her take my kids.

Students choose the correct connecting word with its correct punctuation. In this case, they would choose *so* and write a comma before it to produce this sentence.

> My neighbor wanted to go to Europe in the worst way, so I let her take my kids.

Figure 7.2 shows a sample of a sentence-combining practice sheet with answers included.

Slice 13	Aim: 60 words in 3 minutes—if tool skill < 125 letters per minute, aim is 80% of see/write rate per minute × 3
Chapter 13: Add your own adjectives in front of two nouns in a sentence.	
Combine the sentences to form a single, more informative sentence. Write your combined sentence completely on loose-leaf paper.	

19. The wolf howled at the moon at midnight.
    Add your own word or words that describe a wolf that is wild.
    Add your own word or words that describe a moon that is large.
    The untamed, feral wolf howled at the full moon at midnight.

20. The doctor performed experiments.
    Add your own word or words that describe a doctor who was crazy.
    Add your own word or words that describe experiments that were large in number.
    The mad doctor performed countless experiments.

21. The student tried to retrieve her document when her computer crashed.
    Add your own word or words that describe how the student felt.
    Add your own word or words that describe what kind of computer kept crashing.
    The freaked-out student tried to retrieve her document when her old, undependable computer crashed.

22. The sky was edged with mountains.
    Add your own word or words that describe a sky that was clear.
    Add your own word or words that describe mountains that were beautiful.
    The beautiful blue sky was edged with majestic mountains.

23. The witch had a house on the edge of town.
    Add your own word or words that describe a witch who was scary.
    Add your own word or words that describe a house that was bad.
    The creepy witch had an old, dilapidated house on the edge of town.

24. The gymnast bounced lightly on the balance beam.
    Add your own word or words that describe a gymnast who was excellent.
    Add your own word or words that describe a balance beam that wiggled.
    The agile gymnast bounced lightly on the wobbly balance beam.

FIGURE 7.2. Sample sentence-combining practice sheet answer key. Reprinted with permission of Morningside Press.

Dozens of studies over 30 years show that with at least 20 hours of practice, sentence combining improves grammar and usage skills, increases the complexity of sentences, improves punctuation skills, improves proofreading skills, increases reading levels, and even increases foreign-language learning and the quality of compositions (Daiker, Kerek, & Morenberg, 1979; O'Hare, 1973). Studies have demonstrated these effects with a variety of learners, from fourth graders through college students. In dramatic demonstrations of generativity, two studies compared instruction in a range of composition genres (e.g., descriptive writing, persuasive writing, expository writing) with instruction in sentence combining alone, without genre instruction. They found that sentence-combining students wrote better compositions! (See O'Hare, 1973, with seventh graders, and Daiker, Kerek, & Morenberg, 1979, with college freshmen.) According to Linden and Whimbey (1990, pp. 23–24), a National Council of Teachers of English survey of sentence-combining research concluded that "no other single teaching approach has ever consistently been shown to have a beneficial effect on syntactical maturity and writing quality."

In Linden and Whimbey's prototype construction technology, many of the rules of grammar and punctuation are taught with sentence combining, including the most complicated arrangements of dependent clauses and the use of gerunds as sentence subjects. Prototype construction employs not only sentence combining, but also other techniques such as sentence rearranging, subtracting from sentences, and expanding sentences. Neither teachers nor students must learn or use the technical terms of grammar and linguistics. And as icing on the cake, their humor, illustrated by the example above of going to Europe with children, helps make learning grammar fun. This husband-and-wife pair, working with colleagues, has published a series of textbooks on grammar and sentence writing for middle school, high school, and college learners. (See *www.bgfperformance.com/ttgrammar.html* for a complete listing of works.) Table 7.1 lists the component skills taught with the prototype construction technology.

Anita Archer and colleagues have published a writing program called *REWARDS Writing: Sentence Refinement* (Archer et al., 2008a), which teaches sentence combining to younger learners in the intermediate elementary school grades. Their program also employs sentence subtraction and sentence expansion techniques, as well as paragraph editing, which we describe later.

In sum, to teach sentence-writing skills, we recommend that teachers model patterns for building upon kernel sentences, using sentence combining and other techniques described by Whimbey and Linden (2001). Students then practice to achieve

TABLE 7.1. Component Skills Taught with the Prototype Construction Technology

"To be" verbs	Relative clauses
Nouns	Using helping verbs to extend the meaning of verbs
Adjectives	Using *have* as a main verb, and as a helping verb in forming the perfect tenses
Adverbs	Voice: active and passive
Prepositions	The "to do" verb: tenses, emphasizing ideas, asking questions
Coordinating conjunctions	Noun clauses
Pronouns	
Subordinating conjunctions in complex sentences	

frequency aims, first in isolation, then in cumulative mixes. Morningside Academy and Fit Learners, assessment and tutoring centers in Reno, Nevada and Locust Valley, New York, have compiled three binders full of practice materials for sentence combining and other grammar and usage skills. They are available from Morningside Press.

Frequency and Celeration Aims for Sentence Writing

We set frequency aims for sentence writing in two contexts—composing sentences and editing sentences. Sentence composition fluency depends upon fluency in writing and typing tool skills. Our sentence-writing frequency aim is 20–15 wpm (with words averaging 5 letters each). This calculates to a final output of 100–75 letters written per minute, including time for writing and time for thinking. We allow 20% "think time," which requires a writing tool frequency of 125–90 letters (25–18 five-letter words) written per minute.

Sentence-editing fluency depends primarily upon reading fluency, and to a much lesser extent on writing fluency. Our sentence-editing practice sheets include 20–15 words that need editing for every 100 words read. Accordingly, our frequency aim is 20–15 words edited for every 100 words read. So, to allow 20% "think time" and 10% "write time" during an editing timing, students must read at least 130 wpm for every 100 words to edit.

Both sentence-writing and sentence-editing frequency building require 3- or 5-minute timings, in order for learners to provide enough performance output. One-minute timings allow too few sentences to be written or edited to provide a representative sample of the required skills.

If a learner's writing or typing tool skill does not meet the minimum requirements, we set an intermediate frequency aim to accommodate the deficiency: We multiply the learner's writing or typing rate by 80% to provide "think time." For example, if a learner writes only 50 letters per minute, we would set his or her intermediate sentence-writing frequency aim at 40 letters per minute. We say "intermediate," because there is no guarantee that intermediate performance frequency is fast enough to guarantee fluency—that is, maintenance, endurance, stability, application, and generativity (get the MESsAGe?). As the learner's tool skill frequencies increase, periodic checks for MESsAGe, with additional practice when necessary, will assure that the student's performance will be fluent. Our celeration aim for both sentence writing and sentence editing is ×2.

Teaching Vocabulary Revisited

In Chapter 6, we have described vocabulary frequency-building procedures for reading. There we have focused upon learning new words and their meanings. Vocabulary can also be addressed during writing instruction. Here the emphasis is not on learning new words, but on learning the nuances of familiar, simple words. A unique component of Archer et al.'s (2008a) *REWARDS Writing: Sentence Refinement* program teaches students how to sharpen their word choices. Students start with a simple sentence using mundane words, like this:

> He walked into the big building.

They go on to derive a more interesting sentence, like this:

He wandered into an enormous department store.

Learners edit sentences and paragraphs by replacing common, overused adjectives, verbs, and nouns with sharper, less common, and more engaging choices. Mundane adjectives include *nice, big, bad, pretty, hot, little, smart, cold, good, happy, terrible, funny, dirty, wonderful, scared, sad, old, clean, mean,* and *hard*. Mundane verbs include *made, liked, walked, ran, ate, took, grew, got, went, saw, knew, used, gave, let, said, had, lived, talked, found, stayed, wanted, put, helped, built,* and *thought*.

Archer and colleagues' program includes another book, the *REWARDS Writing: Word Choice Help Book* (Archer et al., 2008b). Precision teachers will have a field day with this supplement. Pinpoints galore can be written; some of ours appear below.

- See mundane words/write (or say) synonyms (for nouns).
  - For example, the learner sees *shoes* and writes *sandals, boots, sneakers, heels, slippers, moccasins, flip-flops, pumps, flats, slip-ons . . .*
- See mundane words/write (or say) comparative and superlative forms (for adjectives).
  - For example, the learner sees *bad* and writes *awful, terrible, atrocious, worthless, imperfect, unacceptable, unsatisfactory, inadequate, faulty, inferior, deficient . . .*
- See mundane words/write (or say) synonyms (for verbs).
  - For example, the learner sees *found* and writes *discovered, detected, spotted, located, pinpointed, identified, uncovered, acquired, encountered, obtained, unearthed . . .*
- See mundane verbs/write (or say) adverbs (for adverbs).
  - For example, the learner sees *spoke* and writes *slowly, quietly, respectfully, honestly, persuasively . . .*

Our frequency aim for these writing pinpoints is 20–15 wpm. Since students can speak faster than they can write, the frequency aim for a "say" performance is 80–60 wpm. Since each word list contains far fewer than 60 words, students can list sharp alternatives for several mundane words in a 1-minute timing. Our celeration aim is ×2.

Three More Sentence-Writing Component Skills

We encourage precision teachers to explicitly teach and establish practice routines for three other sentence-writing components: capitalization; discriminating between sentences and fragments and sentences and run-ons; and spelling. Capitalization can be taught and practiced in a sentence-editing context, using the editing aim parameters and adjustments described above. In order to demonstrate fluency in discriminating sentences from fragments and run-ons, learners must practice reading items and marking each one S for sentence, F for fragment, and R for run-on. Our frequency aim is 20–15 words in sentences marked for every 100 words read, including 20% "think time" and 10% "write time." Thus, for every 100 words in discrimination items, a student must be able to read at least 130 wpm.

Spelling should be practiced until the learner can hear words and spell them without any "think time." A MESsAGe frequency aim for spelling is 125–90 letters written per minute. As with dictation, spelling timings require choreography between the teacher or peer coach and the learner. It is important that the reader state the next word to be spelled as the learner is writing the last letter or two of the previous word. Pausing between words puts a ceiling on the writer's performance, possibly preventing the learner from achieving the frequency aim. Dixon, Engelmann, Bauer, Steely, and Wells's (2007) *Spelling Mastery*, Dixon and Engelmann's (2007) *Spelling through Morphographs*, and Engelmann's (2008) *Reading Mastery Signature Edition* programs group spelling words together that all follow a general rule, such as this:

> When a short word ends CVC (e.g., run), and the part to add next begins with a vowel (e.g., -er), double the final consonant first before adding the ending (e.g., *runner*, not *runer*).

This approach maximizes application. Ten spelling rules in *Spelling through Morphographs* allow the learner to spell more than 30,000 words in the English language!

For learners who struggle with learning how to spell, we build frequency on discrimination tasks: "See words/mark those spelled correctly (or incorrectly)." These spelling–editing fluency exercises depend primarily upon reading fluency. To eliminate performance bias, our spelling–editing practice sheets include 50% correctly spelled and 50% incorrectly spelled words; flashcards can be used as well. To determine the number of words in an exercise and to set a frequency aim, we multiply a student's word list reading frequency by .8 to allow 20% "think time." Our spelling celeration aim is ×2.

COMPOSING PARAGRAPHS, ESSAYS, AND REPORTS

At the paragraph level, composition can be characterized as storytelling or narrative writing; persuasive writing; descriptive writing, including each of the five senses as relevant; expository writing, including summarizing and comparing–contrasting; and practical writing, such as writing business and personal letters, letters of complaint, directions to a location, and invitations to an event. Terry Dodds (2005) has designed extensive rubrics for each writing genre for her program *High Performance Writing*. Each rubric contains 20 features sorted into four aspects: organization, content, style, and mechanics. For example, for persuasive writing content, Dodds lists "Uses supporting statements that include facts, statistics, examples, and expert opinions" and "Anticipates and addresses readers' concerns and counter-arguments." For descriptive writing style, she lists "Uses at least fifteen adjectives to modify nouns" and "Uses figurative language (onomatopoeia, similes, alliteration, metaphors)." Each quality is rated from 0 through 5, with 0 indicating no evidence of the element, 1 indicating the emergent or minimum level, 3 indicating a satisfactory level, and 5 indicating the mastery level. Both teachers and students can learn to use each rubric reliably. The program is written at three levels—beginning, intermediate, and advanced—with increasingly detailed rubrics across levels. (The examples above may be found on page 7 of the *Persuasive Writing* booklet in the advanced-level notebook.) Each level also includes 10 scripted lessons describing the qualities of each genre. Dodds's programs include a "practical writing" module to teach these components, as well as a report-writing module. Report writing may also involve research skills (a repertoire omitted by Dodds and by this chapter). Morningside Academy has created its own rubrics for persuasive, expository, narrative, and descriptive writing.

Our frequency aim for composing is 250–200 words in 15 minutes, "think time" included, and with words averaging 5 letters each. This calculates to 85–65 letters per minute, with a 15-minute endurance. Adding 20% thinking time requires a writing tool frequency of 100–75 letters per minute, with a 15-minute endurance. These aims work well for the average middle school student. For students whose tool skill frequency is below 100–75 letters per minute, we multiply their tool skill aim by .8 (80%), to allow 20% thinking time. Our celeration aim is ×2.

Although Dodds's (2005) program provides highly detailed composing criteria, it does not teach students explicit strategies for achieving them. Archer et al.'s (2008a) *REWARDS Writing: Sentence Refinement* program does teach strategies for editing compositions, which, when mastered, will eventually become part of the learner's initial composing repertoire. The program teaches three editing processes: revising, editing, and proofreading. During revision, the writer focuses on the overall quality of the composition, asking him- or herself questions such as "Did I include all the necessary information or arguments?" and "Is my composition well organized?" During editing, the writer focuses on the quality of the sentences; during proofreading, the writer carefully checks conventions (including spelling, punctuation, etc.). Specifically, Archer et al. teach a strategy they call SCORE. S stands for *sounds good*, C stands for *combine*, O stands for *omit*, R stands for *replace*, and E stands for *expand*. We look forward to future programs by Archer and her colleagues that will provide explicit strategies for teaching each genre.

Sequencing Sentences in Paragraphs and Paragraphs in Compositions

One critical component of composing is sequencing sentences in paragraphs, and paragraphs in compositions. Linden and Whimbey (1990) describe a technology for teaching sentence sequencing, which they call *text reconstruction* (TRC). During TRC exercises, learners order jumbled sentences into paragraphs, and jumbled paragraphs into essays or stories. Let's inspect an example of a TRC exercise.

> *Instructions:* Read all the sentences. Decide which should come first, and number it "1." Then decide which should come second, and number it "2." Continue numbering the sentences in this way.
>
> ___ Therefore, when 19-year-old Michael Grubbs became this year's queen, it shocked no one.
> ___ One year its queen was a dog, and another year a refrigerator.
> ___ Rice University has had some unusual homecoming queens in the past.
> ___ So Michael has agreed to give up his title and escort his runner-up, Nancy Jones, to the festivities.
> ___ But Cotton Bowl rules prohibit a man from being a princess in the parade.

During instruction, teachers demonstrate the reordering process, providing "think-aloud" models. After ordering the sentences, the learner then copies them in order, using the following steps:

1. Read as many words as you believe you can write correctly from memory (usually 5–10 words, except for large or difficult-to-spell words).
2. Write those words from memory, including all capitals and punctuation marks.
3. Check back to the original sentence and correct any errors you made.
4. Read the next group of words and repeat the process.

Transcribing text is a time-honored tradition dating back to the Romans. Linden and Whimbey (1990) trace the roots of transcribing (and link TRC's heritage) to Benjamin Franklin, who worked in his brother's printing shop. His brother was widely recognized for his superior writing, so well-known writers of his time would use his shop. Franklin would take their manuscripts and cut them up into sentences, put the strips in a box, shake the box, and then reorder and copy the sentences. In a variation of the procedure that would eventually become TRC, he would write down only key words from authors' sentences, order the set, and attempt to recall the exact wording of the full sentences during the "copying" phase. Franklin (1944, p. 19) said that "this was to teach me method in the arrangement of thoughts," and claimed that he owed his writing prowess to the practice. Linden and Whimbey also cite Malcolm X's account of another extraordinary program of analytical copying, noting that when he entered prison, his reading and writing skills were very poor. To remedy this, he secured a dictionary to learn new words. He also wanted to improve his handwriting, so he began copying the words and definitions. Then he would repeatedly read his writing aloud to himself. He was in prison long enough to copy the entire dictionary!

The careful inspection contingency inherent in TRC teaches learners to focus upon sentence meaning and the logical relations among sentences. They also learn to recognize many of the transition words employed by effective writers, such as *therefore*, and *but*. The finer discriminations shaped by TRC may also improve reading fluency, spelling, punctuation, other English conventions, and even mastery of facts and concepts. In fact, Linden is currently writing an American history text in TRC jumbled sentences!

As with sentence and composition writing and editing, frequency aims should include 20% "think time," so we multiply a student's reading rate by .8. Our celeration aim is ×2. Table 7.2 is a summary of pinpoints for applying PT to writing.

READING OR LANGUAGE ARTS?

Many schools stop scheduling separate reading and writing blocks after the primary grades, and integrate them into a "language arts block." Language arts blocks are typically shorter than the combined total of previously scheduled reading and writing blocks. By middle school, basic reading and writing skills are expected rather than taught, with literature, social studies, or science topics becoming the primary focus of language arts. Many teachers ask us, "Which is better: separate reading and writing blocks, or a combined language arts block?" Our answer depends upon each student's

TABLE 7.2. Practice Pinpoints for Writing

Pinpoint	Frequency aim	Celeration aim	Tool skill requirements
1. See/write words (transcription tool skill)	*Ultimate aim* 180–160 letters per minute (36–32 words averaging 5 letters each/minute) *Primary grades* 50 letters/minute *Intermediate grades* 100 letters/minute *Middle school* 150–130 letters/minute	×1.25	N/A
2. Hear/write words (dictation tool skill) (middle school and higher)	130–110 letters/minute	×1.25	N/A
3. Hear/write words (spelling)	125–90 letters/minute	×2	Hear/write 125–90 letters/minute
4. See mundane words/write sharp words (vocabulary)	20–15 words written/minute or 80–60 words spoken/minute	×2	N/A
5. See 2–5 short sentences/write 1 sentence by combining, subtracting, and/or adding words	20–15 words written/minute, for 3–5 minutes[a]	×2	See/write 125–90 letters (25–18 words averaging 5 letters each)/minute
6. See paragraphs/write • edit sentences (grammar, punctuation, capitalization, etc.)	20–15 words written (edited) for every 100 words, for 3–5 minutes[a]	×2	See/say >130 wpm
7. See jumbled sentences or paragraphs/write numbers to rank-order them	80% of reading rate	×2	N/A
8. Free/write paragraphs, essays, reports	250–200 words/15 minutes[a]	×2	100–75 letters/minute

[a]Number of words written assumes words averaging 5 letters each. If words average more or fewer letters, adjust accordingly to meet the criterion of 100–75 total letters written per minute.

demonstrated performance and takes a first-things-first approach to learning. If a learner can make expected annual progress in reading and writing with a combined, shortened block that focuses upon application, then such a block is the real-world block of choice. However, if a learner needs more skill building in reading or writing to make expected annual progress, then separate blocks are better. Progress-monitoring data will help you determine which is best for each learner.

CHAPTER 8

Precision Teaching in Mathematics

MR. WOLFSON'S TIER I MATH CLASS

Let's visit Mr. Wolfson's third-grade math class.* It's a Tier 1 class. Each day he schedules 20 minutes of his 75-minute math class for practicing skills, concepts, and principles that he has already taught. It is late October, and his students have just finished a third lesson in multiplying two-digit numbers by two-digit numbers. Since he usually schedules fluency practice after three initial lessons, it's time for practice. "Get your 'See computation problem/write answers' folder, and sit with your partners while I pass out the timers. You have 1 minute to get ready!"

Each folder contains several daily charts stapled to the back cover, a packet of computation worksheets, and several timings charts stapled to an inside cover. The members of each pair have been carefully matched: High performers are paired with high performers, and medium performers are paired with medium or lower performers. Lower performers are never paired with lower performers. Mr. Wolfson hands each pair a timer as the partners sit in their designated seats next to each other.

"We've completed three lessons in multiplying with larger numbers. Now it's time to practice to fluency! Look inside your folders. You'll notice new worksheets related to the new multiplication problems we have been learning to solve. Everyone take a copy of the new multiplication worksheet from your folder and get ready for a timing. You'll have 3 minutes to complete as many problems as you can. After the timing, we'll exchange papers, score them, and chart the results. Look at me when you're ready."

When all of his students are looking, he says, "Remember, it's about a pace, not a race. See if you can keep an even pace as you complete the problems. OK, please begin!" He is careful never to say "Go!" or anything else that would promote racing. Mr. Wolfson circulates during the timing, telling several students not to race, and giving encouraging words to those who are breathing normally and keeping an even pace.

After 3 minutes, Mr. Wolfson says, "OK, please stop. Exchange papers as I pass out the answer key." The key contains completed problems showing all regrouping, intermediate digits, and answer digits. Each student uses the key to score his or her partner's work. Scoring involves circling each incorrect intermediate digit and answer digit the partner has written. "Look at me when you've completed your scoring."

When all students are looking, Mr. Wolfson says, "OK, now count up the number of incorrect digits you've circled and subtract that number from the total number of digits your partner wrote. What's the quick way to do your counting . . . Nick?"

"You can determine the total by first adding up the totals at the end of each row your partner completed, and then adding that number to the number of digits in the last row that was not finished. You'll have to count those digits in that last unfinished row. Then write the correct digit number over the incorrect digit number at the top of your partner's worksheet," Nick says proudly.

"Very good explanation, Nick!" Mr. Wolfson beams. "OK, everyone, count 'em up! Look at me when you're done." (Since students are familiar with this scoring process, having built their frequencies of one-digit by two-digit multiplication problems earlier in the fall, a brief review is all that is necessary.)

As the students complete their adding and counting, Mr. Wolfson checks the accuracy of a few partners who have made errors doing this work in the past. He knows, however, that the counts can be off by a bit and not distort the frequencies plotted on charts, especially those frequencies higher than 20.

When all students are looking, he says, "OK, now take a minute or two to coach your partner's performance." During coaching, partners point to problems with circled error digits one at a time, and students fix up their errors. Coaches review computation steps and math facts as needed. If they are stuck, they call Mr. Wolfson, who helps in the coaching process. Recently, Mr. Wolfson has identified two high performers who assist him with this process.

When everyone has finished, he says, "Everyone is working so well! Now please start a new timings chart for this kind of problem. Label it 'See two-digit times two-digit multiplacation problems/write answers,' and plot your corrects and errors. Work as a team, first charting one partner's performance and then the other's. Then pass your worksheets to the end of your table (or row) and I'll collect them. Look at me when you're done."

When all students are looking, Mr. Wolfson says, "Take out another worksheet. We'll see if you can beat your corrects and reduce your errors in another 3-minute timing. Find the problem that you must complete to beat your first timing, and mark it with a star at the top. How can you figure out which problem it is . . . Lydia?"

"You add the numbers at the end of each row until you're almost at the rate you got on the last timing. Then you add a few more problems until the number of digits is higher than the number you got in your last timing," says Lydia.

"That's right," says Mr. Wolfson. "OK, everyone, mark your problem, and look at me when you're ready." When all students are looking, he says, "Please begin." During the second timing, Mr. Wolfson faces the class and scans each first timing sheet, noting whether errors were due to incorrect math facts or to an incorrect multiplication process. He repeats the timing–scoring–charting–intervention–goal-setting process with a third 3-minute timing, again noting error patterns on the worksheets for the second timing.

After the third timing–scoring–charting–intervention process is complete, Mr. Wolfson says, "OK, now we'll chart our personal bests.[†] Find the blank daily chart underneath the one we've been using ('See one-digit times two-digit multiplication problems/write answers) and start a new daily chart. Label it 'See two-digit times two-digit multiplication problems/write answers,' and chart your best corrects and incorrects with each other. Then pass your folders to the end of the row."

Before school tomorrow, Mr. Wolfson will inspect the third timing performances for error patterns, and check a sample of charts to verify correct charting. He'll also fill each folder with packets of worksheets for the day's practicing.

During the last 10 minutes of math class, he will schedule additional instruction as an intervention for those who made process errors or whose correct digit frequencies did not increase. He will also add "See/write math fact answers" timings and charts as an intervention for those who made more than three math fact errors. Those who need interventions will still complete the three timings in the 20-minute practice block with the rest of the class. Those with no intervention needs will complete an enrichment activity that requires students to tell how many square feet of carpeting to buy for rooms of various sizes.

---

*Thanks to Michael Wolfson and his students for teaching and learning while Kent Johnson summarized this episode.

†The use of the term *personal best* in this context originated in Elizabeth Haughton's kindergarten classroom in the 1970s. Students originally described their progress to parents and siblings by saying, "I went up!", but their listeners did not understand. After Elizabeth taught the students to call the highest frequency they had achieved a "personal best," they began to communicate more clearly—for example, by exclaiming that they "made three personal bests in math today!" Elizabeth warns, however, that an exclusive focus on personal bests may slow learning if teachers and learners shoot for minimum improvement by setting "just one better" as the criterion for rewards. She gives reward tickets for each personal best that also maintains a ×2 celeration.

Figure 8.1 presents our schema of mathematics composites and components broken down into concepts, operations, algorithms, and vocabulary for six domains of foundational mathematics: whole numbers, decimals, simple percentages, fractions, ratios/equations, and algebra. Each domain includes (1) math tool skills, such as early numeracy and math facts; (2) computation; (3) standard word problems with algebraic equations; (4) talk-aloud problem solving (TAPS) for solving complex problems (Whimbey & Lockhead, 1999); and (5) the language of math, including terminology for all math concepts and principles. This analysis parallels the analysis of domains that led to the program requirements of Reading First.[1] Schools that seek funds to improve reading instruction through Reading First must use research-based reading programs that include (1) phonemic awareness, (2) phonics, (3) passage fluency, (4) vocabulary, and (5) comprehension. Our five-part foundational math program is in essence a "Math First" equivalent to Reading First.

Our analysis stands in stark contrast to the content of the most popular mathematics textbooks. These textbooks emphasize the development of reasoning strategies—asking students to reason their way to methods for computation and problem solving, and even going so far as omitting the teaching of standard computation and word problem algorithms. The "do-it-yourself" reasoning approaches students derive are like reinventing the wheel and are most tedious and inefficient. We believe that reasoning should be saved for defining and solving more complex quantitative problems. Efficient

---

[1]The U.S. Department of Education amendment to the No Child Left Behind Act of 2001, to ensure that all children read at grade level by the end of third grade (see *www2.ed.gov/programs/readingfirst/index.html*).

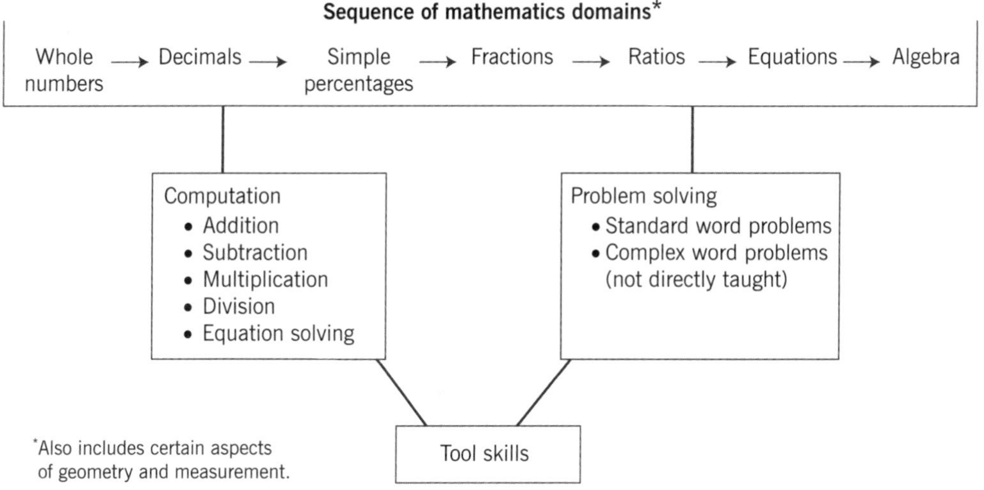

FIGURE 8.1. Tool, component, and composite skills in mathematics.

algorithms are the tools, not the context, for teaching thinking and reasoning; their mastery is essential. Apparently the U.S. Department of Education agrees with us.

Because of the poor performance of U.S. students in mathematics, especially when compared with students from other Western countries (Olson, Martin, & Mullis, 2008), the U.S. Department of Education recently convened a panel to study the current state of mathematics education for students in elementary and secondary schools. The National Mathematics Advisory Panel (NMAP) studied the available scientific evidence and developed six principal recommendations to assist educators in such areas as core principles of mathematics, effective instruction, effective assessment, and the importance of research (NMAP, 2008). The panel's big message: In order to produce mathematically competent adults for the global market, educators must prepare students to be proficient in algebra, the gateway to later mathematical achievement. The routes to algebra proficiency, according to the NMAP (2008), are as follows:

- Fluency with whole numbers.
- Fluency with fractions (including decimals, percents, and negative fractions).
- Fluency with certain key aspects of geometry and measurement.

The NMAP also emphasized the importance of developing conceptual understanding, computation, and problem-solving skills simultaneously.

Two of the panel's six principal recommendations deserve further attention here. First, "The mathematics curriculum in Grades PreK–8 should be streamlined and should emphasize a well-defined set of the most critical topics in the early grades" (NMAP, 2008, p. 11). We heartily agree with this recommendation; many of the mathematics curricula on the market today present an overwhelming number of topics, with no depth of learning each topic. Second,

> Use should be made of what is clearly known from rigorous research about how children learn, especially by recognizing a) the advantages for children in having a strong start; b) the mutually reinforcing benefits of conceptual understanding, procedural fluency, and automatic (i.e., quick and effortless) recall of facts; and c) that effort, not just inherent talent, counts in mathematical achievement. (NMAP, 2008, p. 11)

Indeed! Many students struggle with higher mathematics because they lack basic computational fluency skills. This supports the importance of emphasizing the quick recall of basic mathematics facts. A national survey of algebra teachers revealed that many teachers believe that current curricula do not place a high enough priority on these skills. In fact, the most frequent type of suggestion among the 578 teachers who responded in writing to an open-ended question was for a greater focus in the elementary grades on proficiency with basic mathematics concepts and skills (NMAP, 2008). Miller and Carr (1997) have also supported the importance of the development of computation skills, because ultimately speed and accuracy are integral to successful student performance in mathematics. They sound like precision teachers, don't they?

The myth of inherent talents or abilities in mathematics also needs to be dashed. At Morningside, we wish we had a dollar for every parent who told us, "Well, I was never good in math either."

The NMAP also described "benchmarks for critical foundations in algebra." According to the benchmarks, fluency with math facts and computation of whole numbers must be achieved before the end of the elementary school years. Likewise, by the end of sixth grade, students should be able to perform all basic operations with fractions and decimals, as well as certain aspects of geometry and measurement, proficiently.

Since the 1990s, Morningside Academy has been developing its own math program, *Morningside Mathematics Fluency* (Johnson & Casson, 2005a, 2005b; Johnson, 2005, 2008a). This program develops learner fluency in whole numbers, fractions, decimals, and simple percent operations; shortly, we will add key aspects of geometry and measurement. We are pleased that our plans so closely match the NMAP's recommendations, and we agree that U.S. teachers need to return to arithmetic as a core of mathematics education. Space does not permit a full explication of our program here; rather, we describe our practice procedures related to arithmetic and mathematics. We begin by describing how we build the underlying tool skills required to make rapid progress.

TOOL SKILLS IN MATHEMATICS

Key tool skills that are part of all mathematics include counting, number reading and writing, identifying place value, and math fact proficiency. As in reading, after explicit instruction in each tool skill, the skills are practiced by pairs of students who provide peer coaching to each other. Most of the written timings can be practiced simultaneously, with peers alternating in providing feedback after each timing.

Counting

In *Morningside Mathematics Fluency: Basic Number Skills* (Johnson, 2005), we teach three kinds of counting: *rote counting,* or saying the numbers from 1 to 1,000 in sequence without reference to objects to count; *1:1 counting*, or saying numbers in sequence while touching specific objects being counted; and *counting estimate,* or seeing a group of objects and estimating the number of objects in the group. Our frequency aim for all types of counting is 200–180 digits per minute. Our celeration aim is ×2.

Number Reading

In *Morningside Mathematics Fluency: Basic Number Skills* (Johnson, 2005), students also practice reading numbers sliced by number of digits, in a sequence from one through nine digits. The digits on these slices are in random order. Cumulative review occurs after each new digit slice. For example, slice 1 includes one-digit numbers; slice 2 includes two-digit numbers; cumulative slice 2 includes both one-digit and two-digit numbers; slice 3 includes three-digit numbers; cumulative slice 3 includes one-digit, two-digit, and three-digit numbers; and so on. Our frequency aim for saying numbers is 200–180 digits per minute, or 70–60 periods per minute (a *period* being a set of three digits in a number separated by a comma—hundreds, thousands, millions, etc.). Our celeration aim is ×2.

Number Writing

Our students also practice writing the 10 digits fundamental to all numbers: 0 through 9. Our frequency aim for writing the numbers 0 through 9 is 160–130 per minute. Our frequency aim for taking dictation of multiple-digit numbers is 120–100 digits per minute. Our celeration aim for writing numbers is ×1.25.

Place Value

We present multiple-digit numbers to our students with one digit larger than the others and in boldface. They say the place value (e.g., 1s, 10s, 100s, 1,000s) of the larger, bold digit. For example, they see 1,67**5**,237 and say the place value of the 5 (1,000s). They are fluent when they can say 80–60 place values per minute. Our celeration aim is ×2.

Math Facts

Many students become math "dropouts," failing to master math beyond the primary grades because they never master math facts. They depend on calculators for the simplest operations. Even with calculators they are hampered in their ability to solve sophisticated problems, because they must interrupt their train of thought to punch numbers in the calculators. The result is that they often "lose their place" in the problem-solving algorithm. But without the calculator or counting on their fingers, they arrive at incorrect answers. Math work becomes very tedious, and students lose their motivation to learn math.

In *Morningside Mathematics Fluency: Math Facts* (Johnson, 2008a), we take a conceptual approach by teaching *number families*. For example, the addition and subtraction number family 4, 9, 13 yields two addition facts ($4 + 9 = 13, 9 + 4 = 13$) and two subtraction facts ($13 - 9 = 4, 13 - 4 = 9$). The multiplication and division number family 5, 9, 45 produces two multiplication facts ($9 \times 5 = 45, 5 \times 9 = 45$) and two division facts ($45 \div 5 = 9, 45 \div 9 = 5$). This conceptual system also teaches the complementary processes of addition and subtraction and of multiplication and division. Finally, and most significantly for a vast number of students, it reduces by three-quarters the amount of memorization necessary to master the 400 separate math facts in the traditional addition, subtraction, multiplication, and division math facts tables. Why? Because memorizing only three numbers yields four separate math facts that traditionally required separate memorizing. Figure 8.2 lists the math fact families taught in our program.

Our frequency aim for writing math fact answers is 100–80 answers (one to two digits) per minute, with no more than two errors. Our celeration aim is ×2.

Addition and subtraction		**Multiplication and division**	
2, 2, 4	4, 7, 11	2, 2, 4	4, 7, 28
2, 3, 5	4, 8, 12	2, 3, 6	4, 8, 32
2, 4, 6	4, 9, 13	2, 4, 8	4, 9, 36
2, 5, 7	5, 5, 10	2, 5, 10	5, 5, 25
2, 6, 8	5, 6, 11	2, 6, 12	5, 6, 30
2, 7, 9	5, 7, 12	2, 7, 14	5, 7, 35
2, 8, 10	5, 8, 13	2, 8, 16	5, 8, 40
2, 9, 11	5, 9, 14	2, 9, 18	5, 9, 45
3, 3, 6	6, 6, 12	3, 3, 9	6, 6, 36
3, 4, 7	6, 7, 13	3, 4, 12	6, 7, 42
3, 5, 8	6, 8, 14	3, 5, 15	6, 8, 48
3, 6, 9	6, 9, 15	3, 6, 18	6, 9, 54
3, 7, 10	7, 7, 14	3, 7, 21	7, 7, 49
3, 8, 11	7, 8, 15	3, 8, 24	7, 8, 56
3, 9, 12	7, 9, 16	3, 9, 27	7, 9, 63
4, 4, 8	8, 8, 16	4, 4, 16	8, 8, 64
4, 5, 9	8, 9, 17	4, 5, 20	8, 9, 72
4, 6, 10	9, 9, 18	4, 6, 24	9, 9, 81

FIGURE 8.2. Addition and subtraction, and multiplication and division number families.

COMPUTATION SKILLS

In a series of six Morningside math computation programs (Johnson & Casson, 2005a, 2005b; Johnson & Melroe, 2006a, 2006b, 2009, 2011), students practice the standard operations or algorithms for adding columns of numbers, subtracting with regrouping, long multiplication, and long division. We begin with whole-number computation skills, breaking them into more than 100 subskills. For example, addition computation includes 20 subskills, such as "three-digit number plus three-digit number with carrying." Our program includes methods for teaching these operations, plus plenty of materials for practicing them until they are fluent. Our program also includes about 100 subskills for teaching students to add, subtract, multiply, and divide fractions, decimals, and percents, and to solve ratio equations.

Each student completes diagnostic tests to determine which computation skills are deficient or not fluent. The diagnostic tests also prescribe specific lessons and practice materials for reteaching each problem when students need additional instruction in the algorithms.

When encountering a computation slice for the first time, our students practice in 1-minute timings, building to 5-minute timings. They work in pairs, doing simultaneous timings followed by exchanging their work and alternating feedback and coaching. We set different frequency aims for addition, subtraction, multiplication, and division of whole numbers, fractions, and decimals, which we describe later in this chapter. Our celeration aim is ×2.

Effective Intervention Procedures for Teaching Computation

We have noted earlier in this book that one of our PT mantras is *Discriminate before you generate.* Students who can quickly identify and fix errors in completed computation exercises are much less likely to make those same errors themselves. For example, after using boardwork to teach an algorithm for regrouping in subtraction, we give students a set of completed subtraction problems with errors at each spot where errors typically occur, and ask them to "fix them up." We include both correctly and incorrectly performed problems in the mix. When students can spot and fix errors such as incorrectly regrouping across place values with zeroes almost at the rate it takes to inspect the problems, they have learned a *self-correcting repertoire* that serves them well as they compute problems on their own: If they begin to make a common error, they catch themselves and avoid it. As we have described more fully in Chapter 3, we apply *Discriminate before you generate* to all component skills instruction—from punctuation, to spelling, to decoding, to word problem solving.

SOLVING STANDARD WORD PROBLEMS WITH ALGEBRAIC EQUATIONS

We also teach students how to solve common forms of word problems with algebraic equations. One of us (Kent Johnson) conducted an extensive analysis of nearly 2,000 word problems presented in current elementary math texts, and discerned five types of addition and subtraction word problems, plus four types of multiplication and division word problems.

The five types of addition and subtraction problems include (1) finding the total when we know the original number and the number added, and finding the number left when we know the original number and the number gone; (2) finding how many were added or how many more are needed when we know the original number and the total, and finding the number gone when we know the original number and the number left; (3) finding how many there were to begin with when we know the number added and the resulting total, and finding the original number when we know the number gone and the number left; (4) finding the total number in the class when we know the size of both subclasses, and finding the size of one of the classes when we know the total and the size of one class; and (5) finding the larger quantity when we know (a) the smaller quantity and (b) the difference between the smaller quantity and the larger quantity, and finding the smaller quantity when we know (c) the larger quantity and (d) the difference between the smaller and larger quantity.

Let's briefly examine each of these types of addition and subtraction problems:

> There were nine knights at the Round Table. Six knights went hunting. How many knights stayed at the Round Table?

To solve it, students write and solve this equation:

$9 - 6 = x, x = 3$

How did the students derive this equation? Each problem can be conceptualized as a mini-story—not usually a very interesting story, but a story nonetheless. The first number in the equation corresponds to what happened at the beginning of the story. The second number corresponds to what happened in the middle of the story. The final symbol—*x* for "unknown"—corresponds to what happened at the end of the story.

Here's another type of addition–subtraction word problem:

> Betty had six pieces of candy. She gave some of them away. Then she had four pieces left. How many pieces did she give away?

To solve it, learners write and solve this equation:

$6 - x = 4, - x = -2, x = 2$

Notice that since we do not know what happened in the middle of the story, the *x* serves as the middle term of the equation. (Notice also that students get an early start on understanding negative numbers.)

Here's another type of problem:

> After Sue found three leaves, she had seven leaves in all. How many leaves did Sue have before she found the three?

To solve it, students write and solve this equation:

$x + 3 = 7, x = 4$

Which part of the story—beginning, middle, or end—is unknown?

Some addition and subtraction problems are not stories with a beginning, middle, and end; students can always solve these problems by placing the unknown at the end of the equation, after the "equals" sign. For example:

> The warehouse contained 25 cars and 25 trucks. How many vehicles were in the warehouse?

To solve it, students write and solve this equation:

$25 + 25 = x, x = 50$

Students also solve addition and subtraction word problems that require comparison:

> Mrs. Hill has seven plates. She has four more plates than glasses. How many glasses does she have?

To solve it, students write and solve this equation:

7 (size of larger group) – x (size of smaller group) = 4 (the difference between groups), $-x = -3, x = 3$

All comparative problems are solved this way. After students read a story problem, their first task is to identify the type of problem. Then they use the corresponding equation type to solve it.

We also teach four kinds of multiplication and division word problems, including (1) finding a total when we know the number of groups and number in each group; (2) finding the number in each group when we know the total and the number of groups; (3) finding the number of groups when we know the total and the number in each group; and (4) two kinds of comparison problems.[2] Students also learn to solve all types of problems with distracters in them. The nine kinds of word problems, with examples and equations, are displayed in Table 8.1.

Students practice in pairs, with simultaneous timings and alternating coaching. Our frequency aim is two answers per minute for 3 minutes, or six answers in 3 minutes. We have not yet set a celeration aim for word problems. Students must show all work, including the equations associated with each problem and their solutions. These aims work well with problems averaging about 50 words in length and requiring basic

[2]Word problems involving money, time, and distance, often taught as multiplication and division problems, are best taught as ratio problems—an approach that is more conceptually sophisticated, as well as computationally easier.

TABLE 8.1. Nine Types of Standard Word Problems

Class	Problem	Example	Equation
Five types of addition and subtraction word problems			
1	Finding the total when we know the original number and the number added	John had 9 apples. Tom gave him 3 apples. How many apples did John have then?	$9 + 3 = x$
	Finding the number left when we know the original number and the number gone	John had 12 apples. He ate 3 of them. How many apples did he have then?	$12 - 3 = x$
2	Finding how many were added or how many more are needed when we know the original number and the total	John had 9 apples. Afer Tom had given him some more apples, he had 12 apples. How many apples did Tom give him?	$9 + x = 12$
	Finding the number gone when we know the original number and the number left	John had 12 apples. Then he ate some. He had 9 apples left. How many apples did he eat?	$12 - x = 9$
3	Finding how many there were to begin with when we know the number added and the resulting total	John had some apples. Tom gave him 3 apples. Then he had 12 apples. How many apples did John have to begin with?	$x + 3 = 12$
	Finding the original number when we know the number gone and the number left	John had some apples. He ate 3 of them. Then he had 9 apples left. How many apples did he have to begin with?	$x - 3 = 9$
4 (Classification)	Finding the total number in the class when we know the size of both subclasses	John has 9 apples and 3 oranges. How many fruits does John have?	$9 + 3 = x$
	Finding the size of one of the classes when we know the total and the size of one class	John has 12 fruits. Nine of those fruits are apples. The rest are oranges. How many oranges does John have?	$9 + x = 12$
5 (Comparison)	Finding the larger quantity when we know (a) the smaller quantity and (b) the difference between the smaller quantity and the larger quantity	John has 9 apples. He has 3 more oranges than apples (*or* 3 fewer apples than oranges). How many oranges does he have?	$x - 9 = 3$
	Finding the smaller quantity when we know (a) the larger quantity and (b) the difference between the smaller and larger quantity	John has 12 apples. He has 3 more apples than oranges (*or* 3 fewer oranges than apples). How many oranges does he have?	$12 - x = 3$

(cont.)

TABLE 8.1. *(cont.)*

Class	Problem	Example	Equation
Four types of multiplication and division word problems			
1	Find total when we know the number of groups and number of items in each group	Ann has 2 bags of apples. If there are 3 apples in each bag, how many apples does she have in total?	$2 \times 3 = n$
2	Find the number of items in each group when we know the number of groups and the total	Ann has 6 apples. She wants to divide them in two equal bags. How many apples will go to each bag?	$2 \times n = 6$
3	Find the number of groups when we know the total and number of items in each group	Ann has 6 apples. She wants to put 3 apples in each bag. How many bags will she need?	$n \times 3 = 6$
4	Comparison problems: Find the larger quantity when we know the smaller quantity and the ratio of larger to smaller quantities	Celia is 3 years old. Her mom is 10 times older than her. How old is Celia's mom?	$3 \times 10 = n$
	Comparison problems: Find the smaller quantity when we know the larger quantity and the ratio of larger to smaller quantities	Celia's mom is 30 years old. She is 10 times older than Celia. How old is Celia?	$n \times 10 = 30$

computation. For best results, students should also be able to read the problems without decoding errors at an independent rate of 125 wpm or more.

EFFECTIVENESS OF *MORNINGSIDE MATHEMATICS FLUENCY*

How well does *Morningside Mathematics Fluency* work? Three informal evaluations attest to its effectiveness. Fort Fraser Elementary School, a small rural public school in northern British Columbia, formed a partnership with Morningside. Students' national percentile rankings in reading, mathematics, and writing performance on the Canadian Tests of Basic Skills (CTBS) improved substantially over a 5-year period. One group of students was tracked from fifth grade through their seventh-grade graduation. Another group was tracked from third grade through their seventh-grade graduation. Prior to the Morningside implementation, students performed slightly below the 30th percentile nationally. During the 4 years of implementation, students made steady gains in both mathematics and reading percentile rankings, achieving CTBS scores at national averages (50th percentile) within 2 years. After 4 years, both groups ranked well above average in both CTBS reading and math scores, performing at the 64th percentile nationally in reading and the 75th percentile nationally in math. The school rose from a ranking of 13th in a district of 25 schools, to 2nd in math and 5th in reading. Writing performance was also systematically measured in 1 year of the project. At the beginning of the year, only 39% of students were at grade level. After 9 months, 80% of students were at grade level. Figure 8.3 shows the math achievement gains for Fort Fraser's students.

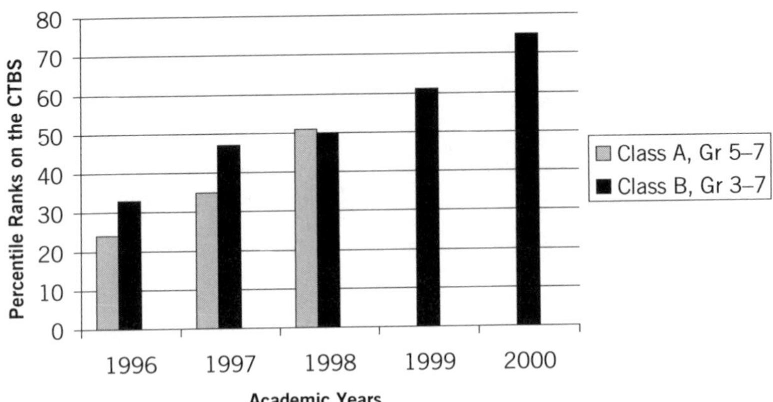

FIGURE 8.3. Math achievement gains in percentile rankings for students at Fort Fraser Elementary School in British Columbia on the nationally normed Canadian Tests of Basic Skills (CTBS) following introduction of *Morningside Mathematics Fluency.*

Morningside Mathematics Fluency has also been effective in urban schools. One example is Emerson Elementary, a public school in Seattle that had over 90% African American students and was the 9th most economically impoverished school of 80 elementary schools in the Seattle School District. Before our program was implemented, only 10% of Emerson's students passed Washington's statewide achievement test in mathematics. Two years after implementing the program, over 60% were passing the state test.

A more recent evaluation of *Morningside Mathematics Fluency* at Morningside Academy produced impressive results. From 2002 to 2007, we tracked the amount of mathematics progress students had attained in school before enrolling at Morningside. On the Iowa Tests of Basic Skills (ITBS), students who were 2 years or more behind their national peers averaged 6 months of growth per year in their previous school years, falling farther and farther behind each year. After their first year at Morningside, these same students made 1.45 years' growth, 2.4 times more growth than they had previously been making (see Figure 8.4). Students who were 1 month to 2 years behind their national peers at the beginning of a school year averaged 7.5 months of growth per year in their previous school years. After their first year at Morningside, these students made 2.4 years' growth, 3.2 times more progress than they had previously been making (see Figure 8.5). Even students whose math progress was equal to or above that of their national peers made more progress after their first year at Morningside than they had previously been making. These students averaged 1.3 years' growth prior to Morningside, and 2.5 years' growth in their first year at Morningside, 1.9 times more progress than they had previously been making (see Figure 8.6). An examination of ITBS math subtest performance showed that these results occurred not only for the two subtests directly related to *Morningside Mathematics Fluency* (Math Computation; Math Problem Solving and Data Interpretation), but also for the subtest not directly addressed by the program (Math Concepts and Estimation). Similar results were obtained on the Math Fluency subtest of the Woodcock–Johnson III Tests of Achievement. Students averaged just under 1 year's growth per year prior to Morningside and averaged 4.1 years'

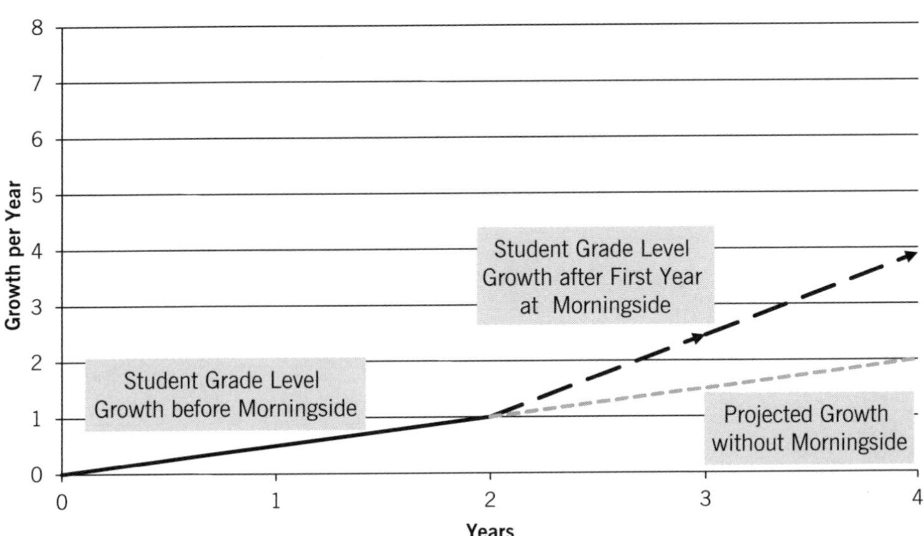

FIGURE 8.4. Average student grade level growth per year for students who were 2 or more years below their grade level prior to entering Morningside Academy and participating in *Morningside Mathematics Fluency*; their projected growth without the Morningside intervention; and their actual growth at the end of the first year of the program. These data reflect growth on the Iowa Tests of Basic Skills (ITBS).

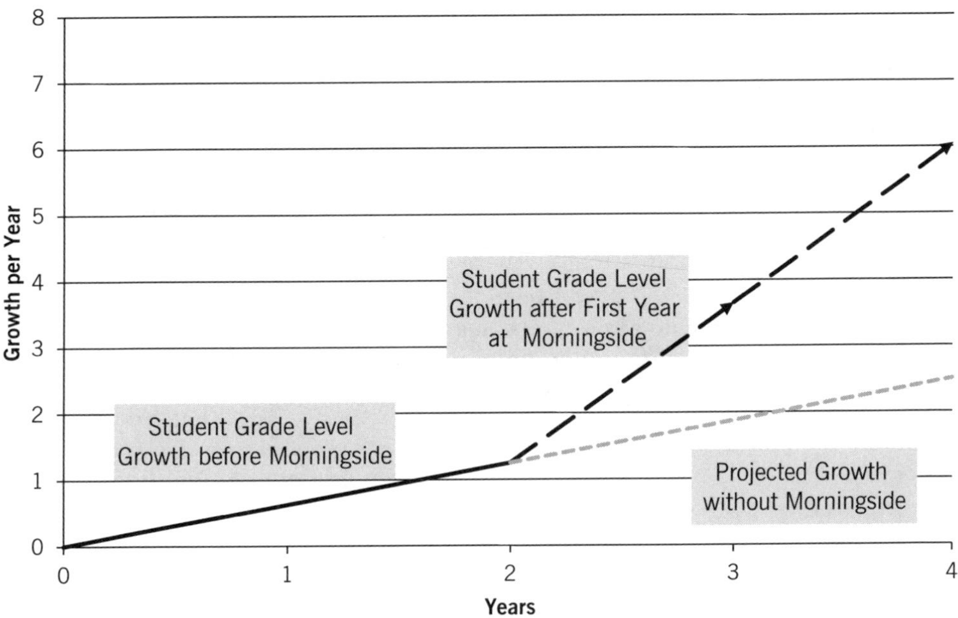

FIGURE 8.5. Average student grade level growth per year for students who were 1 month to 2 years below their grade level prior to entering Morningside Academy and participating in *Morningside Mathematics Fluency*; their projected growth without the Morningside intervention; and their actual growth at the end of the first year of the program. Again, these data reflect growth on the ITBS.

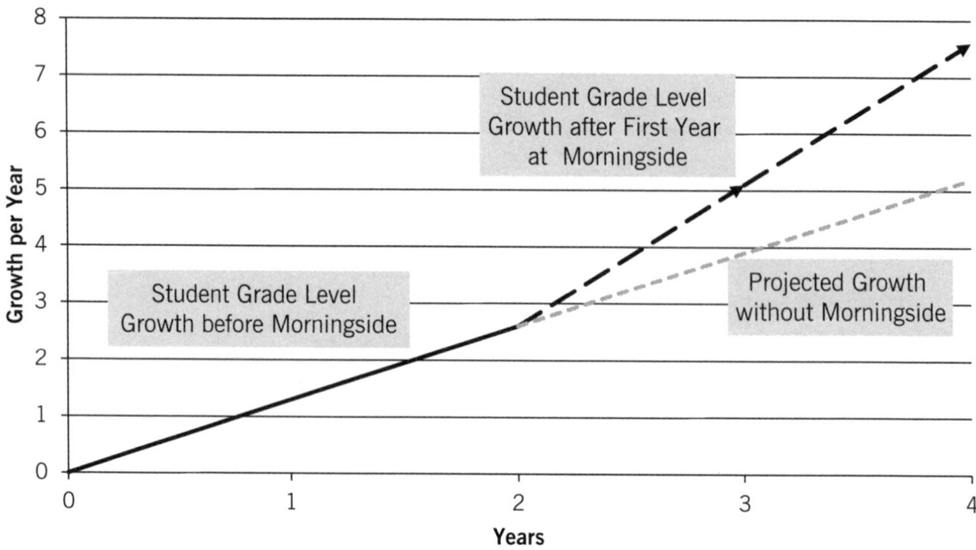

FIGURE 8.6. Average student grade level growth per year for students who were at or above their grade level prior to entering Morningside Academy and participating in *Morningside Mathematics Fluency*; their projected growth without the Morningside intervention; and their actual growth at the end of the first year of the program. Again, these data reflect growth on the ITBS.

progress after their first year, 4.5 times more progress than they had previously been making.

We are currently designing computation algorithms and standard word problems with equations for the core geometry and measurement objectives identified by the NMAP (2008).

Table 8.2 summarizes the pinpoints for applying PT to mathematics, including a few self-explanatory pinpoints that we have not discussed in this chapter. Each frequency aim assumes that the performer's tool skill frequency equals or exceeds our tool skill aims. Intermediate aims can be set at 80% of the learner's current tool skill frequency. As tool skill performance rises, remember to make periodic checks for maintenance of the computation or problem-solving skills.

TABLE 8.2. Practice Pinpoints for Mathematics Foundations

Pinpoint	Frequency aim	Celeration aim
Tool skills		
1. See objects/say • count them in succession	110–90 objects/minute	×2
2. See/say numbers (1–9 digits each)	200–180 digits/minute or 70–60 periods/ minute (e.g., 231, 450, 514 = 3 periods)	×2
3. Write numbers: 0–9	160–130 digits/minute	×1.25
4. See/write math facts	100–80 answers/minute	×2
5. See/say place value	80–60 place names/minute	×2
6. See three-term equation with one unknown/ write • solve equation for unknown	110–90 digits and symbols/minute for 5 minutes (e.g., $23 - x = 9$, $x = 23 - 9$, $x = 14$)	×2
7. See numbers/write greatest common factor	110–90 digits/minute	×2
8. See numbers/write lowest common denominator	110–90 digits/minute	×2
9. See fraction/write decimal, percent, and ratio (all variations of conversions)	110–90 digits/minute	×2
10. See numbers/write • plot on graph	20–15 dots dropped/minute	×2
11. Hear/write numbers	120–100/minute	×1.25
Computation skills		
For 12–17: See problem/write solution as directed, including all steps		
12. Addition of whole numbers, decimal numbers	15–10 answer digits/minute for 5 minutes	×2
13. Subtraction of whole numbers, decimal numbers	25–20 answer digits/minute for 5 minutes	×2
14. Multiplication of whole numbers, decimal numbers	65–60 work and answer digits/minute for 5 minutes	×2
15. Division of whole numbers, decimal numbers	55–50 work and answer digits for 5 minutes	×2
16. Fractions	80 steps in 5 minutes	×2
17. Solving complex equations	110-90 digits and symbols/minute	×2
Problem-solving repertoire		
18. See standard word problem/write • solve with three-term equations	2 answers/minute for 3 minutes	×2
19. See complex problem/say • write solutions with TAPS (problem solution not directly taught)	Not yet determined	

CHAPTER 9

Precision Teaching in the Content Areas

USING PRECISION TEACHING IN COLLEGE-LEVEL STATISTICS

In a college classroom in a small public university, students enrolled in an intermediate statistics class were struggling. Their test performance revealed many areas in which they appeared not to "get it." The professor was convinced that they didn't understand the concepts, and thought that the solution was to arrange study groups where students could ask questions. However, a graduate student in the program—one who was schooled in PT—thought otherwise. He had identified several associations and concepts that students were supposed to have learned in a statistics class that was prerequisite to the current one, and noted that they appeared to have either forgotten them or never really learned them in the earlier class. For example, they appeared to have forgotten the difference between Type I and Type II errors, as well as what symbols like Σ (sum of) stood for. Some even were struggling to discriminate symbols for greater than (>) and less than (<). The graduate student believed that these skill deficits were at the root of their failure to understand concepts in the higher-level class.

The professor, ever willing to gather empirical data, agreed to allow the graduate student to conduct an experiment to test the question. The class was divided into two groups, with students randomly assigned to each group. Half of the class—the PT group—spent 10 minutes at the end of each class day building fluency on these critical associations and concepts. The other half—the Questions group—spent 10 minutes with the graduate teaching assistant, who answered their questions about the content. To decrease the chance of bias, the professor was not told which students were in each group.

In addition to their regular midterm and final examinations, students' knowledge of the content was probed with short tests that incorporated problems similar to those discussed in class. Furthermore, the graduate student conducting the study compared final course grades for the two groups of students. Those in the PT group scored better than those in the Questions group on the probes, with the PT group's advantage growing with each successive probe. In addition, those in the PT group earned a final grade in the class that was, on average, one letter grade higher than those in the Questions group.

The preceding story is true and is recorded in greater detail in Aaron MacKenzie's (1998) master's thesis. MacKenzie had taken classes in which he had learned about component–composite analysis and the important role it plays in instructional design. (See Chapter 3 for more detail on instructional design.) He realized that the students in the intermediate statistics class couldn't be expected to "get it" until they had mastered the key concepts and associations on which "getting it" hinged. He also recognized that the rules of instructional design apply to all areas and at all levels of learning. Much of this book has been devoted to the use of PT to ensure that learners acquire skills that are fundamental to mastery of the traditional "three Rs"—reading, 'riting, and 'rithmetic. We would be remiss, however, if we didn't include a chapter on its use in content areas at the intermediate, middle school, high school, and college levels.

There are several ways teachers can employ PT to improve performance in the content areas. One way is to ensure that students continue to use and maintain the skills they have already acquired. For example, at Morningside Academy, when we teach subject matter content in social studies and science, we incorporate many pinpoints and practice procedures from reading and writing. All students practice retelling passages from text, as well as whole chapters. They also practice building vocabulary fluency with SAFMEDs, a strategy we have described in Chapter 6.[1] Learners write expository paragraphs summarizing sections and whole chapters, and in social studies they may write persuasive compositions defending particular positions.

All students receive instruction in note taking and simultaneously build their transcription rates (from text, blackboards/whiteboards, and transparencies) and their dictation rates (from lectures). It has been our experience that these skills are uniformly underdeveloped among intermediate, middle school, high school, and some college students, and thus some work on these is appropriate for all students. Ideally, these skills should be taught and mastered in the intermediate grades. At the same time, struggling readers continue to practice passage fluency to bring their rates to a frequency that maximizes comprehension—their typical speaking and listening rates.

Teachers in the content areas are encouraged to review their courses to determine the tool and component skills that every student should master in order to be successful. It would be particularly helpful to identify those areas where a reasonably large number of students have struggled in the past and to choose several frequency-building exercises that might engage all students. Some may involve reading (e.g., building vocabulary or reading challenging multisyllable words). Others will involve mathematics (e.g., telling smaller vs. larger exponents; using basic operations with decimals and fractions). And still others may involve writing (e.g., students in an American history class may be able to do well on multiple-choice tests about the content, suggesting that their reading skills are adequate—but they may not do so well on short-essay tests,

[1]For a history of SAFMEDS and explicit instructions about the use of this specialized flashcard strategy, go to *http://standardcelerationcharttopics.pbworks.com/w/page/15573489/SAFMEDS%20on%20the%20Web.*

where they need to collect and organize their thoughts and to write technically correct paragraphs).

However, in addition to extending the skills students have acquired in the "three Rs," there may be content-specific associations or concepts for which fluent repertoires will improve overall learning in the content field. For example, social studies teachers may decide that understanding broader social studies concepts is improved when students have fluent mapping skills. Although in the best of all possible worlds there would be some commonality among the skills identified by teachers of each content-area specialization, teachers may also identify different skills on which to build fluency, based on the aspects of the content field they emphasize. One advantage to having a common set of skills is, of course, that teachers can create worksheets that can be shared.[2]

Similarly, if students enter content-area instruction lacking fluency in basic reading, writing, and arithmetic prerequisites, or in skills that were intended to be acquired in a previous grade, it may save time and improve accuracy and fluency in the current content-specific class to set aside time for PT practice sessions that focus on those skills. This situation is similar to the example at the beginning of the chapter, in which students were not able to benefit from instruction in an intermediate statistics class without having mastered key associations and concepts from the introductory statistics class. In that example, taking 10 minutes a day of instructional time to build fluency on beginning-level skills significantly improved learners' performance on the intermediate-level material. The same might be true in a chemistry class for students who have not yet mastered basic operations, or in a second-year language class for students who lack fluency on material that was to have been mastered in the first-year language class. Similarly, students who have not mastered the locations of countries on a map may have trouble understanding political struggles among countries in a social studies class that emphasizes regional strife.

There are at least three ways in which PT can be applied in content-area classrooms:

- First, it can be used to ensure that association, concept, and principle application skills, which are fundamental to the success of *all* learners, are acquired to levels of fluency that predict learners will have ready access to them.
- Second, it can be used to build fundamental "three Rs" repertoires or other skills that are prerequisite to the content for students who have *acquired* them but have not built *fluent* repertoires around them. That is, they still need to concentrate on them in ways that interfere with their ability to understand the field's more global content.
- Third, it can be used in conjunction with direct instruction to build skills that some learners have not *acquired*, let alone built fluent repertoires around. The lack of such skills will stand in the way of progress in the content area.

Said another way, learners at all three tiers in the RTI framework can continue to benefit from PT when they move from "learning to read" to "reading to learn" and their

[2]As we've noted in other chapters, designing fluency sheets that have the right number and type of slices is challenging work; still, some teachers learn relatively quickly to adapt sheets or to add and subtract slices, based on student performance. Furthermore, as enough teachers come to expect well-designed fluency-building materials for their courses, publishers will invest in developing such materials.

equivalents in mathematics and writing. The differences among the three tiers, as we've described in previous chapters, will be in the intensity of the interventions required to effect change and in the time needed to achieve goals. One could argue that students in Tier 3 may need to spend significant time to remedy skill deficits and appropriately may be pulled out of regular instruction; however, that decision is best left to school personnel and parents.

Content-area teachers may reasonably ask what kinds of skills are appropriate for fluency building. The best answer is any tool or component skill (see Chapter 3) that influences the learner's ability to perform a composite skill with ease. For example, does knowing the properties of the different categories of elements in the periodic table improve the learner's ability to determine how elements will react when combined, and is the latter skill something learners will be asked to do routinely? If yes, then naming the categories and matching properties with categories are important skills for fluency building. An Advanced Placement (AP) chemistry teacher might build one or more fluency-building exercises around skills that predict the learners' ability to do well on the AP Chemistry Curriculum Modules. (See, e.g., *http://apcentral.collegeboard.com/apc/public/repository/curriculum-module-chemical-bonding.pdf*, the module for chemical bonding.)

Teachers can also take advantage of online worksheets, although not all of them provide multiple versions, nor do all of them allow teachers to set parameters for the content. A particularly nice set of worksheets that does both can be found at *www.smart-schools.com*. Another site that provides excellent practice opportunities, but that uses a duration-time counter and provides feedback per item is available at *www.ixl.com*.

In the section that follows, we recommend areas for whole-class fluency building from skills that are typically included in scope and sequence charts of different content areas. However, these lists are in no way prescriptive or exhaustive; as we have already noted, we are not content experts in each field of study.

PINPOINTS IN THE CONTENT AREAS

Mathematics

Mathematics provides countless opportunities to build tool and component skills that enable performance on composite skills. Here are four examples in typical mathematics curricula where all students could benefit from fluency building.

- *"See/change word phrases and sentences into mathematical expressions and equations."* Students' ability to complete seatwork and homework in mathematics content classes is frequently hampered by poor word problem "decoding." Here, however, we use the term *decoding* to refer to the learner's ability to translate word phrases and sentences into mathematical expressions and equations. About 10–15 minutes of timed practice that includes a specified aim (perhaps something a bit short of what the teacher can do) and daily goals could significantly improve learners' facility with this skill and lead to improved problem solving. In this case, the slice of the curriculum that would be set aside for practice would be decoding only, although students might at the same time complete slices on finding the answers to problems that are already decoded. As students achieve facility with both, they might then have timed trials on decoding and answering in a combined slice.

- *"See a shape name/write the formula for area, volume, and perimeter."* Ability to recall formulas is another area where students' facility can improve their concentration on the particulars of problems.

- *"Think/say key geometry theorems."* Many students struggle with proofs in geometry because they do not have a good grasp of the theorems and axioms that can be brought to bear. One such instance involved a college student who was completing her student teaching for an undergraduate degree in math education with high school students who had failed geometry and were taking it again during a summer session. This was during the late 1960s, and PT had not yet taken hold. Even so, she recognized that students' problem-solving ability was hampered because they didn't think of relevant theorems to apply. Thus she had them develop shorthand lists of theorems, which they memorized and rehearsed as they were solving a problem. Despite the very informal manner in which the practice was employed, it effectively bridged the students' skill in knowing *what* the theorems said and deciding *when* to use them. Here's how this might work: Students might first do some fluency building on abbreviations and definitions. For example, learners might use SAFMEDS to develop facility with the relation between the definition and the name of a congruence theorem. In this step, they might learn to say the following definitions among others when they see the names of the theorems:

angle–side–angle	If two angles of one triangle are congruent to the angles of another triangle, the triangles are similar and the ratio of proportionality is equal to the ratio of the included sides (Gorini, 2003, p. 7).
side–side–side	If three sides of one triangle are congruent or proportional to the sides of another triangle, the triangles are congruent or similar (Gorini, 2003, p. 150).
side–angle–side	If two sides of one triangle are congruent or proportional to the sides of another triangle and the included angles are congruent, the triangles are congruent or similar (Gorini, 2003, p. 150).

In a second step, learners might practice associating each abbreviation with its corresponding name. In this example, they would develop fluency with these three relations:

ASA	angle–side–angle
SAS	side–angle–side
SSS	side–side–side

As these and other congruence theorems and their abbreviations are learned, learners might then practice saying the abbreviations as a chain. In this example, they would practice until they had achieved accuracy and speed saying the following chain: ASA–SAS–SSS. Of course, there are more congruence theorems than these as well as other types of theorems that would be similarly learned. Once the chain and the meaning of individual elements are firmly in learners' repertoires, they will have easy access to them when attempting geometric proofs.

- *"See/say exponents less than/greater than other exponents."*Exponents are notoriously difficult for learners to get their heads around. They often find it difficult to discriminate among them on the basis of size. For example, which is larger: 4^2 or 2^3? Softschools (*www.softschools.com/sheets.jsp*) provides worksheets suitable for timed practice of this skill.

Chemistry

- *"See abbreviation/say name or see name/say abbreviation of elements from the periodic table."* There are several obvious frequency-building exercises related to the periodic table. The television show *Jeopardy!* often requires contestants to identify an element by its abbreviation. Similarly, most chemistry teachers would like their students to acquire facility in this skill, and PT provides a mechanism to achieve it. This requires a very straightforward worksheet in which elements are randomly ordered by either name or abbreviation, and the learner tells the one that is missing. Slices can be used to break the list into smaller units, with cumulative slices building to the entire set. Similarly, the location of an element in the table provides information about the type of element it is. Should the teacher expect students to have the skill "See location on the table/say the type of element," he or she may wish to make a copy of the table with regions highlighted and have students say (or write) the type of element (e.g., alkali metals, halogens, and noble gases). Other variations could be derived as well, depending on the class level, since the teacher of an introductory high school chemistry class will have different expectations from the teacher of a higher-level college chemistry class.

Additional candidates among many others that might be appropriate for fluency building in chemistry might include calculating mass relationships in chemical reactions or calculating the quantity of matter in gaseous chemicals and chemical solutions.

Biology

Biology provides a good example of a content area in which a single pinpoint may require fluency in different aspects of it, depending on the level of the class (intermediate, middle school, high school, or college) the student is taking.

- *"See the kingdom, phylum, class, order, family, genus, or species/say its distinguishing features."* Students at a beginning level of biology may be expected to know the distinguishing features of plants and animals by kingdom and phylum, but not by class, order, family, genus, or species. However, students in a college-level class may be expected to make much finer discriminations. Furthermore, teachers at some levels may not think that fluency (translated as automatic and speedy recall) is important for this skill, while those at other levels may recognize the value of not having to think about or look up the information. Thus each teacher needs to decide how the skill will be used before assigning a fluency aim to it.

- *"See a diagram/write the names of the cranial nerves."* Clearly this content is more typical in a college classroom, but it provides a great example of content where facility with a number of component skills benefits mastery of higher-order composites. For example, learners may benefit by being able to do the following:

    - Name cranial nerves, given their location.
    - Identify the location of cranial nerves, given their names.

- Say the function of a cranial nerve, given its name.
- Say the name of a cranial nerve, given its function.

Social Studies

- *"See data/place points on a graph."* Students are often asked to graph data in social studies, and for many it's a struggle, particularly when the graphs vary in the metrics used on the x and y axes. Such students could build fluency in placing points on a graph. Separately, they might practice providing labels for the x and y axes. In yet another practice session, they could practice identifying anchor numbers for the x and y axes. The eventual goal is fluency with reading and creating graphs. For reading graphs, the next pinpoint may also be helpful.
- *"See/say coordinates of points on a graph."* Students could work with a partner and say the coordinates for points on a graph.
- *"Locate countries and other geographic features on a map."* Learners often do not master the relative locations of states, continents, mountain ranges, and oceans, but the skill can be beneficial in understanding geography of specific regions or political strife within a region. Short sprints or full 1-minute timings can build students' mapping repertoires. Blank maps are available in most social studies curricula and online (see, e.g., the blank maps at *www.superteacherworksheets.com/maps.html*).
- *"See/say primary characteristics of different types of government."* Social studies also presents opportunities to practice vocabulary. For example, learners might be given a list of different types of government and practice saying their key characteristics, or vice versa.
- *"Hear an example/say the type of government represented."* Teachers might also ask learners to practice identifying the type of government in use from novel examples or to say the type of government in place in specific countries. Similarly, learners might be asked to hear an example of a political philosophy and say the "-ism" that is best represented.

Literature, Art, and Music

- *"See or hear an example/classify it into the appropriate genre."* This goal is appropriate for literature, art, or music, although it often requires longer than the typical 1-minute timing. Students can listen to novel pieces of music, look at paintings or sculptures, or read a short literary passage and identify the genre and time period it represents. Sprints on choices (for example, classical, baroque, or romantic music among others) or see a genre/say its characteristics can be good preparation for students prior to the classification exercise.

CREATING OR LOCATING FLUENCY SHEETS

As we've noted earlier, the teacher is in the best position to determine the tool and component skills that will enable smoother performance on important composite skills in each discipline. The existence of a worksheet in teacher ancillary materials is a very good indication that PT work may be needed, and almost any worksheet can be redesigned to function within the PT framework. That is, most will need to be reconfigured according to the analyses we describe in Chapter 3 and the design features we describe below.

Teachers can start with online worksheets, several of which have been developed over the last several years to serve the needs of parents who are homeschooling their children (see, e.g., *www.softschools.com*). In a number of key academic areas, this site provides worksheets that allow teachers to set parameters. For example, in a place value worksheet, teachers can set the minimum and maximum numbers for the examples, thus developing curricular slices of increasing difficulty.

Given the increasing emphasis on sustainability in our era, teachers may question the amount of paper that worksheets require. Several strategies are available to address this legitimate concern:

- Teachers can create worksheets on transparencies, or they can provide transparent overlays that can be used with a variety of individual worksheets. Additional time is required to clean the Mylar, but the savings in paper is substantial. Another option is the EduAction Boards (see more about them at *www.facebook.com/pages/Edu-Action/100615503360039*). Working together with Morningside Academy's principal and assistant director, Joanne Robbins, and Morningside teachers, EduAction designed the Engagement Board, which is described at *www.facebook.com/pages/EduAction/0615503360039?v=info#info_edit_sections* as "a classroom tool that students and teachers could use in various lessons and activities. The Engagement Board is made up of a clear and an opaque piece of acrylic separated by a felt strip which allows for worksheets to be slid inside. Students can 'fill-in' the worksheet by writing on the clear side, or write answers to group questions on the opaque side." EduAction also provides a teacher handout and requests teacher feedback to assist in making improvements to this collaborative process. Robbins and her colleagues have found that the best pens for Mylar or Engagement Board use are distributed by Auspen (see more about the pens at *http://auspenmarkers.com*).

- SAFMEDS can reduce the amount of paper needed for some practice by using peer coaches to listen and affirm the correctness of responses. (We describe other benefits of peer coaching in Chapter 5.) In addition, SAFMEDS decks can be randomized easily by shuffling and can be divided into subgroups of gradually increasing difficulty.

- Some online programs are designed to permit students to respond by using the computer keyboard. For example, *Quizlet* (see features at *http://quizlet.com/features*) offers fluency exercises for a variety of content areas and provides a flashcard-making program. Not all exercises are timed, but there is a great deal of flexibility to design sheets according to individual specifications.

- Some online sites that are designed especially for K–12 teachers have a worksheet feature or allow teachers to share self-designed sheets. Some require log-in information, and others charge a nominal fee. Should you decide to use one of these, choose ones that provide a free trial, so that you can check the degree to which the materials provided meet the requirements for good practice activities.

- Some textbook producers also provide worksheet-building pages, although most are for printable sheets, which don't address the cost or the environmental sustainability issue.

FEATURES OF GOOD WORKSHEETS/ PRACTICE OPPORTUNITIES

Remember that from a PT perspective, not all practice opportunities are created equal. Good practice from this perspective includes the following features:

- *All items are of a similar type.* Some authors combine different question types on the same sheet. Some items may require the learner to fill in the blank, while others ask him or her to pick the best answer of four choices. Such variations can hinder rate building; thus typical PT worksheets focus on only one kind of question at a time.
- *Construction-type questions are favored over selection-type questions.* Typical items are fill-in-the-blank question types instead of matching or multiple-choice question types. The exception is early in practice when the "Discriminate before you generate" rule is in effect.
- *Items vary across all relevant features of the pinpoint.* For example, if the goal is to read CVC nonsense words, including words that use all possible combinations of consonants and vowels strengthens the worksheet.
- *Worksheets are organized by slices that allow learners to build the skill from the ground up and that allow practice at each step.* So, for example, if the objective is "See/say or see/write all of the add–subtract number families," the smart teacher will provide worksheets that contain only a few of the families at first. As practice on each new set of families becomes firm, cumulative worksheets will maintain skills on those that were previously acquired. (See Chapter 8 for more on number families.)
- *Worksheets contain more problems than students can reasonably complete in the time allotted, to ensure that they can continue to work throughout the time interval.* Practices in which the response is on the "say" channel (see Chapter 3 for more on learning channels) allow the option of beginning again at the top of the sheet if a learner should finish before the timing period has ended; however, those on a "write" channel do not. In addition, to avoid the very real possibility that students will memorize answers by their order rather than respond to the items, multiple versions are recommended.
- *Items are appropriately calibrated.* That is, each response requires the same type and number of responses, or, when multiple components of a response are required, the count is calculated in the same way for each problem. Take, for example, this problem:

$$\begin{array}{r} 2\ 4\ 3 \\ +\ 7\ 9\ 2 \\ \hline \end{array}$$

The learner engages in nine steps:

- Step 1: Add 3 + 2 = 5. Write the five in the 1s column in the sum.
- Step 2: Add 9 + 4 = 13.
- Step 3: Write the 3 in the 10s column in the sum.
- Step 4: Write the 1 above the 100s column.
- Step 5: Add 1 + 2 = 3.

- Step 6: Add 3 + 7 = 10.
- Step 7: Write the 0 in the 100s column in the sum.
- Step 8: Write the 1 above the 1,000s column.
- Step 9: Bring down the 1 in the 1,000s column in the sum.

However, the convention is that the learner receives a point or a count of 1 for each number written. A completely correct response would look like this and would, by convention, receive a count of 6.

```
1 1
  2 4 3
+ 7 9 2
1 0 3 5
```

- *The procedure specifies a time limit for practice.* To ensure that data across practice sessions are equivalent, the same time limit is used for each session.
- *The worksheet divides the curriculum goal into manageable chunks, or slices, consistent with the learner's needs.* Some learners need smaller chunks of the curriculum than others when building fluency. Thus, while some learners may be able to take on the capitals of all 50 states in the United States, others may benefit by learning and practicing the capitals of the northwestern states; other regions may then be added one at a time, and learners engage in cumulative practice of new slices with all old slices until the entire set is acquired.

SUMMARY

Some students enter content-area instruction deficient in skills that are prerequisites for their success. In addition, other students benefit from well-designed practice to build fluent repertoires in tool and component skills that figure heavily in their ability to master composite repertoires in the content field. Teachers are encouraged to identify and then locate or create practice materials that are well designed to build these fluent repertoires. Although some practice materials are designed for fluency building, many are not. For maximum effect and speediest results, teachers are encouraged to ensure that fluency-building exercises are designed according to the criteria we describe.

CHAPTER 10

Project-Based Learning, Building Complex Repertoires, and Ensuring Real-World Competence

Much of what we've talked about in the first nine chapters of this book describes the ways in which PT can assist in building the tool and component skills that are involved in critical academic skill sets. Sometimes teachers will ask how or whether PT technologies ever lead to more complex repertoires and real-world competence. Indeed they do, if teachers or curriculum designers have done their homework. By this we mean that the same exacting analysis that we have described for the reading, writing, and mathematics curricula must be employed for more complex skills. Others have asked how or whether these technologies overlap with *project-based learning* (PBL), which is so popular in today's schools. Again, the answer is yes: There is an implicit assumption in PBL that learners possess a repertoire of tool and component skills (e.g., reading comprehension, basic mathematics, or computer literacy) that will allow them to complete challenging and personally relevant projects. And as we discuss later in this chapter, learners can adapt the technologies to fluency needs that arise during the course of a project.

In the sections that follow, we:

- Describe two perspectives on educational practice that are at the heart of a debate among educators, and explain how a melding of the two is essential to ensuring that all learners have the opportunity to acquire and perfect complex repertoires.
- Analyze several complex repertoires and show how PT technologies can be used to ensure their acquisition for learners at various skill levels.
- Talk about the benefits of a "right-side-up" world view.

- Explore the benefits of PBL and show how PT technologies can intersect with it.
- Discuss the organic nature of skills learning that occasions more complex repertoires.
- Discuss *generativity*—the emergence of untrained repertoires—and explain how teachers can arrange conditions to promote it.

THE TWO CAMPS

Two seemingly orthogonal perspectives underpin pedagogical conversations among educators. One, which derives most directly from the writings of behavioral psychologist B. F. Skinner (1953, 1968, 1974), is called *instructivism;* another, which derives most directly from the writings of developmental psychologist Jean Piaget (1957) and cognitive psychologist Lev Vygotsky (1978, 1986), is called *constructivism.*

Instructivism is a molecular approach to pedagogy. It favors thorough content analysis, identification of tool and component skills, carefully crafted educational sequences that build elemental knowledge into complex wholes, and an emphasis on building fluency in component skills as a way to encourage the emergence of untaught behaviors. It encourages explicit instruction in the conventions and codes of the culture—for example, the symbolic code for translating oral language into written language or for describing the numeric properties of nature. Although it accepts that these contrived symbolic systems stand for natural processes or describe natural objects and events, it does not view the symbolic systems themselves as "natural" or discoverable. Instructivist practices place the teacher in charge of instruction and learning.

Constructivism is a molar approach to pedagogy. It favors student exploration of content and processes in authentic contexts. It encourages students to construct their own knowledge by testing ideas and integrating new knowledge with preexisting intellectual constructs. It favors the natural ontogenesis of learning consistent with each learner's optimal developmental trajectory. It views knowledge as temporary, developmental, subjective, internally constructed, and socially and culturally mediated. It supposes that learners construct knowledge through cooperative social activity, discourse, and debate. Constructivist practices place the student in charge of his or her own learning, and attempt to reduce the impact of power relationships on what is learned and believed.

The Pragmatic Solution

The rancor of the debate between instructivists and constructivists has led teachers to believe that they must choose one or the other position and align their educational practices with it. We favor a different option—one that was posited by the great philosopher John Dewey, the father of pragmatism and progressive education. Although Dewey is often claimed by constructivists, and his pragmatism shares a number of features with constructivism, his laboratory school was as much instructivistic as it was constructivistic. The laboratory school curricula defined areas of living (e.g., cooking, carpentry) within which the learner's interests and needs to know were addressed (Dewey,

1900/1976b). In Dewey's formulation the teacher is responsible for using and extending those interests and "need-to-knows" in relation to a curriculum agenda. In "The Child and the Curriculum," first published in 1902, Dewey noted that "the child and the curriculum are simply two limits which define a single process. Just as two points define a straight line, so the present standpoint of the child and the facts and truths of studies define instruction" (Dewey, 1902/1976a, p. 278).

In fact, Bringmann, Luck, Miller, and Early's (1997) history of psychology calls Dewey the "philosophical behaviorist" of the 1920s. Dewey's philosophy aligns quite nicely with Skinner's position, emphasizing how important it is for the consequences of learning to be naturally reinforcing to the learner. The role of naturally reinforcing consequences has not received the kind of prominence it should in many presentations of the behavioral approach. Furthermore, the "consequences" aspect of Dewey's pragmatism is not highlighted in modern-day constructivism, nor is the reality base of Dewey's curriculum given much prominence in constructivism.

To combine the two approaches in the real world of the classroom, a teacher begins with teaching basic conventions and symbol systems that learners need to engage in the kind of naturally reinforced learning that is characteristic of PBL and Dewey's progressive education. The combination, which characterizes the Morningside Model of Generative Instruction (Johnson & Street, 2004), results in a continuum that begins with a more technological approach, in which the teacher seeds the repertoires of naïve learners with skills and strategies that are foundational to the culture (e.g., base 10 in mathematics or sound–symbol relations in reading). As students master these foundational skills and process repertoires, the Morningside Model advocates switching to a more Deweyian approach, in which students apply their foundational skills and processes in a personal, democratic, and naturally reinforcing manner. To put it another way, the teacher prepares the learner to analyze the world critically and to engage with it creatively.

In the case of reading, the molecular perspective of instructivism provides the learner with the repertoire to read; the molar perspective of constructivism encourages the learner to discover and read about areas of personal interest. It's arguable that instructivists sometimes do, but should not unduly, shape student interests by constraining the content of the materials used to teach reading. It is also arguable that constructivists sometimes do, but should not, expect students to learn to read by using "unnatural" phonics conventions without levels of instruction and support appropriate to the students' entering repertoires.

In the case of science, the molecular perspective of instructivism would instruct students in the underlying principles of science, its vocabulary, and its current methods of exploration; the molar perspective of constructivism would encourage them to investigate unknown phenomena, to make new discoveries, and to develop new methods of exploration.

You might be asking yourself what, if anything, this work has to do with PT and RTI. It has everything to do with them! Too often students whose entering skill levels place them in Tiers 2 and 3 are relegated to poorly designed instruction that does not prepare them for higher-level thinking and problem solving, even though many of them are capable of it. To correct this tendency, teachers and curriculum designers must do the following:

- Identify the tool and component skills that are involved in socially important complex repertoires and real-world competencies.
- Teach these tool and component skills to levels of fluency that predict their application to new settings.
- Teach students to apply a thinking strategy systematically (e.g., Whimbey & Lockhead's [1999] Talk Aloud Problem Solving [TAPS], mentioned in Chapter 8).
- Provide opportunities for students to engage in complex repertoires that match their underlying skills sets.

In the examples that follow, we describe complex repertoires that have multiple points of entry, depending on the level of the learner's underlying skill set. In both cases, we show how a thorough component–composite analysis identifies the skills individuals need to be successful. We then provide an example of a content analysis and describe the learning channels that are implicated for one of the skills.

TWO EXAMPLES

Example 1: Participating in a Book Club

Let's agree for the sake of argument that participating in a book club is a good way to continue one's learning outside traditional educational settings. Using strategies we've discussed in earlier chapters, let's see how we might set the stage for this behavior.

Component–Composite Analysis

First, we would identify critical composite repertoires. Although others may emerge, our current analysis suggests that there are two: active reading and group participation. Figure 10.1 outlines these composites and their components. The active reading composite includes at least four sets of component skills: decoding words, reading with fluency, self-monitoring while reading, and preparing questions and comments to discuss with the club group.

Each of these sets of component skills has many smaller components. For example, decoding words involves a sounding-out component, in which the learner makes each sound in a word from beginning to end, holding each sound until making the next sound in the word, until all of the sounds have been spoken. Then the learner says the chain of sounds rapidly, as if speaking the word in typical discourse. Other component skills involved in decoding words include all the component letter and word part sounds. Reading with fluency includes components related to speed, intonation, punctuation, and other characteristics of speaking represented by text.

Notice that the terms *component* and *composite* are relative concepts. A component of a larger composite is a composite of a smaller component. For example, decoding is a composite repertoire consisting of sounding-out and sound components. Decoding, in turn, is a component of a composite repertoire, active reading.

Active reading involves a third set of component skills, self-monitoring. Self-monitoring one's reading includes several component skills related to word recognition, word meaning, and tracking the main idea and details. For example, readers who

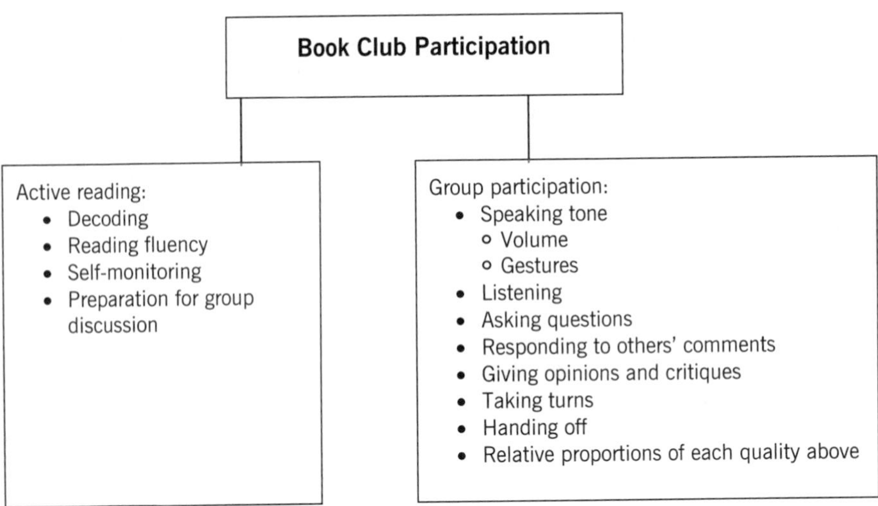

FIGURE 10.1. Component and composite skills for participating in a book club.

self-monitor slow down or speed up, depending upon the words in the text. They also ask themselves whether they have pronounced the words correctly and know their meanings. If the answer is yes, the readers proceed; if not, they may use a dictionary or question another person.

Self-monitoring includes such component skills as examining one's history to make a connection with what is being read, and making inferences about what else may be true in addition to what an author has explicitly written. Authors of fiction, for example, rarely include all of the information about the setting and character of their narrative; they provide some information, but they require readers to make logical inferences about other details to enrich their understanding of the narrative. If an author writes about a cold climate, describing low temperatures and drifts of snow, a reader can infer many other facts about the setting, including barren trees, icy roads, and heavy coats and gloves, even though the author has not described these facts. If an author writes about a frugal character, telling us how Mr. Jones saves his money and operates within a strict budget, the reader can infer many other aspects about the character's behavior in addition to what the author has written, and can make predictions about how Mr. Jones will respond to upcoming events in the narrative (such as refusing to make unplanned contributions to neighborhood canvassers, or refusing to purchase items in a store that are not on his shopping list).

Good self-monitors also notice details that require more clarification and search for clarifying information. They may ask another person clarifying questions. All of these self-monitoring component skills can be taught and practiced to fluency.

Our active reading composite repertoire includes a fourth set of component skills, preparing for group discussion. A book club participant prepares clarifying questions, opinions, alternative viewpoints, critiques of the author's style, and so on. These component skills can also be taught and brought to fluency.

So far we've discussed one large composite repertoire for book club participation, active reading. Being a book club member requires fluency in another large composite repertoire, group participation. Participation in group discussion involves several component skills, including speaking tone, volume, accompanying gestures to make one's speaking easier to comprehend, and so on. Good participation also involves listening, asking questions, responding to others' comments, giving opinions and critiques, taking turns, and handing off one's comments or questions to other participants. Good participators engage in proportions of listening, questioning, and speaking that are optimal for their audience. One group may recognize a reader as an expert in an area and expect more speaking from him or her. In another group, that same reader may not be an expert and may listen more and ask more questions. As with the component skills of active reading, all of the component skills of group participation can also be taught and practiced to fluency. Notice that the intent here is not to teach the content of participation, but rather the act itself, and it is noteworthy that a good teacher must be attentive to this distinction.

Content and Task Analysis

Let us examine one of the component skills of active reading that we have identified to illustrate the process of content and task analysis (Tiemann & Markle, 1990). Active readers are fluent at getting the main idea of paragraphs and passages as they read. Dixon et al. (2008) have designed a task analysis of this component skill. While reading a passage, the learner first notes who or what is mentioned most prominently. At the beginning of the program, the learner actually tallies the number of times an author mentions various people and events in a passage. Second, the learner makes a list of actions or descriptions related to "who or what is talked about the most." Third, the learner classifies the details in the list. For example, one of Dixon et al.'s (2008) paragraphs describes a cat's behavior.

> She tore the drapes to pieces.
> She knocked a box of sugar onto the floor.
> She doesn't always use her litter box. (Level A Student Workbook, p. 16)

A learner then classifies these details by completing this sentence:

> These are all things a cat does if it is ____________.
> (possible answers: a troublemaker, rambunctious, mischievous)

Fourth, the learner writes a main idea sentence. The subject of the sentence is "who or what is talked about the most." The predicate of the sentence is the learner's characterization of the list of details about the subject. In the example above, the learner could write, "The cat was a troublemaker."

Learning Channels Analysis

Students practice the "main idea component skills" by tallying, listing, and characterizing the list. Various pinpoints involving various learning channels are involved:

1. See passage/write characters and events,
2. See passage plus list of characters and events/write (tally) their frequencies.
3. See list of actions and descriptions/write (characterize) the list.

An expert can do all of these, limited only by the difficulty of the content presented.

When students are accurate at tasks across these relevant learning channels, they practice reading passages and writing main idea sentences without having to tally, list, and characterize the list—a "See passage/write main idea" task. They practice this task until they can write main ideas while reading at 80% of their passage frequency rate. They also practice "See passage/say main idea" with a partner.

Putting It All Together

Having put all of these tool and component skills in place doesn't guarantee that learners will choose to participate in a book club—or, if they join a book club, that they will necessarily participate actively. Should book club participation be desirable in a formal educational setting, the teacher's role may shift from curriculum design and direct instruction to arranging circumstances and managing consequences. For example, the teacher may encourage participation in one of several classroom-based book clubs by providing extra credit contingent on participation, or by providing the opportunity for learners of similar interests to select potentially enjoyable books. Students sometimes develop an interest in topics that use an unknown vocabulary, which may limit their ability to benefit. In these cases, the teacher may guide the students toward identifying unfamiliar words, defining them, and perhaps even creating frequency-building exercises, so that the vocabulary becomes fluent and more easily accessible.

Example 2: Designing an Advocacy Brochure

Let's say we want to teach students to write advocacy brochures. A brochure might advocate for a specific environmental or social goal, a specific candidate for political office, or a specific individual or group of individuals who need special services. A component–composite analysis reveals that several styles of writing would be required. The brochure would incorporate descriptive writing about the cause or individual concerned. It could also include narrative writing—that is, actual stories about the specific events or individuals concerned. The brochure would obviously incorporate persuasive writing as well. Each of these styles of writing—descriptive, narrative, and persuasive—requires an analysis of the principles or procedures involved, which we have described in Chapter 7. Other component skills are also required, including grammar, punctuation, and sentence refinement skills (such as sharpening word choices; combining sentences; and expanding sentences through questions such as when, where, why, and how; Archer et al., 2008a, 2008b). For enjoyable brochure writing, fluent writing and typing tool skills are also required.

TURNING THE WORLD VIEW RIGHT SIDE UP

In a quest for making classroom learning relevant to the real world, most approaches to teaching complex behavior have learners immediately practice the identified target composite behavior, with guidance. For example, most approaches to teaching book club participation or brochure writing attempt to teach these complex activities as extended endeavors, in a real-world context, rather than first teaching their components in isolation. Component–composite analysis and its subsequent content and task analyses provide an alternative approach, building up to eventual practice of the composite repertoire.

The analytical procedures we have described so far facilitate the simultaneous programming of multiple complex behaviors that share common component elements. The composite repertoires and component skills involved in book club participation also pertain to many other complex repertoires that require studying materials and engaging in group problem solving, such as planning a dance party or a research study. Similarly, the component skills involved in brochure writing also pertain to many other real-world competencies, such as writing letters to the editor. Our analytical approach turns progressive, real-world education "on its head," but right side up—ending (not beginning) instruction with the complex activities themselves.

Complex Repertoire Mastery as an Organic Process

This is not to say that the forays into complex activities must wait until each component has been brought to full flower. Instead, the teacher can analyze complex activities that arise naturally to identify ways in which learners' current skill levels overlap with these activities' requirements. One might think of the mastery of a complex skill as an organic process—one in which learners can engage in the complex skill with prompts or in a less sophisticated version of it, at the same time as they are acquiring more sophisticated forms of the tool and component skills.

For example, at Morningside Academy students learn a full complement of tool skills related to addition–subtraction and multiplication–division number families. For example, the addition–subtraction number family made up of the numbers 1, 2, 3 can generate four addition/subtraction facts: $1 + 2 = 3$; $2 + 1 = 3$; $3 - 2 = 1$; and $3 - 1 = 2$. However, "word problems" don't wait until all of the number families have been mastered. Instead, once students have mastered a subset (about a third) of all addition–subtraction number families, word problems that incorporate these number families are introduced.

In a similar fashion, a child who is not yet skilled in all components of writing a brochure may be introduced to the idea when a topic of interest to him or her is under public review. Let's say a school district is hoping to build a new elementary school because of overcrowding. Young children may learn about the particulars and may in the end contribute a drawing or a testimonial that makes the brochure more compelling. These naturally occurring opportunities should not be ignored, but less skilled learners may need additional support to contribute in meaningful ways, and thereby to build enthusiasm for acquiring proficiency in skills needed to do the task more independently.

We cannot overemphasize the pressure on teachers and curriculum designers to select carefully just the right composite repertoires and to analyze naturally occurring opportunities. These repertoires need to offer just the right amount of learning challenge to students, and the students need to have adequate tool and composite skills and thinking strategies to master them.

Project-Based Learning

John Dewey's interests in inquiry and active learning were pivotal to the progressive movement in education that his work spawned, and PBL grew out of these interests. Dewey believed that a primary role of education was to create thoughtful citizens, and he posited that the schools can play a role in their development by creating states of "disturbed equilibrium" (Dewey, 1938/1986, p. 34) that encourage exploration of new ideas. He believed that well-conceived projects establish such states and thus provide an environment in which inquiry and active learning thrive.

PBL has been employed in public education for nearly a century, sometimes to good effect and sometimes not. It has been variously and loosely defined and proceduralized, leading some teachers to establish their own definitions and derive their own procedures. Implementation often went far astray from Dewey's original notion and was driven more by students' own interests than by intellectually stimulating questions that grew out of an "areas of living"-driven curriculum. This student-interest-driven approach sometimes lacked the rigor that Dewey envisioned, and over time the approach fell out of favor.

Recent efforts to reinvigorate PBL have added more exacting standards and have tied it more clearly to specified curricular outcomes. Capraro and Slough's (2009) book *Project-Based Learning: An Integrated Science, Technology, Engineering, and Mathematics (STEM) Approach* describes just such an initiative. They clearly see PBL as partially teacher-driven and teacher-monitored; explicitly tied to the curriculum; dependent on tool and component skills and on strategic thinking skills; and based on well-defined questions. Although they divorce themselves from what they appear to see as overly mechanistic behavioral terminology and approaches, a careful review of the strategies they propose makes it clear that successful completion of their types of projects depends on an abundance of expertise in a wide variety of tool and component skills (e.g., reading comprehension and mathematics problem solving). Virtually none of the skills they expect students to have at entry are listed, and yet a careful reading reveals that they are assumed. Two other promising programs that are designed for elementary school instruction are Boss and Krauss's (2007) *Reinventing Project-Based Learning: Your Field Guide to Real-World Projects in the Digital Age* and Bender's (2012) *Project-Based Learning: Differentiating Instruction for the 21st Century.*

Most PBL approaches use timing differently than in typical PT scenarios. They may design modules that must be completed in a week instead of a 1-minute or 10-minute window, and the entire assignment may be designed to take the better part of a quarter, semester, or academic year.

However, some projects may reveal knowledge or skill gaps that could be filled through structured practice. Much as young students of guitar may practice certain "riffs" over and over until they can play them flawlessly at speeds required by the piece they wish to play, we would hope to see parallels in academic tasks. Self-derived fluency-building activities, though not always well proceduralized, are characteristic of active learners. For example, new parents who learn that their child has a major hearing impairment are encouraged to enroll in an immersion sign language class, where they practice sign language conversational skills with other parents. They may recognize that this approach is not building vocabulary at the rate they need; words that are important but infrequently used in the class don't get the kind of practice required for fluency. In response, they may purchase sign language translation flashcards and develop their own practice strategies to build fluency. The benefit for students who have experience with PT technologies is that they have a more systematic way to track their progress and make changes when their improvements aren't adequate.

As a result, students who have learned how to master new skills quickly and efficiently may initiate a frequency-building exercise on their own when they encounter vocabulary, formulae, or other tool or component skills for which their lack of fluency is impeding progress. In such a scenario, they or their teachers recognize when nonfluent repertoires are interfering with critical thinking or productive reasoning, and do what has worked in the past. At Morningside Academy, we've seen exactly this kind of self-initiation.

Generative Instruction and Contingency Adduction

Our experience indicates that when we teach components well, learners will successfully engage in more complex activities that incorporate them, with little or no instruction (Johnson & Layng, 1992, 1994, 1996; Johnson & Street, 2004). We call the model we use to achieve such an outcome *generative instruction*, and the outcome itself we call *generative thinking*. Generative thinking is equivalent to everyday cognitive notions such as "figuring out how to do things without being directly taught them," "gaining insight," "creative problem solving," and so forth.

The generative instruction model assumes that new composite repertoires derive from combinations and recombinations of component skills already learned. Technically speaking, when component behaviors are taught well, some educational requirement or opportunity for reinforcement can easily recruit those component behaviors to form a novel recombination of relevant behaviors that meet the new requirement. The technical term for this recruitment process is *contingency adduction* (Andronis et al., 1997; Johnson & Layng, 1992, 1994, 1996; Kubina, Morrison, & Lee, 2006; Layng, Twymann, & Stikeleather, 2004).

At least three conditions must be in place for composite skills to emerge with little or no instruction:

- The composites' component skills must be taught well.
- Learners must engage in generative thinking repertoires.
- The learning environment must provide opportunities to engage in novel, complex behavior.

By "taught well," we mean that learners must have reached frequency levels that predict fluency. You'll recall our brief discussion of generativity in Chapter 2, where we have talked about it as one of the five kinds of evidence that a behavior is fluent. We have said that frequency is the best proxy we've found for fluency, but the true test of a behavior's fluency is that it:

- Maintains with minimal practice.
- Endures for lengths of time that match real-world requirements.
- Is Stable in the face of distraction.
- Is readily Applied in unfamiliar situations and settings.
- Is Generative.

By "engage in generative thinking repertoires," we mean that learners have mastered robust problem-solving strategies. Although some students appear to develop these strategies without instruction, many do not. That's why teachers at Morningside Academy explicitly teach generative thinking repertoires such as TAPS (Whimbey & Lockhead, 1999) to promote contingency adduction—a topic beyond the scope of this chapter. By "provide opportunities to engage in novel, complex behavior," we mean that teachers and curriculum designers must seed the environment with activities that call on the tools and components previously taught, but in novel combinations.

We call this approach the Morningside Model of Generative Instruction to emphasize these three features: our focus upon teaching component skills and practicing them to fluency; teaching generative thinking; and providing opportunities to engage in novel, complex behavior without direct teaching (Johnson & Street, 2004). When teachers and instructional designers are masterful at generative instruction, learners make many *curriculum leaps,* as component and composite skills in a curriculum ladder emerge with little or no instruction.

It is also our experience that educators steeped in constructivist and holistic traditions readily relate to generative instruction, because it directly addresses complexity. They are also surprised when they learn that behavior analysis—an approach they often discount—is at the heart of our enterprise! By following through from tools and components to composites, we avoid the typical characterization of behavioral instruction as simplistic, splinter-skills development, appropriate for a simpler, more arcane industrial society. And when educators implement generative instruction procedures, they are pleased with their vastly more successful outcomes than those they achieved with their previous holistic attempts.

Precision Decisions for the Timings Chart

Data-Driven Decisions for Performance-Based Measures within Sessions

Deb Brown, MS, BCBA
Stanislaus County Office of Education
Morningside Teachers' Academy

Performance-based measures of a behavior reflect not only the behavior's *correctness,* but the *speed* at which it occurs. The basic unit of measure is *movement per minute* or *count per minute.*

PHASES OF LEARNING AND TEACHING DURING A PROGRAM SESSION

During a student's program session, two phases of learning and teaching occur: (1) instruction/correction and (2) practice (performance-based measure). Total length of the session is no more than 10 minutes, unless otherwise specified.

Instruction/Correction

The instruction/correction phase is based on discrete-trial teaching or direct instruction materials. Instruction may happen at the beginning of each session and between each timing, but not during a timing.

Each set of instructions or corrections is a volley between student and instructor, which has a specific instructional sequence. An elementary instructional sequence is as follows:

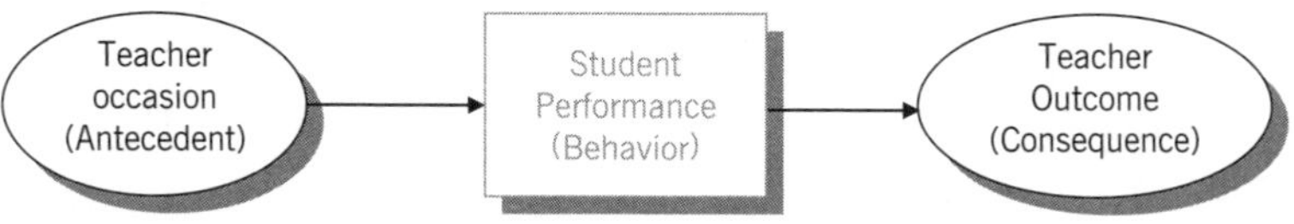

The teacher–student volley is structured around the student's performance behavior. The teacher should adjust the instruction and feedback according to the student's behavior. The teacher should have clear and concise instructions, and the student's behavior must be measurable.

Practice

> **"The learner knows best."**
> **—Ogden Lindsley**

The practice phase is based on Precision Teaching (PT) and frequency building; it consists of performance-based measures. PT is a teaching technology based on the principles of behavior analysis. It is not a curriculum, but rather a way to evaluate specific instructional strategies for each individual student by using behavioral measures. Its foundation is "The learner knows best," as Ogden Lindsley used to say. It looks at a student's behavior concretely, so that it can be measured and recorded quickly in a standardized way (the Standard Celeration Chart). In PT, as long as a student's learning picture is progressing, then the program is appropriate; otherwise, the program needs to be changed in some way. PT does not tell an instructor what to do, just when to try something else.

CHARTING THE STUDENT'S PROGRESS

A student's performance progress is determined from two separate charts: (1) the Daily per minute Standard Celeration Chart and (2) the Timings Standard Celeration Chart. These charts are multiplicative charts, rather than the linear charts so often used. One reason these charts are used is that you can see high-frequency and low-frequency behaviors on the same chart.

Daily per Minute Chart

The Daily per minute Chart is where the student's day-to-day progress is monitored. This is the chart on which overall performance aims are set, starting point is set, and minimum celeration is determined. Daily goal aims can be determined as well.

Timings Chart

The Timings Chart is for making decisions within a program session. The scale that runs up and down on the left indicates the frequency of the behavior being charted. Each vertical line allows for each timed practice during a session. The sessions are broken up by the darker blue lines. Not all lines may be used if a session ends before nine practices.

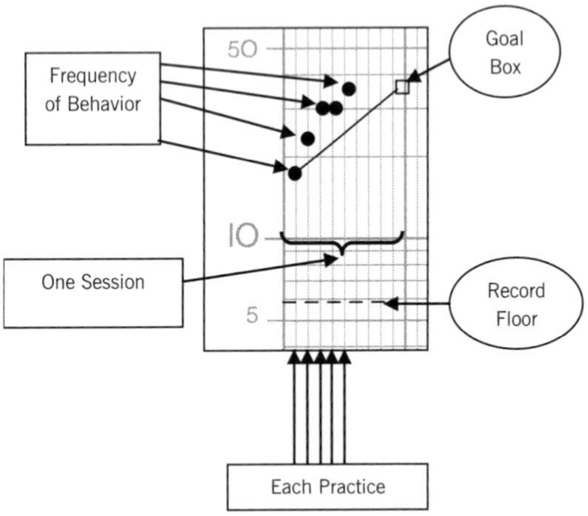

CHARTING THE COURSE ON THE TIMINGS CHART

The Team and Targets

At the bottom of each timings chart, there is space to put information about the student, and the program personnel, and the behavior. *Performer* is generally the student. *Charter* is the person who is charting. *Counted* is the behavior being counted (e.g., "See/say words in isolation"). *Counter* is the person counting the behavior. *Manager* is the person who manages the program. *Advisor* is the person who is advising the manager, and *Supervisor* is the person who runs the organization. The top of the chart should list the month and day the session is being run, the time (if the program is run more than once per day), and the slice or lesson being conducted.

Setting Aim

For a new program, or a major change in a program, the instructor should get the student's baseline and compare it with the performance standard of the program or predetermined goal for the student. The session should be labeled "SET AIM"; three timings should be completed; the best or average performance should be placed on the daily chart (manager's decision); and a minimum celeration line should be determined by the manager. The daily performance goal will be established by the minimum celeration line crossing the specific day of the week. The line will cross at a specific frequency, which is the daily performance goal.

Daily Performance Goal

The daily performance goal may be obtained from the daily chart or otherwise specified by the instructor. A staff member should place a goal box on the timings chart at the correct session block. This daily performance aim is the frequency of correct responding the student should achieve by the end of the session. It is determined by examining past performances.

Record Floor

Each timing is specified by the program for each individual student. A timing may last 10 seconds 15 seconds, 20 seconds, 30 seconds, 1 minute, or longer. Depending on the length of time, there may need to be a conversion to 1 minute to standardize all the charts.

Conversions:

10 seconds → # × 6 = #/minute	30 seconds → # × 2 = #/minute
15 seconds → # × 4 = #/minute	2 minutes → # ÷ 2 = #/minute
20 seconds → # × 3= #/minute	5 minutes → # ÷ 5 = #/minute

The *record floor* is based on the length of the timing. It is the lowest non-zero score that can be obtained, and the number that is needed to a convert to count-per-minute score. For example, if a student was timed for 15 seconds and performed only 1 behavior, to convert this to a count per minute, we would multiply 1 × 4. So the lowest score possible would be 4. Another example (see the adjoining illustration) has the record floor on the 6 line, which means it was a 10-second timing. The first practice score was 3 in 10 seconds (3 × 6 = 18) recorded as 18 per minute. The record floor can be stable or constant for a particular session, or it may change (e.g., four 10-second timings and 1-minute timing). But there's no need to worry: On the right-hand side of the timings chart, there are labels to indicate the correct lines for the most common floors. A line should be drawn just under the corresponding line on the chart (see the illustration).

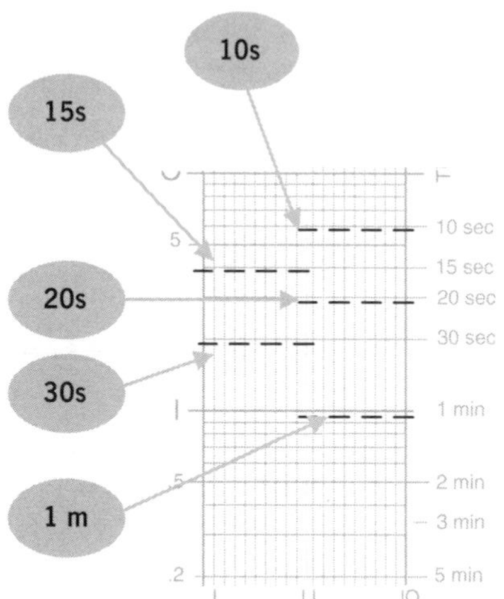

Timing the Target Behavior

After the initial instruction, practice should begin. The program should have a designated time for the practice. The instructor should begin the timing by saying, "Please begin," and start a timer. This is for pacing, not racing. At the end of the time period, the instructor should say, "Please stop." The instructor should count correct responses and incorrect responses (errors).

Plotting the Student's Performance

The instructor should make any conversions to 1 minute if necessary. The timings chart should be marked with a '•' denoting corrects and a '×' denoting errors with conversions. If no errors were made, place a '?' or '×' just below the record floor. (This will note a zero score; there is no zero on the chart.). After each timing, corrects, errors, and the record floor should be plotted on the chart.

After the First Time, Drawing the Line

Every session (except for the "SET AIM" session), after the first timing is completed and the data have been plotted for corrects and errors, draw a line between the correct dot and the goal box. This is the student's minimum celeration line. The goal for the session is to keep the student at or above the line until he or she reaches the frequency recorded in the goal box.

PRECISION DECISIONS

When Do You Stop?

1. When the dot meets the box, you can stop.
   - This means that on any particular timing, if the student meets or exceeds the goal box frequency, the session can stop. If the student meets this on the first timing, the session can still stop. The manager may want to evaluate the student's learning picture for the future.
2. When the time has diminished, you are finished.
   - This means that if the time allotted for the program session is over, even if the student has not met the goal box, you should stop running the program. There probably needs to be a change that the manager needs to consider.

Do You Know When to Go?

3. At or above the line, do another time.
   - This means that the student is progressing toward the goal. He or she is making adequate gains to achieve the daily performance goal. Continue to get appropriate feedback, and provide another timing.
4. Once below the line is just fine.
   - Often one time under the line doesn't mean that the student is not making progress. Make sure that you have the student's attention and that he or she is prepared to go (finger following along, enough materials, etc.).

When Should You Make a Change?

5. Twice below, the reinforcer should go.
   - If the student was making successive approximations toward the goal and then drops off, motivation is generally the key. Rethink the reinforcer. Do a reinforcer survey; is there a more motivating activity or item? Try something new!
   - If a change is being made, draw a phase change line and state the change. In the example chart, the parents changed the reinforcer to a lollipop.

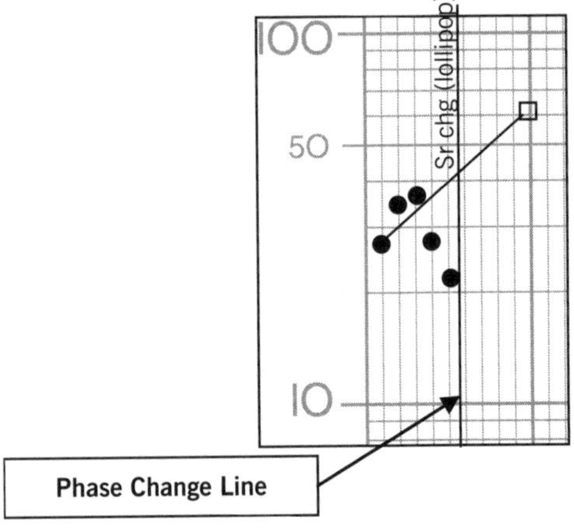

When Do You Ask for Help?

6. Three times or more, the manager must explore.
    - If the student falls below the line three times in a row, ask for help. The teacher or manager should try to vary the program in some way. If the teacher is able to help during a session, be sure to put a phase change line in, and state the change as well. (Stimuli may change, duration of timing, etc.).

END OF THE SESSION

At the end of the session, the best score from the Timings Chart should be transferred to the Daily per minute Chart. If the student is at or just above the celeration line, continue sessions. If the student has met his or her program aim, or the student is below or way above the celeration line, notify the teacher or manager of the situation.

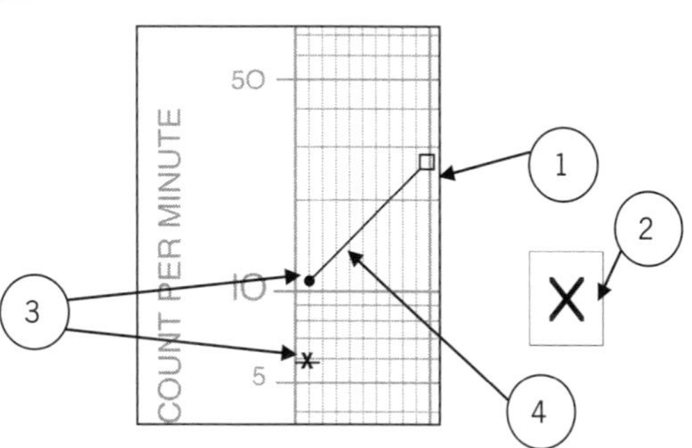

SUMMARY/QUICK TIPS

Within Sessions

Charting the Course

1. Draw the box so the data "talk."
2. Time the target (behavior).
3. Plot the dot (student's performance).
4. After the first time, draw the line.

Precision Decisions

- When do you stop?
    1. When the dot meets the box, you can stop.
    2. When the time has diminished, you are finished.
- Do you know when to go?
    3. At or above the line, do another time.
    4. Once below the line is just fine.
- When should you make a change?
    5. Twice below, the reinforcer should go.
- When do you ask for help?
    6. Three times or more, the manager must explore.

What Should You Do?

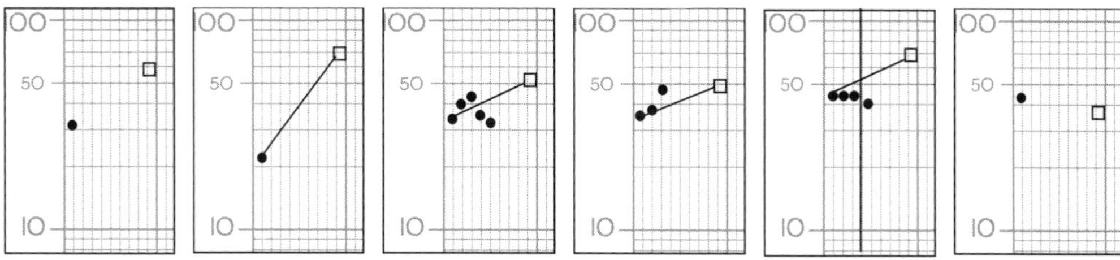

Things to Remember

- Plot both corrects and errors.
- Plot the record floor.
- After each timing, make a decision.
- Don't forget to instruct between timings.
    - Tell the student what he or she is doing right too!
- Always be prepared to vary the possible reinforcers.

APPENDIX 2

Using the Timings Chart to Make Within-Session Decisions

Deb Brown
Stanislaus County Office of Education
Morningside Teachers' Academy

TWO TYPES OF DECISIONS

1. Timings sessions.
   - First level of decision making.
   - Timings Standard Celeration Chart is used.
2. Across sessions.
   - Decisions are based on learning pictures.
   - Daily per Minute Standard Celeration Chart is used.

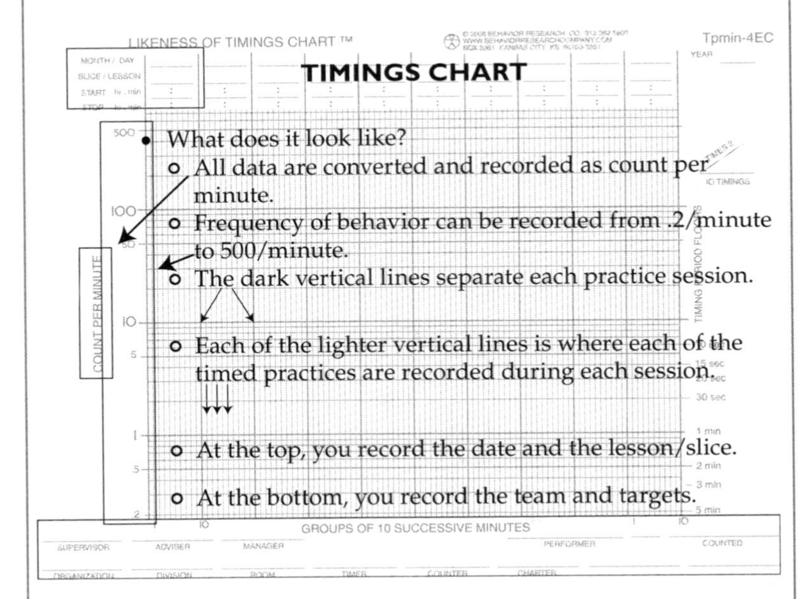

Reprinted with permission from Deb Brown in *Response to Intervention and Precision Teaching: Creating Synergy in the Classroom* by Kent Johnson and Elizabeth Street (The Guilford Press, 2013). Permission to photocopy this appendix is granted to purchasers of this book for personal use only (see copyright page for details). Purchasers may download a larger version of this appendix from the book's page on The Guilford Press website at *www.guilford.com/p/johnson8*.

WITHIN THE SESSION

Decisions to make during practice

RECORD FLOOR

- The record floor is based on the length of the timing.
  - A timing can last 5 minutes, 1 minute, 30 seconds, 10 seconds, etc.
  - The recent floor denotes the lowest possible non-zero score.
  - It is a line just under the counting floor line.
    - Place floor line on correct practice line.

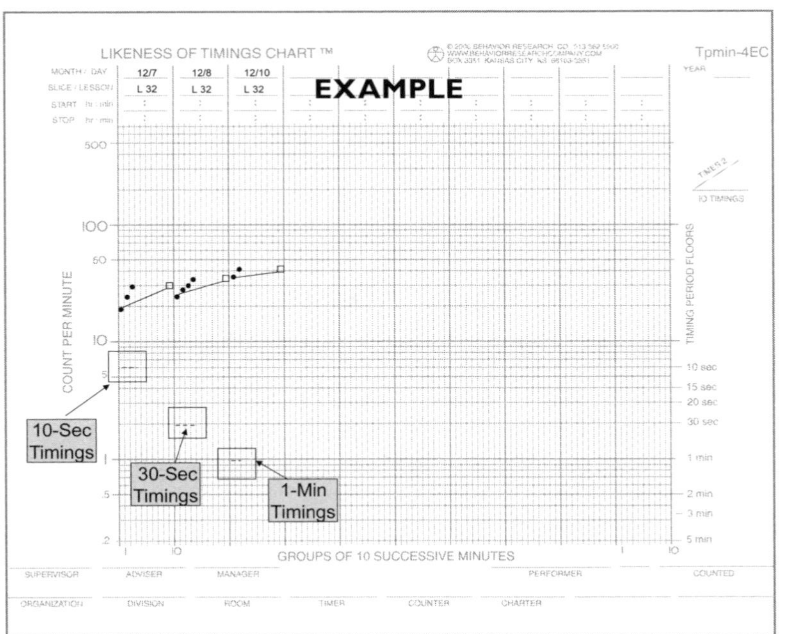

THREE BASIC DECISIONS (BASED ON DATA PATTERNS)

- Stop.
  - Student met goal for day or timed out.
  - Keep going/practicing.
  - Student performance on or above daily performance line.
- Change.
  - Consequences don't seem to be working.
- Ask for help.
  - Student performance dropped below the daily celeration line.

WITHIN SESSIONS, CHARTING YOUR COURSE

1. Draw the box so the data "talk."
2. Time the target.
3. Plot the dots.
4. After the first time, draw the line.
5. Use an incentive to keep the student attentive!

PRECISION DECISIONS

- Stop?
  1. When the dot meets the box.
  2. When the time has diminished, you are finished.
- Do you know when to go?
  3. At or above the line, do another time.
  4. Once below the line is just fine.
- Change?
  5. Twice below the reinforcer should go.
- Ask for help?
  6. Three times or more, the manager must explore.

WITHIN THE SESSION

- Decisions made after every timing
  - Compare student's performance to minimum celeration line.
- Decision about the goal box
  - Manager makes this decision; it's based on daily celeration or previous day's performance.

WITHIN-SESSION DECISION I

- What do you do first?
- What comes next?
- Then what?
- What's your decision?
  - Next?
  - Next?
  - Next?

WITHIN-SESSION DECISION 2

- What do you do first?
- What comes next?
- Then what?
- What's your decision?
  - Next?
  - Next?

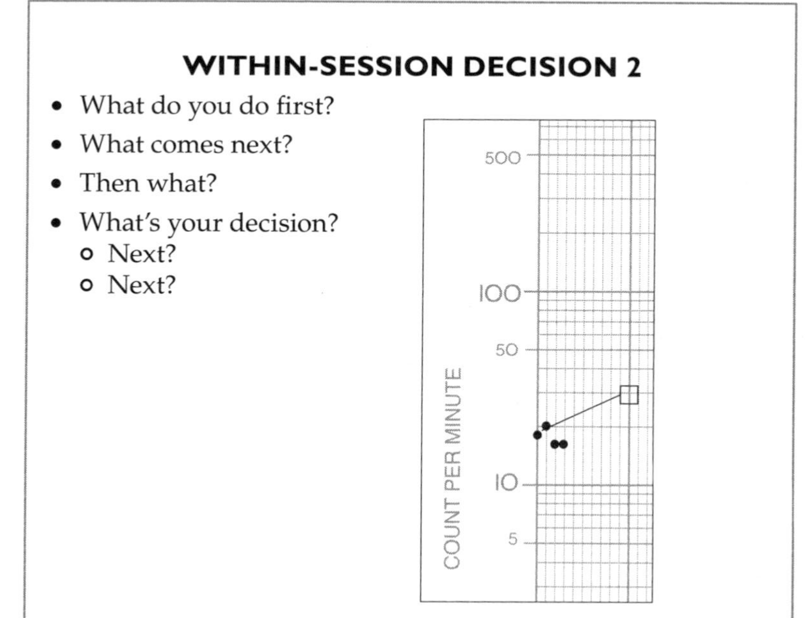

WITHIN-SESSION DECISION 3

What do you do?

APPENDIX 3

A Timings Standard Celeration Chart

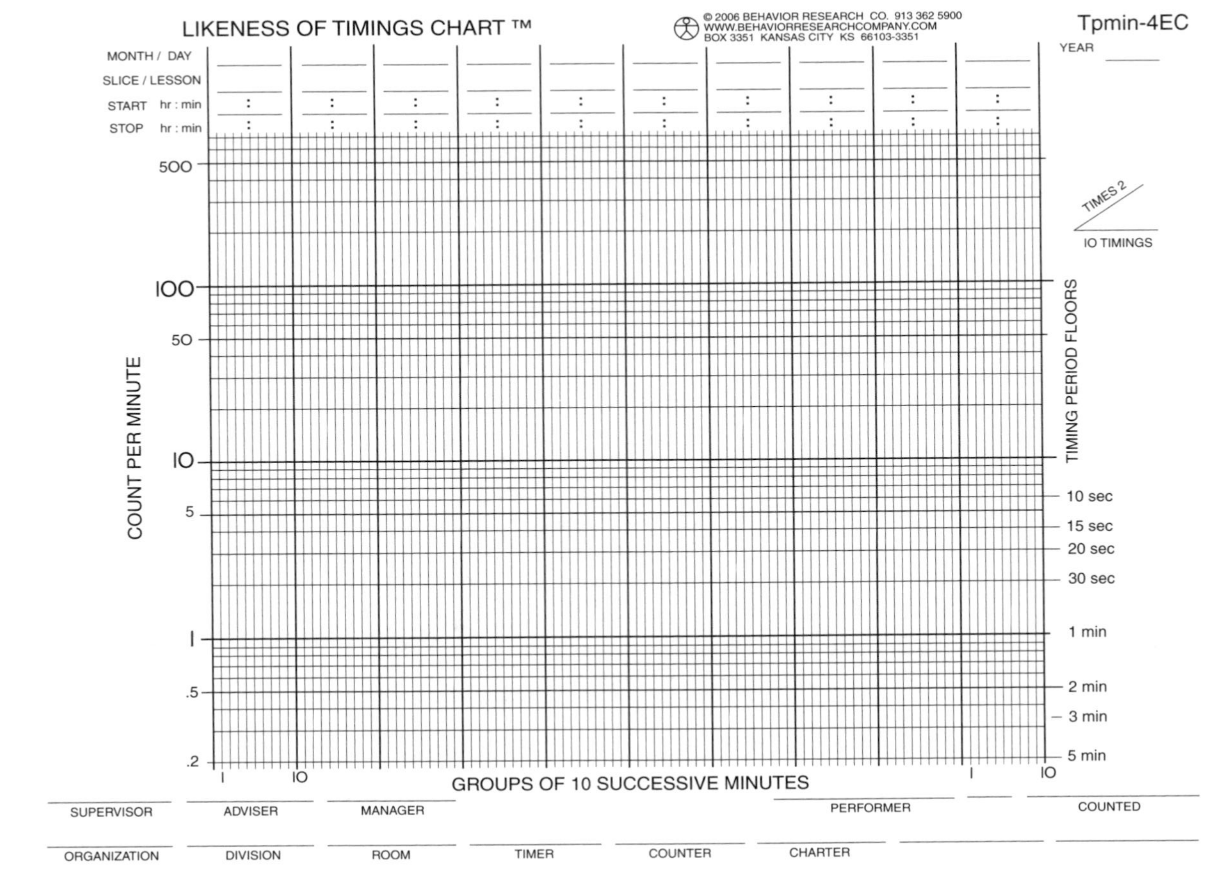

APPENDIX 4

A Daily per Minute Standard Celeration Chart

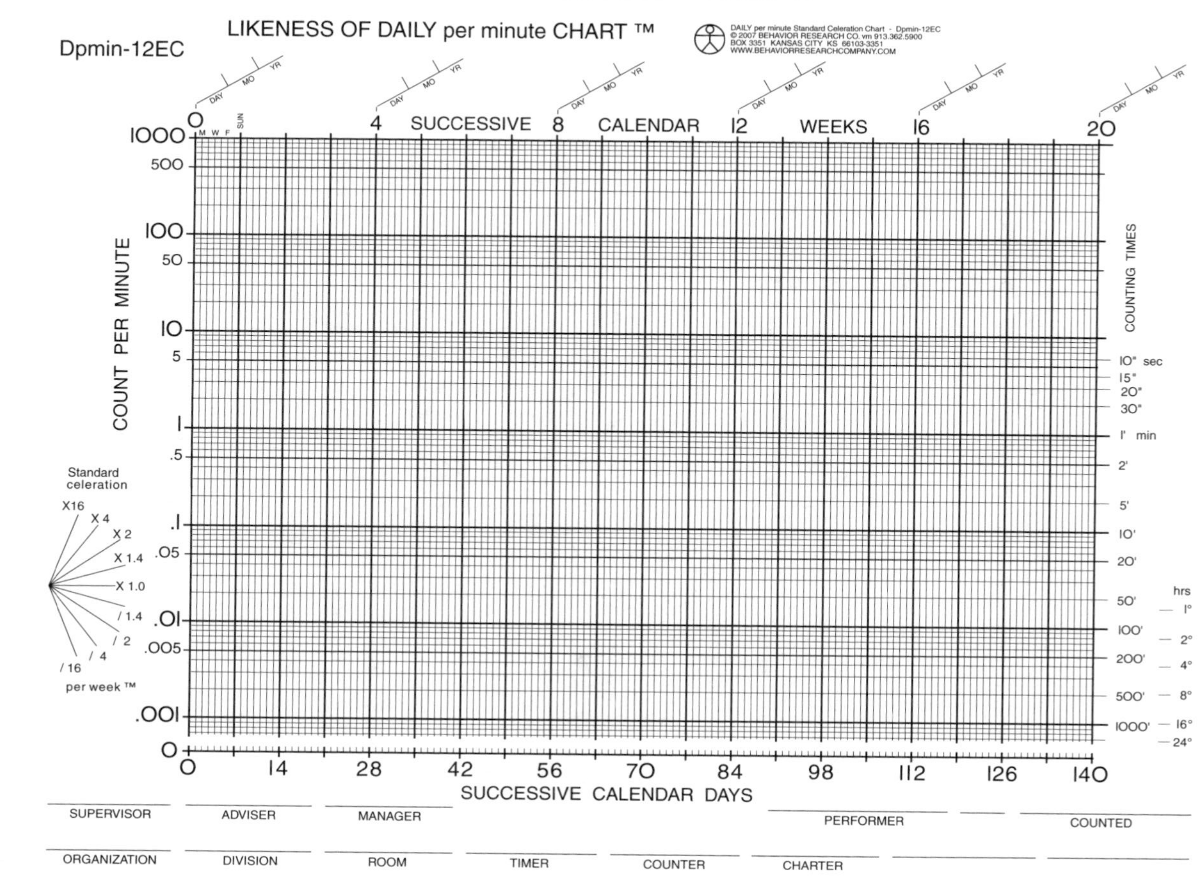

APPENDIX 5

Exercise for Tiemann and Markle's Kinds of Learning

Using this key, identify the kind of learning from Tiemann and Markle's (1990) simple cognitive and complex cognitive domains represented by each example below.

A = Association
Se = Sequence
VR = Verbal Repertoire
C = Concept
PA = Principle Application
St = Strategy

Sometimes a context is required to classify these examples. In that case, describe the context and answer within that context.

Kind of learning	Example
	1. Given a set of sentences, circle the noun.
	2. Use a map to go to a location.
	3. Find a location by using map guide letters and numbers.
	4. Say the meaning of map symbols.
	5. Plot a point by using Cartesian (*x* and *y*) coordinates.
	6. Convert a Fahrenheit temperature to Centigrade.
	7. Convert inches on a map to miles on the ground.
	8. Use a map to find the shortest walking path between two points.
	9. Determine how goods will be distributed fairly among a group of people.
	10. Convert a measurement in English yards or miles to meters or kilometers.
	11. Tell the meaning of metric prefixes (*deca, kilo, mega, giga,* etc.)
	12. Say the names of letters of the alphabet.
	13. Say the letters of the alphabet in order.
	14. Remember "*i* before *e* except after *c*."
	15. Use "*i* before *e* except after *c*" to spell an *ie* word.
	16. Say the Pledge of Allegiance.

Kind of learning	Example
	17. Find novel examples of *biography.*
	18. Say your phone number.
	19. Say your home address.
	20. Identify the artist who created a piece of art you've never seen before.
	21. Identify the hypotenuse of a triangle.
	22. Spell the word *boy.*
	23. Correctly punctuate a sentence.
	24. Say the Japanese equivalents of a series of English words.
	25. Count from 1 to 10 in Spanish.
	26. Tell how to take a person's blood pressure.
	27. Take a person's blood pressure.
	28. Differentiate between cases of addition and cases of subtraction.
	29. Complete a page of addition–subtraction facts.
	30. Select the theorem(s) for solving a geometry problem.
	31. Find the hypotenuse of a triangle, given the opposite and adjacent sides.
	32. Focus a camera.
	33. Tell the formula for mixing a particular color of paint.
	34. Appropriately identify own relatives as uncle, aunt, brother, sister.
	35. Match the gender of a noun and its pronoun.
	36. Match the number of the subject and verb in a sentence.
	37. Tell the meaning of symbols on a TV weather map.
	38. Tell the meaning of Latin abbreviations in reference citations.
	39. Differentiate among synonyms, homophones, and antonyms.
	40. Tell the order of succession to the presidency of the United States.
	41. Determine in a set of sentences those that are complex.
	42. Given two parallel lines that are bisected by a third line and angle *A*, find angle *B*.
	43. Predict what will happen to the price of fruit when a deep freeze destroys a substantial portion of the fruit crop.
	44. Name the state capitals of the United States.
	45. Decide whether to add or subtract in a word problem.
	46. Find the area of a rectangle.
	47. Tell the formula for the area of a rectangle.
	48. Examine a set of sentences, and use a semicolon before any conjunctive adverbs or transitional phrases that connect main clauses.
	49. Write a creative play.
	50. Give a live report of an emerging crisis.

Kind of learning	Example
	51. Tell the meanings of the symbols in the formula for finding the standard deviation of a set of numbers.
	52. Tell the formula for finding the standard deviation of a set of numbers.
	53. Find the standard deviation of a set of numbers by using a formula.
	54. Develop a recycling system that meets the unique needs of your community.
	55. Tell whose style is represented in a particular sculpture.
	56. Name six Impressionist artists.
	57. Select from a set of artworks those that are Impressionistic art.
	58. Observe vignettes of tennis players, and evaluate their grip on the racket.
	59. Differentiate between bacteria and viruses.
	60. String a guitar.
	61. Tell the order of pitches of guitar strings.
	62. Tune a guitar.
	63. Differentiate between major and minor chords.
	64. If your fire alarm sounds, take the appropriate action.
	65. Given a stroke volume and cardiac rate, calculate the cardiac output.
	66. Add fraction problems.
	67. Identify the appropriate rule to solve for x in problems of the sort "$x + b = c$" and "$ax = b$."
	68. Choose the appropriate filter to adjust the color in a photograph.
	69. Find x in statements of the type "$x + b = c$."
	70. Retell the story of *Much Ado about Nothing*.

EXAMPLES OF KINDS OF LEARNING—KEY

A = Association
Se = Sequence
VR = Verbal Repertoire
C = Concept
PA = Principle Application
St = Strategy

Variations may be acceptable, depending upon the context the student describes.

Kind of learning	Example
C	1. Given a set of sentences, circle the noun.
PA	2. Use a map to go to a location.
PA	3. Find a location by using map guide letters and numbers.
A	4. Say the meaning of map symbols.
PA	5. Plot a point using Cartesian (x and y) coordinates.
PA	6. Convert a Fahrenheit temperature to Centigrade.

Kind of learning	Example
PA	7. Convert inches on a map to miles on the ground.
PA	8. Use a map to find the shortest walking path between two points.
Sr	9. Determine how goods will be distributed fairly among a group of people.
PA	10. Convert a measurement in English yards or miles to meters or kilometers.
A	11. Tell the meaning of metric prefixes (*deca, kilo, mega, giga,* etc.)
A	12. Say the names of letters of the alphabet.
Se	13. Say the letters of the alphabet in order.
Se	14. Remember "*i* before *e* except after *c*."
PA	15. Use "*i* before *e* except after *c*" to spell an *ie* word.
Se	16. Say the Pledge of Allegiance.
C	17. Find novel examples of *biography.*
Se	18. Say your phone number.
Se	19. Say your home address.
C	20. Identify the artist who created a piece of art you've never seen before.
C	21. Identify the hypotenuse of a triangle.
A or Se	22. Spell the word *boy.*
PA	23. Correctly punctuate a sentence.
A	24. Say the Japanese equivalents of a series of English words.
Se	25. Count from 1 to 10 in Spanish.
Se	26. Tell how to take a person's blood pressure.
PA	27. Take a person's blood pressure.
C	28. Differentiate between cases of addition and cases of subtraction.
A	29. Complete a page of addition–subtraction facts.
PA/St	30. Select the theorem(s) for solving a geometry problem.
PA	31. Find the hypotenuse of a triangle, given the opposite and adjacent sides.
PA	32. Focus a camera.
Se	33. Tell the formula for mixing a particular color of paint.
A	34. Appropriately identify own relatives as uncle, aunt, brother, sister.
C/PA	35. Match the gender of a noun and its pronoun.
C/PA	36. Match the number of the subject and verb in a sentence.
A	37. Tell the meaning of symbols on a TV weather map.
A	38. Tell the meaning of Latin abbreviations in reference citations.
C	39. Differentiate among synonyms, homophones, and antonyms.
Se	40. Tell the order of succession to the presidency of the United States.
C	41. Determine in a set of sentences those that are complex.

Kind of learning	Example
PA	42. Given two parallel lines that are bisected by a third line and angle *A*, find angle *B*.
PA	43. Predict what will happen to the price of fruit when a deep freeze destroys a substantial portion of the fruit crop.
A	44. Name the state capitals of the United States.
C	45. Decide whether to add or subtract in a word problem.
PA	46. Find the area of a rectangle.
Se	47. Tell the formula for the area of a rectangle.
C	48. Examine a set of sentences, and use a semicolon before any conjunctive adverbs or transitional phrases that connect main clauses.
St	49. Write a creative play.
St (although for experienced newscasters, could be PA)	50. Give a live report of an emerging crisis.
A	51. Tell the meanings of the symbols in the formula for finding the standard deviation of a set of numbers.
Se	52. Tell the formula for finding the standard deviation of a set of numbers.
PA	53. Find the standard deviation of a set of numbers by using a formula.
St	54. Develop a recycling system that meets the unique needs of your community.
C	55. Tell whose style is represented in a particular sculpture.
A	56. Name six Impressionist artists.
C	57. Select from a set of artworks those that are Impressionistic art.
C/PA	58. Observe vignettes of tennis players, and evaluate their grip on the racket.
C	59. Differentiate between bacteria and viruses.
PA	60. String a guitar.
Se	61. Tell the order of pitches of guitar strings.
PA	62. Tune a guitar.
C	63. Differentiate between major and minor chords.
PA	64. If your fire alarm sounds, take the appropriate action.
PA	65. Given a stroke volume and cardiac rate, calculate the cardiac output.
PA	66. Add fraction problems.
C	67. Identify the appropriate rule to solve for x in problems of the sort "$x + b = c$" and "$ax = b$."
PA	68. Choose the appropriate filter to adjust the color in a photograph.
PA	69. Find x in statements of the type "$x + b = c$."
VR	70. Retell the story of *Much Ado about Nothing*.

References

Adams, M. (1990a). *Beginning to read: Thinking and learning about print.* Cambridge, MA: MIT Press.

Adams, M. (1990b). *Beginning to read: Thinking and learning about print. A summary.* Urbana-Champaign, IL: Center for the Study of Reading, University of Illinois at Urbana–Champaign.

Adams, M. (1998). *Phonemic awareness in young children.* Baltimore: Brookes.

Afflerbach, P., Blachowicz, C., Dawson, C., Boyd, A. E., Juel, C., Kame'enui, E., . . . Wixson, K. K. (2008, 2011). *Scott Foresman Reading Street* [Curriculum program]. Glenview, IL: Pearson Education.

AIMSWeb. (2006). *Oral reading fluency norms* [Data file]. Available from *www.aimsweb.com*

Andronis, P. T., Layng, T. V. J., & Goldiamond, I. (1997). Contingency adduction of "symbolic aggression" by pigeons. *Analysis of Verbal Behavior, 14,* 5–17.

Archer, A., Gleason, M., & Isaacson, S. (2008a). *REWARDS Writing: Sentence Refinement* [Curriculum program]. Longmont, CO: Sopris West.

Archer, A., Gleason, M., & Isaacson, S. (2008b). *REWARDS Writing: Word Choice Help Book* [Curriculum program]. Longmont, CO: Sopris West.

Archer, A., Gleason, M., & Vachon, V. (2004). *REWARDS Plus: Reading Strategies Applied to Social Studies Passages* [Curriculum program]. Longmont, CO: Sopris West.

Archer, A., Gleason, M., & Vachon, V. (2005a). *REWARDS: Multisyllabic Word Reading Strategies* [Curriculum program]. Longmont, CO: Sopris West.

Archer, A., Gleason, M., & Vachon, V. (2005b). *REWARDS Plus: Reading Strategies Applied to Science Passages.* Longmont, CO: Sopris West.

Armbruster, B. B., Lehr, F., & Osborn, J. (2001). *Put reading first—The research building blocks for teaching children to read: Kindergarten through grade 3.* Washington, DC: Partnership for Reading. Retrieved from *www.nichd.nih.gov/publications/pubs/upload/PRFbooklet.pdf*

Barrett, B. H. (1979). Communitization and the measured message of normal behavior. In R. York & E. Edgar (Eds.), *Teaching the severely handicapped* (Vol. 4, pp. 301–318). Seattle, WA: American Association for the Education of the Severely/Profoundly Handicapped.

Batsche, G., Elliott, J., Garden, J. L., Grimes, J., Kovaleski, J. F., Prasse, D., . . . Tilly, W. D. (2006). *Response to intervention: Policy considerations and implementation.* Alexandria, VA: National Association of State Directors of Special Education.

Beck, I. L., McKeown, M. G., & Kucan, L. (2002). *Bringing words to life: Robust vocabulary instruction.* New York: Guilford Press.

Becker, W. C. (1986). *Applied psychology for teachers: A behavioral cognitive approach.* Chicago: Science Research Associates.

Beebe-Frankenberger, M., Ferriter-Smith, T., & Hunsaker, D. (2008). *Montana response to intervention: RTI framework.* Helena: Montana Office of Public Instruction. Retrieved from *www.opi.mt.gov/pub/RTI/Framework/RTIFrameworkGUIDE.pdf*

Begeny, J. C. (2009). *Helping Early Literacy with Practice Strategies (HELPS): A one-on-one program designed to improve students' reading fluency* [Curriculum program]. Raleigh, NC: HELPS Education Fund. Retrieved from *www.helpsprogram.org*

Begeny, J. C. (2011). Effects of the Helping Early Literacy with Practice Strategies (HELPS) reading fluency program when implemented at different frequencies. *School Psychology Review, 40,* 149–157.

Begeny, J. C., Schulte, A. C., & Johnson, K. (2012). *Enhancing instructional problem-solving: An efficient system for assisting struggling readers.* New York: Guilford Press.

Bender, W. N. (2012). *Project-based learning: Differentiating instruction for the 21st century.* Thousand Oaks, CA: Corwin Press

Benson, V., & Cummins, C. (2000). *The power of retelling: Developmental steps for building comprehension.* Bothell, WA: Wright Group/McGraw-Hill.

Bergan, J. R. (1977). *Behavioral consultation.* Columbus, OH: Merrill.

Binder, C. (1985). *The effects of explicit timing and performance duration on academic performance frequency in elementary school children.* Unpublished doctoral dissertation, Columbia Pacific University.

Binder, C. (1988). Precision teaching: Measuring and attaining exemplary academic achievement. *Youth Policy, 10*(7), 12–15.

Binder, C. (1993, October). Behavioral fluency: A new paradigm. *Educational Technology,* pp. 8–14. Also available from *www.binder-riha.com/behav_fluency_new_paradigm.pdf*

Binder, C. (1996). Behavioral fluency: Evolution of a new paradigm. *The Behavior Analyst, 19,* 163–197.

Bloom, B. S. (1956). *Taxonomy of educational objectives: Handbook I. The cognitive domain.* New York: McKay.

Boss, S., & Krauss, J. (2007). *Reinventing project-based learning: Your field guide to real-world projects in the digital age.* Eugene, OR: International Society for Technology in Education.

Bringmann, W. G., Luck, H. E., Miller, R., & Early, C. D. (Eds.). (1997). *A pictorial history of psychology.* Chicago: Quintessence.

Brown-Chidsey, R., & Steege, M. W. (2010). *Response to intervention: Principles and strategies for effective practice* (2nd ed.). New York: Guilford Press.

Capraro, R. M., & Slough, S. W. (2009). *Project-based learning: An integrated science, technology, engineering, and mathematics (STEM) approach.* Rotterdam, The Netherlands: Sense.

Carnine, D. W., Silbert, J., Kame'enui, E. J., & Tarver, S. G. (2003). *Direct instruction reading* (4th ed.). Upper Saddle River, NJ: Pearson.

Chemero, A. (2009). *Radical embodied cognitive science.* Cambridge, MA: MIT Press.

Cooper, J. O., Heron, T. E., & Heward, W. L. (2007). *Applied behavior analysis* (2nd ed.). Upper Saddle River, NJ: Pearson.

Daiker, D. A., Kerek, A., & Morenberg, M. (1979). *Sentence combining and the teaching of writing: Selected papers from the Miami University conference, Oxford, Ohio, October 27 & 28, 1978.* Conway, AR: L&S Books.

Deno, E. (1970). Special education as developmental capital. *Exceptional Children, 37,* 229–237.

Deno, S. L. (1985). Curriculum-based measurement: The emerging alternative. *Exceptional Children, 52,* 219–232.

Deno, S. L. (2002). Problem-solving as "best practice." In A. Thomas & J. Grimes (Eds.), *Best practices in school psychology IV* (pp. 37–56). Bethesda, MD: National Association of School Psychologists.

Deno, S. L. (2003). Developments in curriculum-based measurement. *Journal of Special Education, 37,* 184–192.

Dewey, J. (1896). The reflex arc concept in psychology. *Psychological Review, 3,* 357–370.

Dewey, J. (1976a). The child and the curriculum. In J. A. Boydston (Ed.), *John Dewey: The middle works, 1899–1924. Vol. 2: 1902–1903* (pp. 271–291). Carbondale: Southern Illinois University Press. (Original work published 1902)

Dewey, J. (1976b). The school and society. In J. A. Boydston (Ed.), *John Dewey: The middle works, 1899–1924. Vol. 1: 1899–1901* (pp. 1–109). Carbondale: Southern Illinois University Press. (Original work published 1900)

Dewey, J. (1981). Experience and nature. In J. A. Boydston (Ed.), *John Dewey: The later works, 1925–1953. Vol. 1: 1925* (pp. 1–326). Carbondale: Southern Illinois University Press. (Original work published 1925; rev. ed., 1929)

Dewey, J. (1986). Logic: The theory of inquiry. In J. A. Boydston (Ed.), *John Dewey: The later works, 1925–1953. Vol. 12: 1938* (pp. 1–527). Carbondale: Southern Illinois University Press. (Original work published 1938)

Dixon, R., Boorman, L., Conrad, L., Klau, K., & Muti, K. (2008). *Reading Success* [Curriculum program]. Columbus, OH: McGraw-Hill Education.

Dixon, R., & Engelmann, S. (2007). *Spelling through Morphographs* [Curriculum program]. Columbus, OH: McGraw-Hill Education.

Dixon, R., Engelmann, S., Bauer, M. M., Steely, D., & Wells, T. (2007). *Spelling Mastery* [Curriculum program]. Columbus, OH: Science Research Associates.

Dodds, T. (2005). *High Performance Writing* [Curriculum program]. Columbus, OH: McGraw-Hill Education.

Dubuque, E. M., & Kubina, R. M. (2013). *The chart app.* [Mobile Application Software]. Available at *www.behaviorscience.org.*

Engelmann, S. (2008). *Reading Mastery Signature Edition* [Curriculum program]. Columbus, OH: McGraw-Hill Education.

Engelmann, S., & Carnine, D. W. (1991). *Theory of instruction: Principles and applications.* Eugene, OR: ADI Press.

Engelmann, S., Engelmann, O., Davis, K. L. S., & Hanner, S. (1998). *Horizons: Reading to Learn* [Curriculum program]. Columbus, OH: Science Research Associates.

Engelmann, S., & Osborn, J. (2008a). *Language for Learning* [Curriculum program]. Columbus, OH: McGraw-Hill Education.

Engelmann, S., & Osborn, J. (2008b). *Language for Thinking* [Curriculum program]. Columbus, OH: McGraw-Hill Education.

Ericsson, K. A. (Ed.). (1996). *The road to excellence: The acquisition of expert performance in the arts and sciences, sports, and games.* Mahwah, NJ: Erlbaum.

Ericsson, K. A. (2006). The influence of experience and deliberate practice on the development of superior expert performance. In K. A. Ericsson, N. Charness, P. Feltovich, & R. R. Hoffman (Eds.), *Cambridge handbook of expertise and expert performance* (pp. 685–706). Cambridge, UK: Cambridge University Press.

Fabrizio, M. A., & Moors, A. L. (2003). Evaluating mastery: Measuring instructional outcomes for children with autism. *European Journal of Behavior Analysis, 4,* 23–36.

Ferster, C., Culbertson, S., & Boren, M. C. P. (1975). *Behavior principles* (2nd ed.). Englewood Cliffs, NJ: Prentice-Hall.

Ferster, C., & Skinner, B. F. (1957). *Schedules of reinforcement.* New York: Appleton-Century-Crofts.

Fien, H., Baker, S. K., Smolkowski, K., Smith, J. L. M., Kame'enui, E. J., & Beck, C. T. (2008). Using nonsense word fluency to predict reading proficiency in kindergarten through second grade for English learners and native English speakers. *School Psychology Review, 37,* 391–408.

Franklin, B. (1944). *The autobiography of Benjamin Franklin and selections from his writings.* New York: Random House. Also available from *www.ushistory.org/franklin/autobiography/page06.htm*

Fuchs, D., & Fuchs, L. S. (1994, 2008). *PALS Reading* [Curriculum program]. Available from *www.kc.vanderbilt.edu/pals*

Fuchs, D., & Fuchs, L. S. (2006). Introduction to response to intervention: What, why, and how valid is it? *Reading Research Quarterly, 41,* 93–99.

Fuchs, D., Fuchs, L. S., Mathes, P. G., & Simmons, D. C. (1997). Peer-assisted learning strategies:

Making classrooms more responsive to diversity. *American Educational Research Journal, 34,* 174–206

Fuchs, L. S., Powell, S. R., Seethaler, P. M., Cirino, P. T., Fletcher, J. M., Fuchs, D., . . . Zumeta, R. O. (2009). Remediating number combination and word problem deficits among students with mathematics difficulties: A randomized control trial. *Journal of Educational Psychology, 101,* 561–576.

Gagné, R. M. (1985). *The conditions of learning and theory of instruction* (4th ed.). New York: Holt, Rinehart & Winston.

Gagné, R. M., Briggs, L., & Wagner, W. (1992). *Principles of instructional design.* Fort Worth, TX: Harcourt Brace Jovanovich.

Gibson, J. (1966). *The senses considered as perceptual systems.* Boston: Houghton Mifflin.

Gilbert, T. (1962a). Mathetics: The technology of education. *Journal of Mathetics, 1*(1), 7–74.

Gilbert, T. (1962b). Mathetics II: The design of teaching exercises. *Journal of Mathetics, 1*(2), 7–56.

Good, R. H., & Kaminski, R. A. (2002). *Dynamic Indicators of Basic Early Literacy Skills* [Test instrument]. Austin, TX: PRO-ED.

Gorini, C. A. (2003). *The facts on file geometry handbook.* New York: Facts on File.

Graf, S. A. (1994). *How to develop, produce and use SAFMEDS in education and training.* Poland, OH: Zero Brothers Software.

Gresham, F. M. (2007). Evolution of the response-to-intervention concept: Empirical foundations and recent developments. In S. R. Jimerson, M. K. Burns, & A. M. VanDerHeyden (Eds.), *Handbook of response to intervention: The science and practice of assessment and intervention* (pp. 10–24). New York: Springer.

Gresham, F. M., MacMillan, D. L., Beebe-Frankenberger, M. E., & Bocian, K. M. (2000). Treatment integrity in learning disabilities intervention research: Do we really know how treatments are implemented? *Learning Disabilities Research and Practice, 15,* 198–205.

Haring, N., Liberty, K., & White, O. (1980). Rules for data-based strategy decisions in instructional programs: Current research and instructional implications. In W. Sailor, B. Wilcox, & L. Brown (Eds.), *Methods of instruction for severely handicapped students* (pp. 159–192). Baltimore: Brookes.

Haughton, Elizabeth. (2002). *Rapid Automatic Naming: RAN* [Curriculum program]. Jackson, CA: Haughton Learning Center.

Haughton, Elizabeth, & Freeman, G. (1999a). *Phonological Coding: Phonemic Awareness* [Curriculum program]. Jackson, CA: Haughton Learning Center.

Haughton, Elizabeth, & Freeman, G. (1999b). *Phonological Coding: Word and Syllable Awareness* [Curriculum program]. Jackson, CA: Haughton Learning Center.

Haughton, Eric. (1971). Great gains from small starts. *Teaching Exceptional Children, 3,* 141–146.

Haughton, Eric. (1972). Aims: Growing and sharing. In J. B. Jordan & L. S. Robbins (Eds.), *Let's try doing something else kind of thing* (pp. 20–39). Arlington, VA: Council for Exceptional Children.

Haughton, Eric. (1980). Practicing practices: Learning by activity. *Journal of Precision Teaching, 1,* 3–20.

Heistad, D. (2009). RTI and universal screening: Establishing district benchmarks [PowerPoint presentation slides]. Retrieved from *www.rti4success.org/pdf/rtianduniversalscreening_color.pdf*

Heller, K. A., Holtzman, W. H., & Messick, S. (1982). *Placing children in special education: A strategy for equity.* Washington, DC: National Academy Press.

Hosp, M. K., Hosp, J. L., & Howell, K. W. (2007). *The ABCs of CBM: A practical guide to curriculum-based measurement.* New York: Guilford Press.

Johnson, K. (2003). Contributions of Precision Teaching. *European Journal of Behavior Analysis, 4,* 66–70.

Johnson, K. (2005). *Morningside Mathematics Fluency: Basic Number Skills* (Vols. 1–3) [Curriculum program]. Seattle, WA: Morningside Press.

Johnson, K. (2008a). *Morningside Mathematics Fluency: Math Facts* (Vols. 1–6) [Curriculum program]. Seattle, WA: Morningside Press.

Johnson, K. (2008b). Precision Teaching. In N. Salkind (Ed.), *Encyclopedia of educational psychology* (Vol. 2, pp. 809–813). Thousand Oaks, CA: Sage.

Johnson, K., & Casson, S. (2005a). *Morningside Mathematics Fluency: Addition and Subtraction* (Vols. 1–2) [Curriculum program]. Seattle, WA: Morningside Press.

Johnson, K., & Casson, S. (2005b). *Morningside Mathematics Fluency: Multiplication and Division* (Vols. 1–2) [Curriculum program]. Seattle, WA: Morningside Press.

Johnson, K., Casson, S., Street, E., Kevo, H., & Melroe, K., (2005). *Morningside Phonics Fluency: Basic Elements* [Curriculum program]. Seattle, WA: Morningside Press.

Johnson, K., & Fabrizio, M. A. (2006, October). *Language foundation skills and reading comprehension success for learners with autism spectrum disorders.* Workshop conducted at the annual conference of the Organization for Autism Research, Arlington, VA.

Johnson, K., & Layng, T. V. J. (1992). Breaking the structuralist barrier: Literacy and numeracy with fluency. *American Psychologist, 47,* 1475–1490.

Johnson, K., & Layng, T. V. J. (1994). The Morningside Model of Generative Instruction. In R. Gardner, D. Sainato, J. Cooper, T. Heron, W. Heward, J. Eshleman, & T. Grossi (Eds.), *Behavior analysis in education: Focus on measurably superior instruction* (pp. 173–197). Belmont, CA: Brooks/Cole.

Johnson, K., & Layng, T. V. J. (1996). On terms and procedures: Fluency. *The Behavior Analyst, 19,* 281–288.

Johnson, K., & Melroe, K. (2006a). *Teaching Computation Skills: A Diagnostic and Prescriptive Instructional Sequence: Addition and Subtraction* (Vols. 1–2) [Curriculum program]. Seattle, WA: Morningside Press.

Johnson, K., & Melroe, K. (2006b). *Teaching Computation Skills: A Diagnostic and Prescriptive Instructional Sequence: Multiplication and Division* (Vols. 1–2) [Curriculum program]. Seattle, WA: Morningside Press.

Johnson, K., & Melroe, K. (2009). *Teaching Computation Skills: A Diagnostic and Prescriptive Instructional Sequence: Fractions* (Vols. 1–3) [Curriculum program]. Seattle, WA: Morningside Press.

Johnson, K., & Melroe, K. (2011). *Teaching Computation Skills: A Diagnostic and Prescriptive Instructional Sequence: Decimals* (Vols. 1–2) [Curriculum program]. Seattle, WA: Morningside Press.

Johnson, K., & Street, E. M. (2004). *The Morningside Model of Generative Instruction: What It Means to Leave No Child Behind.* Concord, MA: Cambridge Center for Behavioral Studies.

Johnson, K., & Street, E. M. (2012). From the laboratory to the field and back again: Morningside Academy's 32 years of improving students' academic performance. *The Behavior Analyst Today, 13,* 20–40.

Joyce, B., & Showers, B. (1980). Improving inservice training: The messages of research. *Educational Leadership, 37,* 379–385.

Joyce, B., & Showers, B. (1995). *Student achievement through staff development: Fundamentals of staff development.* White Plains, NY: Longman.

Kame'enui, E. J., & Baumann, J. F. (Eds.). (2012). *Vocabulary instruction: Research to practice* (2nd ed.). New York: Guilford Press.

Kauffman, J. M. (1989). The Regular Education Initiative as Reagan–Bush education policy: A trickle-down theory of education of the hard-to-teach. *Journal of Special Education, 23,* 256–278.

Koutsoftas, A. D., Harmon, M. T., & Gray, S. (2009). The effect of Tier 2 intervention for phonemic awareness in a response-to-intervention model in low-income preschool classrooms. *Language, Speech, and Hearing Services in Schools, 40,* 116–130.

Kubina, R. M., Morrison, R. S., & Lee, D. (2006). Behavior analytic contributions to the study of creativity. *Journal of Creative Behavior, 40,* 223–242.

Kubina, R. M., & Yurich, K. K. L. (2012). *The precision teaching book.* Lemont, PA: Greatness Achieved.

Larson, J. (1994). Violence prevention in the schools: A review of selected programs and procedures. *School Psychology Review, 23,* 151–164.

Layng, T. V. J., Twyman, J. S., & Stikeleather, G. (2004). Engineering discovery learning: The contingency adduction of some precursors of textual responding in a beginning reading program. *Analysis of Verbal Behavior, 20,* 99–109.

Lewkowicz, N. K. (1985). Attacking longer words: Don't begin at the beginning. *Journal of Reading, 29,* 226–237.

Lewkowicz, N. K. (1994). *Word workout.* Yellow Springs, OH: Word Workshop.

Linden, M., & Whimbey, A. (1990). *Why Johnny can't write.* Hillsdale, NJ: Erlbaum.

Lindsley, O. R. (1971). Precision teaching in perspective: An interview with Ogden R. Lindsley (A. D. Duncan, interviewer). *Teaching Exceptional Children, 3,* 114–119.

Lindsley, O. R. (1972). From Skinner to Precision Teaching: The child knows best. In J. B. Jordan & L. S. Robbins (Eds.), *Let's try doing something else kind of thing* (pp. 1–11). Arlington, VA: Council for Exceptional Children.

Lindsley, O. R. (1990). Precision Teaching: By teachers for children. *Teaching Exceptional Children, 22,* 10–15.

Lindsley, O. R. (1991). Precision Teaching's unique legacy from B. F. Skinner. *Journal of Behavioral Education, 1,* 253–266.

Lindsley, O. R. (1992). Precision Teaching: Discoveries and effects. *Journal of Applied Behavior Analysis, 25,* 51–57.

Lindsley, O. R. (1999, November). *Celeration and agility for the 2000s.* Paper presented at the International Precision Teaching and Standard Celeration Conference, Provo, UT.

MacKenzie, A. (1998). *The effect of fluency building compared to traditional tutoring on students' statistics performance.* Unpublished master's thesis, Central Washington University.

Mannis, F. R., & Freeman, L. (2002). The relationship of naming speed to multiple reading measures in disabled and normal readers. In M. Wolf (Ed.), *Dyslexia, fluency, and the brain* (pp. 65–92). Timonium, MD: York Press.

Markle, S. M. (1990). *Designs for instructional designers.* Champaign, IL: Stipes.

Mayer, G. R., Sulzer-Azaroff, B., & Wallace, M. (2011). *Behavior analysis for lasting change* (2nd ed.). Cornwall-on-Hudson, NY: Sloan.

Miller, J. H., & Carr, S. C. (1997). Error ratio analysis: Alternative mathematics assessment for general and special educators. *Assessment for Effective Intervention, 23,* 225–231.

Moors, A., Weisenburgh-Snyder, A., & Robbins, J. (2010). Integrating frequency-based mathematics instruction with a multi-level assessment system to enhance response to intervention frameworks. *The Behavior Analyst Today, 11,* 226–244.

National Center on Response to Intervention. (2010). *Essential components of RTI: A closer look at response to intervention.* Washington, DC: Author. Retrieved from *www.cldinternational.org/Articles/rtiessentialcomponents.pdf*

National Mathematics Advisory Panel (NMAP). (2008). *Foundations for success: The final report of the National Mathematics Advisory Panel.* Washington, DC: U.S. Department of Education. Retrieved from *www2.ed.gov/about/bdscomm/list/mathpanel/report/final-report.pdf*

National Reading Panel. (2000). *Teaching children to read: An evidence-based assessment of the scientific research literature on reading and its implications for reading instruction.* Bethesda, MD: National Institute of Child Health and Human Development. Retrieved from *www.nichd.nih.gov/publications/nrp/upload/smallbook_pdf.pdf*

Neuhaus, G. F., Foorman, B. R., Francis, D. J., & Carlson, C. D. (2001). Measures of information processing in rapid automatized naming (RAN) and their relation to reading. *Journal of Experimental Child Psychology, 78,* 359–373.

Newell, M., & Kratochwill, T. R. (2007). The integration of response to intervention and critical race theory–disability studies: A robust approach to reducing racial discrimination in evaluation decisions. In S. R. Jimerson, M. K. Burns, & A. M. VanDerHeyden (Eds.), *Handbook of response to intervention: The science and practice of assessment and intervention* (pp. 65–79). New York: Springer.

O'Hare, F. (1973). *Sentence combining: Improving student writing without formal grammar instruction.* Urbana, IL: National Council of Teachers of English.

Olson, J. F., Martin, M. O., & Mullis, I. V. S. (Eds.). (2008). *Trends in international mathematics and science study (TIMSS) 2007 technical report.* Washington, DC: International Association for the

Evaluation of Educational Achievement. Retrieved from *http://timss.bc.edu/timss2007/PDF/TIMSS2007_TechnicalReport.pdf*

Pennypacker, H. S., Gutierrez, A., & Lindsley, O. R. (2003). *Handbook of the standard celeration chart, deluxe edition.* Concord, MA: Cambridge Center for Behavioral Studies.

Piaget, J. (1957). *The construction of reality in the child.* London: Routledge & Kegan Paul.

Poldrack, R. A., Sabb, F. W., Foerde, K., Tom, S. M., Asarnow, R. F., Bookheimer, S. Y., & Knowlton, B. J. (2005). The neural correlates of motor skill automaticity. *Journal of Neuroscience, 25,* 5356–5464.

Power, T. J., Blom-Hoffman, J., Clarke, A. T., Riley-Tillman, T. C., Kelleher, C., & Manz, P. (2005). Reconceptualizing intervention integrity: A partnership-based framework for linking research with practice. *Psychology in the Schools, 42,* 495–507.

"Precision Teaching." (n.d.). [*"Most Effective Mastery Teaching Methods"* web page]. Retrieved from *http://mastermindprep.com/online-learning/test-prep*

Reynolds, C. R., & Shaywitz, S. E. (2009). Response to intervention: Ready or not? Or, from wait-to-fail to watch-them-fail. *School Psychology Quarterly, 24,* 130–145.

Roksa, J., Jenkins, D., Jaggers, S. S., Zeidenberg, M., & Cho, S. (2009). *Strategies for promoting gatekeeper course success among students needing remediation: Research report for the Virginia Community College System.* New York: Columbia University. Retrieved from *www.achievingthedream.org/Portal/Modules/38e74ad4-0402-4087-97ce-f5d5d0612ccc.asset*

Rosner, J. (1993). *Helping children overcome learning difficulties.* New York: Walker.

Ryle, G. (1949). *The concept of mind.* Chicago: University of Chicago Press.

Sandomierski, T., Kincaid, D., & Algozzine, B. (2007). Response to intervention and positive behavior support: Brothers from different mothers or sisters with different misters? *Positive Behavior Interventions and Supports Newsletter,* 4(2). Retrieved from *www.pbis.org/pbis_newsletter/volume_4/issue2.aspx*

Sanetti, L. M. H., & Kratochwill, T. R. (2009). Treatment integrity assessment in the schools: An evaluation of the Treatment Integrity Planning Protocol (TIPP). *School Psychology Quarterly, 24,* 24–35.

Scholastic. (2007). *Scholastic Reading Inventory* [Test instrument]. New York: Author.

Science Research Associates (SRA)/McGraw-Hill. (2006). *Specific Skills Series* [Curriculum materials]. New York: McGraw-Hill.

Segen, J. C. (2006). *Concise dictionary of modern medicine.* New York: McGraw-Hill.

Share, D. L., & Stanovich, K. E. (1995). Cognitive processes in early reading development: Accommodating individual differences into a model of acquisition. *Issues in Education: Contributions from Educational Psychology, 1,* 1–57.

Shinn, M. R. (Ed.). (1989). *Curriculum-based measurement: Assessing special children.* New York: Guilford Press.

Showers, B., Joyce, B., & Bennett, B. (1987). Synthesis of research on staff development: A framework for future study and a state-of-art analysis. *Educational Leadership, 45,* 77–87.

Simmons, D. C., & Kame'enui, E. J. (2003, March). *A consumer's guide to evaluating a core reading program grades K–3: A critical elements analysis.* Eugene, OR: Institute for the Development of Educational Achievement. Retrieved from *http://reading.uoregon.edu/cia/curricula/core_program.php*

Skinner, B. F. (1938). *The behavior of organisms.* Englewood Cliffs, NJ: Prentice-Hall.

Skinner, B. F. (1953). *Science and human behavior.* New York: Macmillan.

Skinner, B. F. (1968). *The technology of teaching.* New York: Appleton-Century-Crofts.

Skinner, B. F. (1974). *About behaviorism.* New York: Knopf.

Stanovich, K. E. (1993). Romance and reality. *Reading Teacher, 47,* 280–291.

Steege, M. W., & Watson, T. S. (2009). *Conducting school-based functional behavioral assessments: A practitioner's guide* (2nd ed.). New York: Guilford Press.

Stein, M., Kinder, D., Silbert, J., & Carnine, D. W. (2006). *Designing effective mathematics instruction: A direct instruction approach* (4th ed.). Upper Saddle River, NJ: Prentice Hall.

Sugai, G. (2007, December 6). RTI: Reasons, practices, systems, & considerations [PowerPoint presentation slides]. Keynote address to the Response to Intervention Summit, Washington, DC. Retrieved from *www.rti4success.org/pdf/rti_summit_keynote_sugai_2007%20.pdf*

Sugai, G., & Horner, R. H. (2005). School-wide positive behavior supports: Achieving and sustaining effective learning environments for all students. In W. H. Heward (Ed.), *Focus on behavior analysis in education: Achievements, challenges, and opportunities* (pp. 90–102). Upper Saddle River, NJ: Pearson Prentice Hall.

Sugai, G., & Horner, R. H. (2008). What we know and need to know about preventing problem behavior in schools. *Exceptionality, 16*, 67–77.

Sugai, G., Horner, R. H., Dunlap, G., Hieneman, M., Lewis, T. J., Nelson, C. M. . . . Wilcox, B. (2000). Applying positive behavioral support and functional behavioral assessment in schools. *Journal of Positive Behavioral Interventions, 2*, 131–143.

Tiemann, P. W., & Markle, S. M. (1990). *Analyzing instructional content: A guide to instruction and evaluation* (4th ed.). Champaign, IL: Stipes.

Tucci, V., & Johnson, K. (2012). *Fluency FlashCards.* [Computer Tablet Application Software]. Available at *www.tuccisolutions.com*

University of Texas System/Texas Education Agency. (2005). *Introduction to the three-tier reading model* (4th ed.). Austin, TX: Author. Retrieved from *www.meadowscenter.org/vgc/downloads/3tier/Intro3TierModel_4ed.pdf*

VanDerHeyden, A. M., & Burns, M. K. (2010). *Essentials of response to intervention.* Hoboken, NJ: Wiley.

Villa, R. A., & Thousand, J. S. (Eds.). (1995). *Creating an inclusive school.* Alexandria, VA: Association for Supervision and Curriculum Development.

Vygotsky, L. S. (1978). *Mind in society: The development of higher mental processes.* Cambridge, MA: Harvard University Press.

Vygotsky, L. S. (1986). *Thought and language.* Cambridge, MA: Harvard University Press.

Walker, H. M., Horner, R. H., Sugai, G., Bullis, M., Sprague, J. R., Bricker, D., & Kaufman, M. J. (1996). Integrated approaches to preventing antisocial behavior patterns among school-age children and youth. *Journal of Emotional and Behavioral Disorders, 4*, 194– 209.

Walker, H. M., & Shinn, M. R. (2002). Structuring school-based interventions to achieve integrated primary, secondary, and tertiary prevention goals for safe and effective schools. In M. R. Shinn, H. M. Walker, & G. Stoner (Eds.), *Interventions for academic and behavior problems II: Preventive and remedial approaches* (pp. 1–25). Bethesda, MD: National Association of School Psychologists.

Whimbey, A., & Linden, M. (2001). *Teaching and learning grammar: The prototype-construction approach.* Chicago: BGF Performance Systems.

Whimbey, A., & Lockhead, J. (1999). *Problem solving and comprehension* (6th ed.). Mahwah, NJ: Erlbaum.

White, O. R., & Haring, N. G. (1980). *Exceptional teaching* (2nd ed.). Columbus, OH: Merrill.

Will, M. (1986). Educating children with learning problems: A shared responsibility. *Exceptional Children, 51*, 33–51.

Wolfensberger, W. (1972). *Normalization: The principles of normalization in human services.* Toronto: National Institute on Mental Retardation.

Ysseldyke, J. E. (1973). Diagnostic–prescriptive teaching: The search for aptitude–treatment interactions. In L. Mann & D. Sabatino (Eds.), *The first review of special education* (pp. 5–31). Philadelphia: JSE Press.

Ysseldyke, J. E. (2006, April). *Using continuous progress monitoring data to make accountability decisions.* Paper presented at the annual meeting of the National Association of School Psychologists, Anaheim, CA.

Ysseldyke, J. E. (2008). *Frequently asked questions about response to intervention (RtI).* Wisconsin Rapids, WI: Renaissance Learning.

Ysseldyke, J. E., & Bolt, D. M. (2007). Effect of a technology-enhanced continuous progress monitoring system on math achievement. *School Psychology Review, 36*, 453–467.

Ysseldyke, J. E., Burns, M. K., Scholin, S. E., & Parker, D. C. (2010). Instructionally valid assessment within response to intervention. *Teaching Exceptional Children, 42*, 54–61.

Index

Note. Page numbers in *italics* indicate figures and tables. An "n" following a page number indicates a footnote.

D

E

F

G

H

I

K

L

M

N

O

P

Q

R

S

T

U

V

W